THE EUROPEAN UNION SERIES

General Editors: Neill Nugent, William E. Paterson

The European Union series provides an authoritative library on the European Union, ranging from general introductory texts to definitive assessments of key institutions and actors, issues, policies and policy processes, and the role of member states.

Books in the series are written by leading scholars in their fields and reflect the most up-to-date research and debate. Particular attention is paid to accessibility and clear presentation for a wide audience of students, practitioners and interested general readers.

The series editors are **Neill Nugent**, Emeritus Professor of Politics at Manchester Metropolitan University, UK, and **William E. Paterson**, Honorary Professor in German and European Studies, University of Aston. Their co-editor until his death in July 1999, **Vincent Wright,** was a Fellow of Nuffield College, Oxford University.

Feedback on the series and book proposals are always welcome and should be sent to Stephen Wenham, Palgrave, 4 Crinan Street, London N1 9XW, or by e-mail to s.wenham@palgrave.com

---

General textbooks

Published

Laurie Buonanno and Neill Nugent **Policies and Policy Processes of the European Union**
Desmond Dinan **Encyclopedia of the European Union** [Rights: Europe only]
Desmond Dinan **Europe Recast: A History of the European Union (2nd edn)** [Rights: Europe only]
Desmond Dinan **Ever Closer Union: An Introduction to European Integration (4th edn)** [Rights: Europe only]
Mette Eilstrup Sangiovanni (ed.) **Debates on European Integration: A Reader**
Simon Hix and Bjørn Høyland **The Political System of the European Union (3rd edn)**
Dirk Leuffen, Berthold Rittberger and Frank Schimmelfennig **Differentiated Integration**
Paul Magnette **What is the European Union? Nature and Prospects**
John McCormick **Understanding the European Union: A Concise Introduction (6th edn)**
Brent F. Nelsen and Alexander Stubb **The European Union: Readings on the Theory and Practice of European Integration (4th edn)** [Rights: Europe only]
Neill Nugent (ed.) **European Union Enlargement**
Neill Nugent **The Government and Politics of the European Union (8th edn)**
John Peterson and Elizabeth Bomberg **Decision-Making in the European Union**
Ben Rosamond **Theories of European Integration**
Magnus Ryner and Alan Cafruny **A Critical Introduction to the European Union and Global Capitalism**
Sabine Saurugger **Theoretical Approaches to European Integration**
Ingeborg Tömmel **The European Union: What it is and How it Works**
Esther Versluis, Mendeltje van Keulen and Paul Stephenson **Analyzing the European Union Policy Process**
Hubert Zimmermann and Andreas Dür (eds) **Key Controversies in European Integration**

Forthcoming

The European Union and Global Politics
The Political Economy of European Integration

Visit Palgrave Macmillan's EU Resource area at www.palgrave.com/politics/eu/

The major institutions and actors

Published

Renaud Dehousse **The European Court of Justice**
Justin Greenwood **Interest Representation in the European Union (3rd edn)**
Fiona Hayes-Renshaw and Helen Wallace **The Council of Ministers** (2nd edn)
Simon Hix and Christopher Lord **Political Parties in the European Union**
David Judge and David Earnshaw **The European Parliament (2nd edn)**
Neill Nugent and Mark Rhinard **The European Commission (2nd edn)**
Sabine Saurugger and Fabien Terpan **The Court of Justice of the European Union and the Politics of Law**
Anne Stevens with Handley Stevens **Brussels Bureaucrats? The Administration of the European Union**
Wolfgang Wessels **The European Council**
Sabine Saurugger and Fabien Terpan **The Court of Justice of the European Union and the Politics of Law**

Forthcoming

Ariadna Ripoll Servent **The European Parliament**

The main areas of policy

Published

Karen Anderson **Social Policy in the European Union**
Michael Baun and Dan Marek **Cohesion Policy in the European Union**
Michele Chang **Monetary Integration in the European Union**
Michele Chang **Economic and Monetary Union**
Michelle Cini and Lee McGowan **Competition Policy in the European Union (2nd edn)**
Wyn Grant **The Common Agricultural Policy**
Martin Holland and Mathew Doidge **Development Policy of the European Union**
Jolyon Howorth **Security and Defence Policy in the European Union (2nd edn)**
Johanna Kantola **Gender and the European Union**
Stephan Keukeleire and Tom Delreux **The Foreign Policy of the European Union (2nd edn)**
Brigid Laffan **The Finances of the European Union**
Malcolm Levitt and Christopher Lord **The Political Economy of Monetary Union**
Janne Haaland Matláry **Energy Policy in the European Union**
John McCormick **Environmental Policy in the European Union**
John Peterson and Margaret Sharp **Technology Policy in the European Union**
Handley Stevens **Transport Policy in the European Union**
Maren Kreutler, Johannes Pollak and Samuel Schubert **Energy Policy in the European Union**
Tom Delreux and Sander Happaerts **Environmental Policy and Politics in the European Union**

Forthcoming

Sieglinde Gstöhl and Dirk de Bievre **The Trade Policy of the European Union**
Christian Kaunert and Sarah Leonard **Justice and Home Affairs in the European Union**
Paul Stephenson, Esther Versluis and Mendeltje van Keulen **Implementing and Evaluating Policy in the European Union**

Also planned

Political Union

The member states and the Union

Published

Carlos Closa and Paul Heywood **Spain and the European Union**
Andrew Geddes **Britain and the European Union**
Alain Guyomarch, Howard Machin and Ella Ritchie **France in the European Union**
Brigid Laffan and Jane O'Mahoney **Ireland and the European Union**

Forthcoming

Simon Bulmer and William E. Paterson **Germany and the European Union**
Brigid Laffan **The European Union and its Member States**

Issues

Published

Senem Aydın-Düzgit and Nathalie Tocci **Turkey and the European Union**
Derek Beach **The Dynamics of European Integration: Why and When EU Institutions Matter**
Christina Boswell and Andrew Geddes **Migration and Mobility in the European Union**
Thomas Christiansen and Christine Reh **Constitutionalizing the European Union**
Tuomas Forsberg and Hiski Haukkala **The European Union and Russia**
Robert Ladrech **Europeanization and National Politics**
Cécile Leconte **Understanding Euroscepticism**
Steven McGuire and Michael Smith **The European Union and the United States**
Wyn Rees **The US–EU Security Relationship: The Tensions between a European and a Global Agenda**

Forthcoming

Graham Avery **Enlarging the European Union**
Thomas Christiansen, Emil Kirchner and Uwe Wissenbach **The European Union and China**
Desmond Dinan, Neill Nugent and William E. Paterson (eds) **The European Union in Crisis**

Also planned

European Disintegration?

The Court of Justice of the European Union and the Politics of Law

Sabine Saurugger
Fabien Terpan

First published 2017 by
PALGRAVE

Palgrave in the UK is an imprint of Macmillan Publishers Limited, registered in England, company number 785998, of 4 Crinan Street, London, N1 9XW.

Palgrave is a global imprint of the above companies and is represented throughout the world.

Palgrave® and Macmillan® are registered trademarks in the United States, the United Kingdom, Europe and other countries.

ISBN 978–1–137–32027–8 hardback
ISBN 978–1–137–32026–1 paperback

This book is printed on paper suitable for recycling and made from fully managed and sustained forest sources. Logging, pulping and manufacturing processes are expected to conform to the environmental regulations of the country of origin.

A catalogue record for this book is available from the British Library.

A catalog record for this book is available from the Library of Congress.

Contents

List of Boxes, Figures and Tables

Boxes

Figures

Tables

List of Cases

1/54 French Republic vs. High Authority of the ECSC
8/55 Fédéchar vs. High Authority of the ECSC
25/62 Plaumann & Co. vs. Commission
26/62 Van Gend en Loos
28 and 30/62 Da Costa
31 and 33/62 Lütticke et al. vs. Commission
90 and 91/63 Commission vs. Luxembourg and Belgium
6/64 Costa vs. ENEL
57/65 Lütticke
13/68 Salgoil vs. Italian Ministry of Foreign Trade
11/70 Internationale Handelsgesellschaft
22/70 ERTA
25/70 Koester
80/70 Defrenne
5/71 Schöppenstedt vs. Council
6/72 Continental Can
30/72 Commission vs. Italy
4/73 Nold
166/73 Rheinmühlen-Düsseldorf
167/73 Commission vs. France
2/74 Reyners
8/74 Dassonville
41/74 Van Duyn
36/75 Rutili
43/75 Defrenne II
Opinion 1/76
3, 4 and 6/76 Kramer
75/76 Ianelli & Volpi SpA vs. Ditta Paolo Meroni
106/77 Simmenthal
149/77 Defrenne III
92/78 Simmenthal IV
120/78 Cassis de Dijon
148/78 Ratti
232/78 Commission vs. France
44/79 Hauer

138/79 Roquettes frères vs. Council, 'Isoglucose'
8/81 Becker
60/81 International Business Machines Corporation vs. Commission
115 and 116/81 Adoui and Cornouaille vs. Belgium
283/81 C.I.L.F.I.T.
13/83 Parliament vs. Council
14/83 von Colson
240/83 ADBHU
293/83 Gravier
294/83 'Les Verts' vs. Parliament
142 and 156/84 British American Tobacco
152/84 Marshall vs. Southampton and South-West Hampshire Area Health Authority
170/84 Bilka-Kaufhaus Gmbh vs. Weber von Harz
205/84 Commission vs. Germany
222/84 Johnston
59/85 Netherlands vs. Reed
149/85 Wybot vs. Faure
180/85 Drake vs. Chief Adjudication Officer
24/86 Commission vs. Greece
34/86 Council vs. Parliament
302/86 'Danish Bottles'
302/87 'Comitology'
377/87 Parliament vs. Council
C–39/88 Commission vs. Ireland
C–64/88 Commission vs. France
C–70-88 'Chernobyl'
C–145/88 Torfaen Borough Council vs. B&Q plc
C–177/88 Dekker
C–179/88 Herz
C–246/89 Commission vs. UK – Nationality of Fishermen
C–262/88 Barber
C–213/89 Factortame
C–300/89 'Titanium Dioxide'
C–309/89 Codorniu vs. Council
C–312/89 Conforama
C–332/89 Marchandise
C–6/90 Francovich vs. Italy
T-28/90 Asia Motor France and Others vs. Commission
C–65/90 Parliament vs. Council
C–208/90 Emmott

C–271, 281 and 289/90 Spain, Belgium and Italy vs. Commission
C–295/90 Parliament vs. Council
Opinion 1/91
C–45/91 Commission vs. Greece
C–155/91 'Waste Directive'
C–169/91 Stoke-on-Trent City Council vs. B&Q plc
C–267 and 268/91 Keck and Mithouard
C–320/91 Corbeau
C–96/92 Comité Central d'Entreprise de la Société Générale des Grandes Sources vs. Commission
C–388/92 Parliament vs. Council
C–393/92 Almelo
C–421/92 Habermann-Belterman vs. Arbeiterwohlfahrt
C–12/93 Vittel vs. Commission
C–32/93 British Webb
C–187/93 Parliament vs. Council
C–415/93 Bosman vs. Royal Club Liégeois
C–417/93 Parliament vs. Council
C–450/93 Kalanke
C–13/94 P v S & Cornwall County Council
C–21/94 Parliament vs. Council
C–80/94 Wielockx
C–107/94 Asscher
C–140 and 142/94 Dip Spa
C–44/95 Regina vs. Secretary of State for the Environment Lappel Bank
C–120/95 Decker
C–392/95 Parliament vs. Council, 'Chernobyl'
C–158/96 Kohll
C–326/96 Levez
C–189/97 Comité d'entreprise de la Société Française de Production vs. Commission
C–311/97 Royal Bank of Scotland
C–414/97 Commission vs. Spain
C–190/98 Volker Graf vs. Filzmoser Maschinenbau
C–285/98 Kreil
C–352/98P Bergadem et al. vs. Commission
C–377/98 Netherlands vs. Commission and Parliament
C–466, 467, 468, 469, 471, 472, 475 and 476/98 'Open Skies'
C–122/99P and C–125/99P D. and Sweden vs. Council
T-342/99 Airtours

C–503/99 Commission vs. Belgium
C–11/00 Commission vs. ECB
C–50/00 Unión de Pequeños Agricultores
C–453/00 Kühne and Heitz
C–280/00 Altmark
C–206/01 Arsenal Football Club vs. Matthew Reed
T-5/02 Tetra Laval Sidel
C–25-02 Rinke
C–304/02 Commission vs. France, 'French Fisheries II'
C–105/03 Criminal Proceedings against Maria Pupino
T-351/03 Schneider Legrand
C–540/03 Parliament vs. Council of the European Union
T-16/04 Arcelor case
C–27/04 Commission vs. Council
C–144/04 Mangold
C–277/04 Lindorfer
C–317 and 318/04 Parliament vs. Commission
C–442/04 Spain vs. Council
C–112/05 Commission vs. Germany
C–303/05 Advocaten voor de Wereld VZW vs. Leden van de Ministerrad
C–337/05 Commission vs. Italy
C–341/05 Laval
C–402/05 and C–415/05 P Kadi and Al Barakaat International Foundation vs. Council and Commission
C–411/05 Palacios de la Villa
C–438/05 ITWF & FSU vs. Viking
C–444/05 Aikaterini Stalemaki vs. NPDD Organismos Asfaliseos Eleftheron Epangelmation
C–228/06 Soysal and Savatli
C–242/06 Sahin
C–267/06 Maruko
C–294/06 Payir and Others
C–319/06 Commission vs. Luxembourg
C–346/06 Rüffert
C–46/07 Commission vs. Greece
C–54/07 Feryn
C–92/07 Commission vs. The Netherlands
C–465/07 Elgafaji vs. Staatssecretaris van Justitie
C–58/08 Vodafone
C–14/09 Hava Genc

C–208/09 Sayn-Wittgenstein
C–399/09 Landtová
C–149/10 Chazi
C–188 and C–189/10 Melki and Aldeli
C–615/10 InsTiimi Oy
C–95/12 Commission vs. Germany ('Volkswagen')
C–370/12 Pringle
Opinion 2/13
C–62/15 Gauweiler et al. vs. Deutscher Bundestag

List of Abbreviations

AJE	Association des Juristes Européens
BVGh	Bundesverfassungsgericht
CAP	Common Agricultural Policy
CSDP	Common Security and Defence Policy
CFI	Court of First Instance
CFSP	Common Foreign and Security Policy
CJ	Court of Justice
CJEC	Court of Justice of the European Communities
CJEU	Court of Justice of the European Union
CST	Civil Service Tribunal
EAW	European Arrest Warrant
EC	European Communities
ECB	European Central Bank
ECHR	European Convention on Human Rights
ECtHR	European Court of Human Rights
ECJ	European Court of Justice
ECSC	European Coal and Steel Community
EDA	European Defence Agency
EDC	European Defence Community
EEC	European Economic Community
EFSF	European Financial Stability Facility
EMU	Economic and Monetary Union
EOC	(UK) Equal Opportunities Commission
EP	European Parliament
ERTF	European Roma and Traveller Forum
ESM	European Stability Mechanism
EU	European Union
EWL	European Women's Lobby
FCC	(German) Federal Constitutional Court
FIDE	Fédération Internationale pour le Droit Européen
GC	General Court
ICC	Italian Constitutional Court (Corte constituzionale)
ICJ	International Court of Justice
JHA	Justice and Home Affairs
LGBT	Lesbians, Gays, Bisexuals and Transgender

NEVER	Nederlandse Vereniging voor Europees Recht
NGOs	Non-Governmental Organizations
OMC	Open Method of Coordination
OMT	Outright Monetary Transactions
ONIC	Office National Interprofessionnel des Céréales
RSPB	Royal Society for the Protection of Birds
TEC	Treaty Establishing the European Community
TEU	Treaty on European Union
TFEU	Treaty on the Functioning of the European Union
TSCG	Treaty on Stability, Coordination and Governance
UEF	Union of European Federalists
WGE	Wissenschaftliche Gesellschaft für Europarecht

Acknowledgements

Writing this book was a fantastic challenge for both of us. As a legal scholar and a political scientist, respectively, we had to question our certainties, or cognitive frames – our understanding of European integration to which law and political science offer different tools. The result is a book that we hope offers a new approach, bringing together the best the two disciplines can offer.

We would not have succeeded without a number of colleagues and professionals. Steven Kennedy nudged us into the adventure, with his unbelievable skill and incredible knowledge of both worlds, and left us to finish the book with Stephen Wenham's great professionalism. Neill Nugent, Willie Paterson and two anonymous reviewers read previous versions of the manuscript and made extremely constructive, thoughtful and challenging suggestions and provided support whenever needed.

A number of colleagues read parts of the book and/or commented on aspects and controversies despite their overfull agendas, and we would like to express our gratitude for that: Christian Adam, Michael Bauer, Michael Blauberger, Gareth Davies, Stéphane Gervasoni, Thomas Gschwend, Charlotte Halpern, Miriam Hartlapp, Dorte Martinsen, Juan Mayoral, Susanne Schmidt, Iyiola Solanke, Sebastian Sternberg, Lisa Vanhala and Marlene Wind.

Our ever-so-congenial colleague and specialist in public policy Paul Stephenson read the whole book twice, questioning us on English grammar, syntax and style while providing comments and suggestions and question marks where we became too theoretical or too legal. Our book would be very difficult to read without him.

Renaud Dehousse's book on the European Count of Justice was an important model for this book, and our students of our Law & Politics Seminar at Sciences Po Grenoble are a constant source of constructive criticism. Special thanks to Fiona Schnell for valuable research assistance and research input, as well as to Alexandra Mendrek-Laske and Dimitri Pouradier Duteil for preparing the graphs.

Any remaining errors remain, of course, our own.

Chapter 1

Introduction

Courts are key actors in any democratic political and legal system. In recent decades, their one influence has increased hugely in many democratic states, with an impact on literally every aspect of daily life. Understanding how courts 'speak the law' and, in so doing, influence politics at the level of the state, is crucial for every student of political science and law. However, international courts – courts established beyond the realm of the state – have traditionally played a lesser role. Their influence varies and is dependent on the good will of states to recognize and adhere to Court decisions in global governance.

In this general dichotomy, the Court of Justice of the European Union (CJEU) (Box 1.1) is an exception. It is considered an unusually powerful actor that has furthered European integration. The CJEU has attracted considerable interest from both scholars and the public. Legal scholars and political scientists, and more recently, historians, have studied the Court as one of the main actors in the integration process. Those who saw European integration as 'integration through law' (Cappelletti, Seccombe & Weiler, 1986, 1987) originally considered the Court to be the core element driving this process. At crucial moments, the Court's case law has shaped market integration, the balance of power among EU institutions and the 'constitutional' boundaries between supranational and national competences. Whether dealing with Dutch customs rights (*Van Gend en Loos* 26/62), Italian electricity production (*Costa vs. ENEL* 6/64), French liqueur (*Cassis de Dijon* 120/78), Belgian stewardesses (*Defrenne* 43/75, 149/77) or, more recently, age discrimination (*Mangold* 144/04) and the European Stability Mechanism (ESM) (*Pringle* C-370/12), the Court's rulings have significantly influenced European integration. In recent years, the CJEU has seen its jurisdiction broadened to new policy areas such as justice and home affairs, welfare provisions, citizenship, labour law and fiscal coordination. In light of these developments,

Box 1.1 The structure and nomenclature of the Court of Justice of the European Union (CJEU)

The 'Court of Justice of the European Union' (CJEU) since 2009			**In this book referred to as:**
formerly the 'Court of Justice of the European Communities' (CJEC) and commonly referred to in the English-language academic literature as the European Court of Justice (ECJ)			'The CJEU' or 'The European Court' or 'The Court'
It actually comprises different courts			
'Court of Justice' (CJ)	'Court of First Instance' (CFI) since 1988, then 'General Court' (GC) since 2009	'Civil Service Tribunal' (CST) from 2004 to 2016	**In this book referred to as:** **'The courts'**
Since 2016			
'Court of Justice' (CJ)	'General Court' (GC)		**In this book referred to as:** **'The courts'**

The 'Court of Justice of the European Union' (CJEU) is made up of two courts: the 'Court of Justice' (CJ) and, since 1988, the 'General Court' (GC). A third court, the 'Civil Service Tribunal' (CST), was added in 2004. The Treaty of Lisbon (2009) has brought two main modifications regarding the appellation of these jurisdictions: CJEU is now used instead of 'Court of Justice of the European Communities' (CJEC), while 'General Court' has replaced the former 'Court of First Instance' (CFI). The third Court, the Civil Service Tribunal, is to be merged with the General Court as soon as 2016.

For the purposes of this book, we will use the current terms – 'CJEU' rather than 'CJEC' and 'GC' rather than 'CFI' – regardless of the period in time, whether it is before or after the Treaty of Lisbon. In the English-language academic literature, the term 'European Court of Justice' (ECJ) has been applied either to the CJEU/CJEC or to the CJ. However, we have opted for the use of the Lisbon acronym 'CJEU' and therefore will abstain from using ECJ.

For reasons of style and fluidity of the text, we will sometimes mention the 'Court' or the 'European Court' as synonyms of the CJEU, and use the 'courts' when referring to the different jurisdictions making up the CJEU (CJ, GC and CST).

the Court is considered instrumental in building up 'Eurolegalism' (Kelemen, 2011) and developing an adversarial rights-based legal system similar to the United States.

While scholars have sought to evaluate judicial activism at the European Union (EU) level (Schmidt, 2012; de Witte, Muir & Dawson, 2013), some have taken a more critical perspective to expose the pro-integration agenda of the Court (Adam et al., 2013; Beck, 2012; Conway, 2014) and to open, at the EU level, the debate on a 'government of judges'.

The judicial activism of the Court or 'judicialization' of the European political system is not confined to the European realm. Generally it refers to a process through which judges and judicial institutions act as policy-makers, thereby complementing, substituting or competing with political actors. At the European level, this trend may have its origins in the Court itself but may equally be explained by a general trend of judicialization at both the domestic and the international level (Bulmer, 1997; Joerges & Neyer, 1997a; Stone Sweet, 2004; Alter, 2014). Arguably, the significance of the CJEU's impact on its legal and political environment rivals that of the world's most powerful national supreme courts or national constitutional courts (Stone Sweet, 2012).

In recent years, however, the Court has not always been a central actor of European integration. While 'integration through law' remains a powerful narrative in the academic field of European studies, the Court's decisions have not always remained unchallenged.

This view of the Court as being less central to European integration is based on two developments in the scholarship. On the one hand, research findings based on various analytical approaches – from rational choice to post-positivist – suggest that 'integration through law' since the beginning of European integration has been a far less straightforward process than we have otherwise been led to believe. Scholars assert that the Court has been constrained by political, administrative and constitutional counteractions since its establishment in 1952 (Vauchez, 2010; Nowak, 2010; G. Davies, 2012; Rasmussen, 2013; Carrubba & Gabel, 2014; Martinsen, 2015a; Larsson & Naurin, 2016; Larsson et al., 2016).

On the other hand, scholars have identified a number of developments in the integration process from the early 1990s, including the Maastricht Treaty (Treaty on European Union), that explain why the Court's role has come into question.

First, the extension of the CJEU's legal competences to new policy areas has led to increasing political sensitivity, and as a result, scholars have questioned whether the member states and European institutions continue to comply with the Court's rulings. The Court has recently ruled on issues linked to redistributive policies such as health and social policy, but also sensitive regulatory policies such as civil rights and defence procurement. Member states such as Germany and the Czech Republic have been critical of the Court's interventionism in these fields.

Second, since the Maastricht Treaty, new areas of legal competence have been established where the Court previously has had few powers. This is the case for both the Common Foreign and Security Policy (CFSP) and those policy areas covered by the so-called 'new modes of governance' (Dawson, 2011), including parts of social policy, macro-economic policy coordination and education policy. Contrary to directives and regulations, which are compulsory for member states at the domestic level, these new modes of governance are based on policy instruments such as recommendations, peer review, information exchange and structured cooperation, without the provision to control implementation through the Court and its potential sanctions. The more these new modes of governance develop, the more the CJEU is left aside.

Third, for those who see recent developments in the European Union as a new form of intergovernmentalism (Bickerton, Hodson & Puetter, 2015), with deliberation and consensus among member states becoming the guiding norm of day-to-day decision-making at all levels – and hence excluding both the European Commission and the Parliament – the CJEU is now subject to greater stress (Granger, 2015).

Finally, some authors have argued that the CJEU has exercised self-restraint since the early 1990s (Dehousse, 1998; Keeling, 1998; Alter, 2012). Activist rulings have become less frequent, and the Court's case law seems to have become more cautious (Alter, 1996; Dehousse, 1998, p. 148; Keeleng, 1998; Saurugger & Terpan, 2015) in a legal context where supranational institutions face increasing resistance and scepticism from the member states and their citizens. The Court is now less inclined to provide bold interpretations of the treaties and instead sticks to the letter of the texts rather than acting as a 'policy-maker'.

In other words, both academic research and political and legal developments since the 1990s give reason to view the Court as taking a more constrained role. This is a trend that seems, paradoxically, to contradict the development of other international tribunals, such as the International Criminal Court and the Dispute Settlement Body, and Case-Specific Panels of the World Trade Organization, whose role and decisions have become more salient, that is to say more present in the public debate.

In light of these features of the Court, and its role in European integration, the aim of this book is twofold. Its first objective is to explain the establishment, workings and impact of the CJEU as a central institution in the European political system. Its establishment by the founding treaties of the 1950s, its enormous impact during the 1960s and its changing role after the Maastricht Treaty require in-depth analysis. A second objective is to analyse the role of the Court as an embedded actor through the study of the dynamic relationship between legal and political integration, or what Weiler (1986) termed the 'dual character of supranationalism'. While the study of formal rules and norms at the EU level in the post-war period was largely the preserve of legal scholars, during the 1980s and 1990s political scientists began to investigate various aspects of legal regulation. As the co-authors of this book – a legal scholar and a political scientist – we aim to transcend the ever visible, albeit diminished, divide between law and politics (Shaw & More, 1995; Stone Sweet & Sandholtz, 1997; Armstrong & Shaw, 1998; Alter, 2010; Stone Sweet, 2012).

An analysis of the Court in its political and legal context will help us to understand the developments that have taken place in

EU law and the way in which they have influenced the domestic level. Studies on the Court must not focus solely on the impact of the Court's case law on national law (as legal scholars mostly do), nor on the Court's positions with regard to European institutions, member states and non-state actors (as political scientists are prone to do). On the contrary, we need conceptual lenses that allow us to understand, on the one hand, how the Court's actions are embedded in the legal framework of EU law and, on the other, how the Court uses the law to position itself with regard to other actors.

The Court's rulings are based on a legal interpretation of the case – the doctrine that constrains the judges' ability to act – but there are also strategic decisions with regard to the external political, social and economic environment, to which the Court must respond. Hence the Court is not simply a political activist, nor is it an 'automaton agent of formalistic application' (Everson & Eisner, 2007, p. 44).

In this book, beyond the history of the Court and its internal workings, we analyse the construction of the Court's legal doctrine through the study of landmark rulings. We consider how these rulings are embedded in the Court's relationship with other actors – European institutions, member states and interest groups. The CJEU gives the impression of being a unitary actor since the judges' individual positions are not known, contrary to the US Supreme Court. It is, however, also an institution, and one that socializes law professionals. Through this socialization process it creates a specific means of making law (Scheingold, 2004, p. 153; Bobek, 2013). In its rulings we can see the doctrine and understanding of the Court's members, judges and advocates-general, supported by *referendaires* (judicial assistants), as well as the Court's positioning with regard to other actors.

This approach to the Court is similar to strategic or actor-centred constructivist approaches in political science and comparative political economy (McNamara, 1998; Jabko, 2006; Blyth, 2002; Saurugger, 2013). Actors are seen to be embedded in a specific 'logic of appropriateness' – in our case the legal framework – whereby a common understanding of a problem or idea emerges; this understanding can in turn be used strategically by the same actors to reach particular political objectives. Understanding the Court's internal structure and the Court's interaction with its environment will enable readers of this book to analyse how both legal frames *and* strategic actions of the Court define its own political role in the EU's wider political system. Combining law and politics, and considering the changing role of the Court in a wider institutional context, helps to better analyse the CJEU and the 'politics of law'.

The Court has not evolved in a political vacuum. Its contribution to the integration process has been influenced by sociological, political, institutional and economic factors that have varied over time. This mix of factors needs to be considered when examining the Court's place and influence in the European politics of law. We hope this book will help readers understand the Court's functions and institutional development. Furthermore, analysing the politics of law allows us to grasp the transformation of the EU political system as a whole. The book is structured in line with these two objectives, explaining the Court's place in the European political system, while linking legal and political approaches to analysing its evolution and function.

The second chapter examines the role of the Court in the history of European integration, and contextualizes the Court in the broader context of the workings of the European Union. The CJEU is first and foremost an institution and, as such, is engaged in interpreting and shaping perceptions of the law. The aim of this chapter is to chart both its establishment and its evolving role in the history of European integration.

The third chapter presents the members and organization of the Court, which have evolved considerably since its creation. We concentrate on the three courts that made up the CJEU until 2016. While the Court of Justice of the European Communities gained its jurisdiction in the 1950s, its increasing caseload led to the establishment of two other courts: the General Court – formerly called the Court of First Instance (created in 1988) – and the Civil Service Tribunal (created in 2004 and merged with the General Court in 2016). This chapter explains the structure of the three courts and the way in which their members – judges and advocates-general – are appointed. Complementing this institutional dimension, the chapter offers a sociological perspective, focusing on the social characteristics of the judges and how they influence the Court's decision.

As underlined above, the Court is embedded in a larger political system. The Court's duty, as defined in the treaties, is to ensure that EU law is interpreted and applied correctly by the institutions and member states. Chapter 4 examines how the Court reviews the legality of acts adopted by the EU institutions, how it ensures that member states comply with obligations under the treaties and how it interprets EU law at the request of national courts and tribunals. Two different types of review are analysed – those concerning the EU institutions and those concerning the member states. It also introduces comparative elements in order to distinguish the Court's role and its rulings from those of other national and international courts, including the European Court of Human Rights (ECtHR).

The fifth chapter looks at the context in which the judiciary exerts influence and in particular its relations with national courts. We show that while in general the legal transformation of Europe has been backed up by national high courts, some have been anxious to protect national law and reluctant to accept key doctrines such as *primacy* or *direct effect* (Davies, 2012). This resistance has considerably decreased over time, but an important remaining exception is primacy over national constitutions, which is still a controversial issue.

Discussing the politics of law in the EU, without considering how non-state actors such as interest groups, non-governmental organizations (NGOs) and firms interact with the Court, would result in an incomplete picture of the Court's role in the EU political system. Chapter 6 explains how the Court has achieved greater impact due to the involvement of other private and public actors, which have used the CJEU as a means to advance their own position, creating a 'virtuous circle' that has in turn reinforced the integration process.

Chapter 7 looks at the influence of the Court's legal doctrines on integration. It shows how through its audacious rulings the Court has helped the EU transform into a polity and how its active jurisprudence has helped transform the treaties into a sort of *de facto* European constitution (Stein, 1981). It also examines the role the CJEU has played in helping to establish the institutional setting of the EU, shaping the balance of power between the Commission, Parliament and Council, and its role in strengthening the protection of human rights.

While Chapter 7 focuses on judicial activism at the constitutional (treaty) level, Chapter 8 looks at the legislative aspect of the Court's activism. It argues that the Court has not limited itself to a few constitutional principles, but competed with the EU co-legislators – Council and Parliament – in many fields of European integration. It looks at the areas of policy in which the rulings of the Court have had the most impact and asks whether the impact of the European Court can be described as one of law-making

(Alter & Helfer, 2010) and whether the Court, by making law, is transforming itself into a policy-maker.

The aim of Chapter 9 is to make sense of, and embrace, a framework for analysing these empirical developments. It examines how the key theoretical accounts of European integration have understood the role of the Court before arguing that only a combination of legal and political science approaches, that pay due attention also to historical and sociological factors, can allow us to understand the changes in the status of European law within the EU political system.

Overall, this book aims to equip the reader with the tools necessary to understand the development, functioning and limitations of the CJEU's influence in the European political system. These tools are crucial for grasping the complexity of the supranational and intergovernmental dimensions of the EU as a political and legal system today. We hope to have made European legal integration and the Court's role in this process comprehensible and useful for students, teachers and researchers alike.

Chapter 2

The Court in the History of the European Union

To understand the role and function of the Court of Justice of the European Union (CJEU) in the EU's legal and political institutional framework, and the debates surrounding its significance and scope for independent action, we need to consider it as an institution evolving from its origins through almost seven decades of European integration. This chapter tells the story of the Court, of the judges and advocates-general working in it and of its landmark rulings.

The Court was created in 1952 by the ECSC Treaty (Treaty of Paris) in order to control the High Authority of the European Coal and Steel Community (ECSC) and protect the sovereignty of the member states. After a little more than a decade, two new treaties, adopted in 1957 in Rome – the EEC Treaty and the Euratom Treaty – began to transform it into a supranational jurisdiction, independent of the member states. Its inherent authority has strengthened over time, thanks to the Court's own rulings, which have helped bolster its institutional legitimacy over time. Originally, the Court was partially contested at the national level by constitutional and other high courts. However, the combined efforts of the lowest-level national courts, lawyers' networks utilizing European law and the incremental acceptance of European law by administrative actors enabled the Court to exert influence (Alter, 1996, 2009).

Since the early 1990s some scholars have argued that the Court has limited its own influence in EU law and policy-making (Alter, 1996; Dehousse, 1998, p. 148; Keeleng, 1998; Saurugger & Terpan, 2015). Indeed, the Court does not seem to have advanced European integration as markedly as it did in the 1960s and 1970s. Different factors may account for this: the increase in intergovernmental rule-making in the EU, the growing use of soft law instruments in the EU realm and increased media attention and public scrutiny, all of which have put pressure on the Court. The Court has not fully retreated from activism however. Its caseload is ever increasing, even if there are doubts over the impact of its rulings since the 1990s (S. Obermaier, 2008). The aim of this chapter is to situate the debate on the Court's influence and to provide the reader with the tools to better understand the more in-depth discussions developed in later chapters.

Covering the different phases of the Court's history, the chapter is divided into three sections. The first focuses on the initial years of activism when the Court was searching to determine its basic role. In the second section, we discuss what the Court achieved in its heyday of the 1960s and 1970s, before a period of rather slow European integration, known as the years of 'Eurosclerosis'. The third and final section debates whether the Court has retreated from activism since the early 1990s.

The Court's incremental search for a role (1952–58)

The Court was created in 1952 as one of the institutions of the ECSC to ensure that 'in the interpretation and application of this Treaty and of rules laid down for the interpretation thereof, the law is observed'. Its first role was to protect the member states and firms by ensuring that the supranational High Authority – merged with the EEC Commission by way of the Brussels Treaty of 8 April 1965 – did not exceed its competences. In its first years, prior to the Treaty of Rome, the Court's aim was not yet to control member state compliance with Community law.

The Court and the Treaty of Paris

The Court between federalism and unionism

To understand the Court's role in these early years it is useful to take a step back to the interwar (1918–39) and immediate post-Second World War years (1945–51). At that time, a number of federalist movements, such as the Union of European Federalists (UEF) created in 1946 and the European Parliamentary Union founded in 1947 on the initiative of Count Coudenhove-Kalergi, had emerged. Legal scholars became involved in these movements, which gave rise to several proposals for institutional schemes within a new political system where a European Court of Justice would play a central role (Guieu, 2012, p. 334).

The Schuman Declaration of 9 May 1950, inspired and for a large part drafted by Jean Monnet, only contained proposals for a weak, ad hoc appeal system for the decisions made by the central executive institution of the ECSC, the High Authority (Tamm, 2013). Convinced that the High Authority was key to the project's success, the French authors of the Schuman Plan placed it at the very centre of the initiative. According to the plan, the High Authority would be comprised of independent members, representing European, not national, interests. The Council of Minister's decision-making procedures, representing the member states' interests, were to be based on majority voting – later 'qualified majority voting' (QMV). Its decisions would be binding upon the member states. With regard to judicial control, the plan merely stated that 'appropriate measures would be provided for means of appeal against decisions of the Authority'.

On the basis of this plan, Germany, Italy and the Benelux countries (Belgium, the Netherlands and Luxembourg) accepted the French invitation to negotiate an intergovernmental agreement and develop an organization to collectively manage member countries' coal and steel production. While the Schuman Declaration was very cautious with regard to the institutional system, and in particular the establishment of a judicial organ, the German delegation headed by the German law professor and high-level civil servant, Walter Hallstein (he would become the first European Commission President in 1958), and his legal advisor, Carl F. Ophüls, were in favour of a permanent Court of Justice (Rasmussen, 2010, 2012; Boerger-de Smet, 2012). Except for Jean Monnet's legal advisor, Paul Reuter, none of the federalist-minded lawyers of the interwar and war period played a direct role in taking those first steps of integration. Reuter had already been at the heart of the Schuman proposal and now led a committee tasked to consider institutional questions linked with the creation of the ECSC. Its memorandum of August 1950 referred to a permanent Court of Justice balancing the High Authority as a strong executive body. The German and Benelux governments particularly supported the idea, which introduced legal certainty to the ECSC. Thus, the right to bring an action against the High Authority was seen as an important legal guarantee against any arbitrary decision-making, and subsequently, a decisive part of the Treaty of Paris (Tamm, 2013).

We can identify three positions taken during negotiations leading to the establishment of a permanent court. First, the Benelux delegation argued in favour of a court that could determine questions of legality (conformity with the law) and discretion (the power of a judge to make decisions based on her opinion within general legal guidelines). However, Benelux countries advocated that only member states, not individuals, should have access to it. Second, the Germans wanted a constitutional court that was accessible to private firms, with the jurisdiction to hear cases relating to conflicts between the Community's organs, and with the monopoly on legal interpretations of the treaty. Walter Hallstein, the president of the first European Commission, argued that the emerging institutions should be seen as the first step towards a federal organization, structured according to the classical separation of powers doctrine (Boerger-de Smet, 2012). Finally, the French delegation, in an attempt to find a compromise, favoured a court with the right to determine the legality of national decisions. However, the idea that private litigants might be able to sue the European Commission in the court was an idea too far.

In autumn 1950 Monnet replaced his legal advisor with Maurice Lagrange, whose ideas for a European court were closer to his own than those of Reuter. Lagrange came to play a central role in the way the Court was constructed on the institutional model of the French *Conseil d'État*. The French delegation was particularly keen to avoid the establishment of a federalist *gouvernement des juges* (government of judges), which could potentially overrule the major decisions of the High Authority: the Court should not jeopardize the success of the High Authority as the main executive body. The French system also provided a model for the office of advocate-general as an independent legal advisor to the judges of the Court. According to historians working on the Court (Boerger-de Smet, 2012; Tamm, 2013), the decision to create such a central legal position within the Court proved of the utmost importance when it came to 'integration through law', based on the judgements of the Court. The opinions of the advocates-general proved useful as guidelines helping the Court to rule on a case and as valuable information concerning specific legal questions raised by national courts.

Another crucial question was whether the potentially dissenting opinions of the judges should be published (Tamm, 2013). Some in favour of doing so argued that legal theory could be developed more openly. Yet others felt that both the authority of the Court and the independence of its judges would be better protected if dissenting opinions remained secret. The member states finally agreed that opinions of advocates-general should be published, but not the individual, dissenting opinions of the judges.

The provisions of the Treaty of Paris concerning the Court of Justice were finally based on a compromise between the French model, German wishes for a constitutional court and the position of the Benelux countries that only the member states should be able to call upon the Court, and that access by firms should remain very limited.

The role of the first Court

The Court got underway in December 1952. While the European Commission was based in Brussels, the member states decided to locate the Court in Luxembourg, in order to share out the location of the main institutions among countries.

The aim of the Treaty establishing the ECSC, as stated in article 2, was to contribute through the common market for coal and steel to economic expansion, the growth of employment and a higher standard of living. The institutions had to ensure a steady supply of goods to the common market by providing equal access to the sources of production, low prices and improved working conditions, and all this accompanied by growth in international trade and modernization of production. The Court would ensure that in the application and implementation of the treaties the law would be observed.

The four official languages – French, Italian, German and Dutch – were considered to be equal. However, from the very beginning French was, and still is, the internal working language of the Court. Two arguments can explain the use of French. First, having one language allows the Court to avoid using interpreters during deliberations, and to preserve secrecy. Secondly, no English-speaking country was a member state of the Community, at a time when French was the language of diplomacy (Robertson, 2015, p. 35; see also Chapter 3).

The Court of Justice consisted of seven judges each nominated for six years by common agreement among the governments of the member states. On 1 December 1952 the member states decided on the composition of the first Court. The president was Italian, while the Netherlands appointed two judges in order to make an uneven number of judges, and both France and Germany appointed one advocate-general each. In this way parity was achieved between the two biggest member states. It is important to note, however, that this way of working was not stipulated in the treaty, but was conceived of as an unwritten but fundamental principle.

Far from all being established lawyers or professors of law, the first judges of the Court had various backgrounds (Box 2.1). This situation changed slowly: today, the majority of judges have a legal background in EU and internal law (Chapter 3).

First cases

The cases to be heard by the Court were initially of a technical nature, and did not attract that much attention from the outside world. The first case brought before the Court was by France in April 1953. The French government was concerned by the decision of the High Authority to grant concessions to German steel

Box 2.1 The composition of the first Court

The Court's first president from 1952 to 1958, **Massimo Pilotti** (1879–1962), was president of the Italian Court of Cassation. The Dutch members were **Petrus Serrarens** (1888–1963), a former Secretary General of the World Confederation of Labour, and **Adrianus van Kleffens** (1899–1973), a senior civil servant and judge of the ECSC Court in 1952–1958. The German **Otto Riese** (1894–1977) had been professor at the University of Lausanne and vice president of the German Constitutional Court. He continued as a judge until 1963. **Louis Delvaux** (1895–1976) was a Belgian lawyer, journalist and politician, who served as a judge until 1967. The Frenchman **Jacques Rueff** (1896–1978) was a professor of economics and member of the French Academy. He continued as a judge until 1962. **Charles Léon Hammes** (1898–1967) from Luxembourg was a judge and professor in Brussels. He continued as judge of the Court till 1967, in the period between 1964 and 1967 acting as President of the Court. The first advocates-general were the French **Maurice Lagrange** and the German **Karl Roemer** (1899–1984), who were both lawyers and served in the Court from 1953 to 1973.

companies. France felt that this special treatment enabled German companies to sell their steel (after the end of the steel boom caused by the Korean War in 1952–53) at prices that breached existing European law. It was not until December 1954 that a Court ruling partially annulled the High Authority's decision (*French Republic vs. High Authority of the ECSC* 1/54).

It is important to highlight that in its first ruling, the Court stated that its decisions should not be based on individual articles alone. It argued that the articles themselves did not 'provide any decisive argument in one way or another [...] Therefore it is necessary to go further; the question in this dispute must be examined in relation to the Treaty in its entirety' (*French Republic vs. High Authority of the ECSC*, Opinion of the advocate-general, 1/54). Furthermore, the Court began to use terms such as the 'Charter of the Community' and 'constitutionality' (Rasmussen, 2008, 2010; *Fédéchar vs. High Authority of the ECSC* 8/55, cited in Tamm, 2013), which would take on particular significance in later years.

The Treaty of Rome and the Court

The Court and the relaunch of European integration

The treaty establishing a European Defence Community (EDC) was rejected by the French Assembly in August 1954. It appeared that enthusiasm for supranationalism had already disappeared, at least in France where Gaullists and communists defended sovereignty. By May 1955, however, the Benelux countries had taken the initiative to breathe new life into what was then not a particularly successful common project. At the Messina Conference in June 1955 the member states' foreign ministers agreed to call for a new intergovernmental conference, but remained hesitant to give it any particular institutional direction. The French government, wary of upsetting its national parliament and eager to avoid a political 'debacle' in the wake of the rejection of the EDC, sought to reduce the role of the supranational institutions. In particular, it was concerned about the degree of interventionism of the High Authority and the Court of Justice.

In May 1956 the six national ministers of Foreign Affairs adopted the Spaak Report (named after the Belgian foreign minister Paul Henri Spaak, who chaired the working groups). The report set out the general provisions for the establishment of a Common Market and proposed an institutional structure based on the Council of

Ministers, a Commission (instead of the High Authority), an Assembly and a Court. The report already signalled a shift in power from the Commission towards the Council of Ministers, which would soon become the main decision-making body, while the Commission was tasked with submitting proposals to the Council.

However, negotiations stalled over the legal provisions of the Spaak Report. A compromise was eventually found in November 1956 between the French Prime Minister Guy Mollet and the German Chancellor Konrad Adenauer, enabling negotiations to continue. France agreed to discuss institutional options beyond the mere idea of a non-permanent court of arbitration staffed by technical experts (Boerger-de Smet, 2012, p. 349), finally accepting the creation of a permanent judicial body (the Court), as well as an Assembly (later Parliament). The two institutions were to be shared with the ECSC to avoid the proliferation of institutions.

The member states agreed to create two Communities: the European Atomic Energy Community (Euratom) and the European Economic Community (EEC). A group of legal experts, also known as *Groupe de rédaction*, was established at the end of 1956 in order to draft the legal and institutional provisions of the treaties establishing these organizations. Both treaties, the Euratom Treaty and the EEC Treaty, were adopted in Rome on 25 March 1957. Although some of the members of the *Groupe* championed supranationalism (in particular the German, Ernst Wohlfahrt; Italian, Nicola Catalano; Luxembourger, Pierre Pescatore; and French member, Michel Gaudet), others such as the Germans (Joseph Mühlenhöfer and Hubert Ehring) and Dutch (William Riphagen) were more hesitant. In the final report, however, constitutional elements were introduced that would prove crucial for the future development of EU law (Rasmussen, 2010; Boerger-de Smet, 2012, p. 354). They were subsequently introduced in the Treaties of Rome, in particular the treaty establishing the EEC.

Powers deriving from the Treaty of Rome (EEC Treaty)

Certain legal components of the treaty paved the way for the Court's activism, including four key specific provisions. These were not consensual decisions, but harshly negotiated compromises. They are a clue in understanding the kind of resistance later encountered, and the opportunities for the Court to further legal integration from the 1960s onwards, which are analysed throughout this book.

The first provision refers to the preliminary ruling mechanism (art. 177 EEC, now art. 267 TFEU), which was introduced to remedy one of the crucial problems of European integration, the uniform implementation of Community law across the member states. This mechanism allows national courts, even sometimes obliges them, depending on the situation, to submit preliminary questions to the Court when experiencing difficulty interpreting European law. Article 41 ECSC provided a similar provision of a more limited scope insofar as it gave the Court exclusive jurisdiction to give preliminary rulings only on the validity of Community acts. It left the interpretation of the treaty to national judiciaries. However, the fear of conflicting interpretations led the committee in charge of discussing legal issues during the negotiation of the treaties to transform the procedure. The committee rejected the idea of transforming the Court into a constitutional body with exclusive jurisdiction over Community law (Boerger-de Smet, 2012, p. 352), but agreed that national courts, when faced with questions of how to interpret Community law, could or had to refer to the European Court through the preliminary procedure.

The second provision granted the Court the power to review the legality of Community acts (art. 173 EEC, now art. 263 TFEU). Contrary to article 33 of the ECSC Treaty, both the acts adopted by the Commission (High Authority in the ECSC) and those adopted by the Council could be brought before the Court.

Thirdly, the new treaty included an infringement procedure to ensure member states' compliance with Community law. The Court's role was substantially strengthened with an extension of competences beyond those in the ECSC Treaty. In the ECSC, control of the member states was left to the High Authority; the Court did not review legal breaches but merely controlled the way the High Authority fulfilled its task at the request of the member states. In the legal framework of the EEC, the Commission (or a member state) could request the Court to review member states' compliance with the treaty. In the event of such a request, a two-step procedure was introduced that enabled the Commission to deliver a reasoned opinion to a member state failing to fulfil its treaty obligation. If the state refused to comply, the Commission could approach the Court.

However, the EEC's judicial system was weaker than the ECSC's on one specific point: whether or not the High Authority could sanction the member states. Under the ECSC Treaty, the High Authority with the consent of the Council could decide by a two-thirds majority vote to stop financing any member state that breached Community law. Under the EEC Treaty (art. 169, 170 and 171 EEC, now art. 258, 259 and 260 TFEU), these competences were not transferred to the Court, which was not allowed to levy fines, though this would eventually change with the Maastricht Treaty.

From Rome to Maastricht: activism at the Court (1958–93)

Landmark rulings in the 1960s: the building of a legal order

The significance of early Court case law comes down to two main principles: *direct effect* and *primacy*. Direct effect enables individuals to immediately invoke a European provision before a national court. Primacy means that European law has precedence over national law. Both principles are based on landmark rulings that can be explained by three factors: the activism of the Court's judges; the conviction of national courts that European law would help them to gain a larger influence; and the willingness of private litigants and their advocates to use European law in order to defend their rights. The Court and its rulings, of course, did not go unchallenged by the member states and their highest jurisdictions, as we will see more specifically in Chapter 5.

The 1960s and 1970s were an exciting period for the Court, during which it increased its powers in the Community institutional system. The two landmark rulings that are discussed below were not the only ones given by the Court in the 1960s. Yet while the Court was also active in the field of fundamental rights (*Stauder* 29/69), the acts of the institutions (*Mandelli* 3/67; *Plaumann vs. Commission* 25/62) and the free movement of goods (*Commission vs. Italy* 'Italian statistical data' 24/68; *Diamantarbeiders* 2 and 3/69), it was the *van Gend en Loos* and *Costa vs. ENEL* rulings that were the most fundamental in laying the path of future European integration and the construction of a European legal order.

Van Gend en Loos and the direct effect of Community law

Classic international law principally governs inter-state relations. International agreements are binding upon the states that ratify them, but only directly impact citizens in their daily lives when ratified through an act of parliament. The European Community's doctrine of direct effect goes much further. It was made possible via a number of interrelated Court rulings, the first and most famous of which was *van Gend en Loos* (26/62).

In this ruling, issued in 1963, the Court allowed a private Dutch importer to invoke the common market provisions of the EEC Treaty directly, to counter the Dutch government's attempt to impose customs duties on specified imports. The issue itself was rather unspectacular: a Dutch transport firm brought a complaint against Dutch customs for increasing the duty on a product imported from Germany, although article 12 of the EEC Treaty prohibited the increase of duties. The Dutch Court made a preliminary reference to the Court, asking whether the provision had 'direct application' in the national legal order.

While seemingly unexciting in itself, the *van Gend en Loos* ruling allowed for the institutionalization of a number of mechanisms put in place by the Treaty of Rome. The Court declared that in order to answer the question brought to it by a national court, it had to first examine 'the spirit, the general scheme and the wording' of the treaty, which allowed for an expansive interpretation of Community law (see Chapter 7 for further details on the interpretative methods used in this case).

The Court argued that treaty provisions might have immediate and direct effect within the different national legal orders, while the Treaty of Rome only explicitly provided for the direct effect of regulations (one of several specific types of secondary legislation adopted by EU institutions on the basis of the treaty). Furthermore, in a fundamental phrase, the Court stated that:

> the Community constitutes a new legal order of international law for the benefit of which the states have limited their sovereign rights, albeit within limited fields, and the subjects of which comprise not only the member states but also their nationals. Independently of the legislation of the Member States, Community law therefore not only imposes obligations on individuals but is also intended to confer upon them rights which become part of their legal heritage. (*Van Gend en Loos* 26/62)

The Court's later rulings (*Lütticke* 57/65, *Reyners* 2/74, *Van Duyn* 41/74, as well as *Ratti* 148/78 and *Becker* 8/81) reinforced this argument (see Chapter 5) and preserved the integration momentum, despite the inability of the European institutions to achieve the degree of legislative harmonization intended by the treaty.

While based on a legal logic formulated by the treaty, the *Van Gend en Loos* ruling was also made possible by the Court's judges. Two new judges entered the Court in 1962, the Frenchman Robert Lecourt and the Italian Alberto Trabucchi, both of whom were in favour of the Court interpreting the treaty system as a whole. Lecourt and Trabucchi were followed by the Italian Rino Rossi and the Belgian Louis Delvaux, and formed a narrow majority (Tamm, 2013). In addition, the legal service of the Commission headed by the French lawyer Michel Gaudet was strongly in favour of the idea of interpreting the relevant provisions at the domestic level in a uniform way, and had actively promoted it from the mid-1950s. Moreover, Court members tried to convince national judges that it was desirable to use the preliminary reference procedure. Burley and Mattli (1993, pp. 62–3) underline this 'narrative of empowerment' in the following way: 'Through seminars, dinners, regular invitations to Luxembourg, and visits around the Community, the EC judges put a human face on the institutional links they sought to build.' They used congresses of Europeanized lawyers as a venue to disseminate the idea and use of European law. Thus the 1963 Congress of the FIDE (International Federation for European Law) provided an opportunity to make the case in public to European-minded lawyers on the landmark nature of the *Van Gend en Loos* ruling. Three of the nine Court judges and five of the nine *referendaires* attended the meeting. The final resolution of the Congress agreed on the importance of ensuring that all member states recognized the principle of direct effect (Alter, 2009; Vauchez, 2014). In *Van Gend en Loos*, as well as in other cases, such as the 1978 *Simmenthal* ruling (106/77), the Court appealed to national courts to protect individual rights and uphold Community law in respect of the Court.

Costa vs. ENEL and the primacy of European law

The *Van Gend en Loos* ruling was followed in 1964 by the *Costa vs. ENEL* case (6/64), which bolstered the 'new legal order', effectively establishing its superiority over national legal orders (the primacy principle). The CJEU stated that:

> the law stemming from the Treaty, an independent source of law, could not, because of its special and original nature, be overridden by domestic legal provisions, however framed,

> without being deprived of its character as community law and without the legal basis of the community itself being called into question.

As important as direct effect might seem, it was ultimately useless if national law could trump European law. In the *Costa vs. ENEL* case, the Court ruled that the member states had definitively transferred their sovereign rights to the Community and that its law could not be overruled by domestic law. No article in the Treaty of Rome had actually addressed this issue. Article 5 simply stated that member states shall take 'all appropriate measures, whether general or particular, to ensure fulfilment of the obligations arising out of this Treaty'.

Thus, the relationship between national law and European law was actually rather vague and needed interpreting. This is precisely what the Court did with its *Costa vs. ENEL* ruling after a question was referred to the Court by a lower Italian court in Milan. A shareholder in a nationalized electricity company challenged the 1962 Italian nationalization law on the grounds that it broke several provisions of the Treaty of Rome. The Italian government felt the Italian judge should simply apply the new national law adopted domestically after 1958, and hence, after the entry into force of the Treaty of Rome. Although working at a lower-level jurisdiction, the judge chose to refer the problem to the European Court. As was the case with *Van Gend en Loos,* the Court interpreted the law in the spirit of the treaty, arguing that: 'By contrast with ordinary international treaties, the EEC Treaty has created its own legal system which, on the entry into force of the Treaty, became an integral part of the legal systems of the member states and which the courts are bound to apply.' According to the Court, it was crucial to apply Community law uniformly over the whole EEC territory: 'The executive force of Community law cannot vary from one state to another in deference to subsequent domestic laws without jeopardising the attainment of the objectives of the Treaty.' Relying on a bold definition of sovereignty as the sum of legal competences, some of which had been transferred to the European Community, the Court ruled that national sovereignty was thus permanently limited: 'The transfer by the States from their domestic legal system to the Community legal system of the rights and obligations arising under the Treaty carries with it a permanent limitation of their sovereign rights, against which a subsequent unilateral act incompatible with the concept of the Community cannot prevail.'

A few years later, in *Internationale Handelsgesellschaft* (11/70) and *Simmenthal* (106/77), the Court was even more explicit: any provision of a national legal system and any legislative, administrative or judicial practice which might impair the effectiveness of European law by withholding from the national court having jurisdiction to apply such law was incompatible with those requirements which are the very essence of European law. Thus, European law enjoyed absolute *primacy* over all national provisions.

These two landmark decisions made in the 1960s – *Van Gend en Loos* and *Costa vs. ENEL* – became part of a legal tradition the member states would find hard to ignore. It is crucial to remember that these decisions took place at a time when the European integration project was itself coming under pressure due to the debate over national 'sovereignty' that culminated with the 'empty chair' crisis in 1965–66. French president De Gaulle believed that national governments should be the motors of integration, while other member states were more supportive of the Commission's supranationalist initiatives. France fiercely opposed the Commission during the budget negotiations for the Common Agricultural Policy (CAP). While De Gaulle supported the creation of the CAP, he disagreed with the Commission's budget proposals for financing the CAP. Most of all, he could not accept that decisions, in this field as in others, could be taken by majority voting. If France was to participate in the European Community, then a right to veto had to be possible. When de Gaulle was not granted this veto right, France's representative left the Council of Ministers. This event was not resolved until the 'Luxembourg Compromise' of January 1966, which in practice granted every member state a de facto veto power in cases where its vital interests were threatened.

Van Gend en Loos and *Costa vs. Enel* were issued in 1963–64, prior to the 'empty chair' crisis, but the context was very similar. The French government had already expressed concerns over supranationalism. Thus, the first landmark rulings of the European Court were by no means neutral when it came to debates over national sovereignty.

Landmark rulings from the 1970s to the Maastricht Treaty

The 1970s are often seen as a period of 'Eurosclerosis', with supranational European institutions playing a limited role in the integration process and with member states' power increasing. One might point to the establishment of the European Council in 1974 as evidence of this mood. Nonetheless, the Commission took many initiatives during this period, the Parliament was granted budgetary powers and, as discussed below, the Court was actually very active in four areas in particular: first, fundamental rights, which was not a competence of the European Community at that time; second, the establishment of the internal market; third, fostering social policy; and fourth, the constitutionalization of the European Community.

Thus, contrary to the perception of inaction at the EU level, the 1970s and 1980s were a period when the Court succeeded in shaping European law by adopting an active stance to law-making (Table 2.1).

TABLE 2.1 *Landmark rulings, 1960s to 1980s*

Primacy of EU law	**6/64 Costa vs. ENEL** Community law takes precedence over the member states' own domestic law.
Primacy of EU law	**106/77 Simmenthal II** Duty to set aside provisions of national law, including constitutional law, which are incompatible with Community law.
Primacy of EU law	**C–213/89 Factortame** National courts have the duty to secure the full effectiveness of Community law, even where it is necessary to create a national remedy where none had previously existed.
Direct effect	**26/62 Van Gend en Loos** Treaty provisions may have an immediate and direct effect within the different national legal orders, while the Treaty of Rome only explicitly provided for the direct effect of regulations.
Direct effect	**41/74 Van Duyn** The Court extends its jurisprudence on direct effect to directives that have not been transposed (or correctly transposed) in due time.

→

Direct effect	**148/78 Ratti** Member states are precluded by their failure to implement a directive properly from refusing to recognize its binding effect in cases where it is pleaded against them, thus they cannot rely on their failure to implement the directive in time.
Fundamental rights	**11/70 Internationale Handelsgesellschaft** Fundamental rights are an integral part of the general principles of law, the observance of which the Court ensures. These general principles draw from the constitutional traditions of the member states.
Fundamental rights	**4/73 Nold** When protecting fundamental rights, the Court is bound to draw inspiration from constitutional traditions common to the member states, and it cannot therefore uphold measures that are incompatible with fundamental rights, as recognized and protected by the constitutions of those states. The Court can also draw on international human rights treaties to which member states have collaborated or are signatories.
Internal market/Free movement of persons	**41/74 Van Duyn** States could exclude a national from another state on public policy grounds based only on the personal conduct of that individual.
Internal market/Free movement of persons	**36/75 Rutili** The principle of proportionality shall be considered as a general principle of EU law when dealing with freedom of movement. The Court further defines the extent to which the notion of public order could limit a person's freedom of movement.
Internal market/Free movement of persons/Social policy	**43/75 Defrenne vs. Sabena** Article 119 of the EEC Treaty (now art. 157 TFEU), stating that 'Each member state shall ensure that the principle of equal pay for male and female workers for equal work or work of equal value is applied', has a horizontal direct effect, and therefore is enforceable not merely between individuals and the government, but also between private parties.

→

TABLE 2.1 *(Continued)*

Internal market/Free movement of goods	**8/74 Procureur du roi vs. Benoît et Gustave Dassonville** The Court states that: 'All trading rules enacted by Member States which are capable of hindering, directly or indirectly, actually or potentially, intra-Community trade are to be considered as measures having an effect equivalent to quantitative restrictions.'
Internal market/Free movement of goods	**120/78 Rewe-Zentral AG ('*Cassis de Dijon*')** A regulation applying both to imports and to domestic goods (an 'indistinctly applicable measure') that produces an effect equivalent to a quantitative import restriction is held to be an unlawful restriction on the free movement of goods. The major outcome of this case is the principle of mutual recognition: the Court holds that there is no valid reason that a product lawfully marketed in one member state should not be introduced in another member state.
Constitution	**294/83 '*Les Verts*' vs. European Parliament** This case, based on an audacious interpretation of the treaties, included the European Parliament in the constitutional framework and referred to the treaty as 'the basic constitutional charter' of the Community.
Constitution	**C – 6/90** Francovitch vs. Italy The member states are liable to compensate for damages resulting from a breach of EU law.

Protecting fundamental rights

While fundamental rights were (and continue to be) dealt with by the European Convention on Human Rights (ECHR) – implemented by the Council of Europe and controlled by the European Court of Human Rights (ECtHR), two institutions which are entirely independent of the EU's political system – the Court has issued a number of landmark rulings that introduced fundamental rights as part of the European legal order.

The historical legacy of the Second World War led the member states, and specifically Italy and Germany given their fascist past, to foster the idea that the CJEU's activities should go beyond the protection of economic rights to include fundamental rights and the principles of citizenship (Dehousse, 1998). In particular, the German Federal Constitutional Court (FCC) set about examining the compatibility of European law with the provisions of the German Basic Law laying down fundamental rights (1 BvR 248/63 and 216/67, judgement of October 1967) (see Chapters 5 and 7).

The 1970 *Internationale Handelsgesellschaft* ruling (11/70) is considered to be a partial response to the FCC's concern. The case dealt with the forfeiting of a deposit lodged in connection with the issue of export licences for maize meal. According to German law, the deposit was lost if the exportation did not take place as required. This was considered by a German firm (Internationale Handelsgesellschaft mbH) as a disproportionate violation of their right under the German constitution to conduct business.

European judges reviewed an earlier European decision and had the opportunity to rule on a possible violation of national fundamental rights. The European Court decided that it could not apply national law, but instead chose to treat national constitutional rights as an indirect source of European law:

> respect for fundamental rights forms an integral part of the general principles of law protected by the Court of Justice [...] the protection of such rights, whilst inspired by the constitutional traditions common to the member states, must be ensured within the framework of the structure and the objectives of the Community.

The *Nold* ruling (4/73) also resulted from pressure exerted by the FCC, which questioned the jurisprudence of the Court (Rasmussen, 1986, p. 397). *Nold* was decided only two weeks before the FCC's *Solange I* decision where the FCC declared that *as long as* ('solange' in German) the Community had not codified fundamental rights in a satisfactory manner, it would continue to recognize the fundamental rights of Germany as supreme and reserve the right to ensure that European law did not violate fundamental rights contained in the Basic Law (2 BvL 52/71 Internationale Handelsgesellschaft, 'Solange I', 1974).

In *Nold*, the Court underlined that it took human rights provisions included in national constitutions very seriously. The Court upheld that it:

> had already stated (that) fundamental rights form an integral part of the general principles of law, the observance of which it ensures. In safeguarding these rights, the Court is bound to draw inspiration from constitutional traditions common to the member states, and it cannot therefore uphold measures, which are incompatible with fundamental rights recognized and protected by the constitutions of those states. Similarly, international treaties for the protection of human rights on which the member states have collaborated or of which they are signatories, can supply guidelines which should be followed within the framework of Community law.

However, the FCC was not satisfied with this argument, as its famous *Solange I* decision shows (see also Chapter 5). As a consequence, during the 1970s the European Court gradually built up an autonomous system for the protection of fundamental rights. This system was based on general principles of European law, which mainly derived from the constitutional principles of the member states and the ECHR.

After *direct effect* and *primacy* of EU law had been established, the Court's next step was the 'constitutionalization of fundamental rights' (Rasmussen, 2012), which helped alter the relative position of the German Court and lowered its resistance to the primacy of European law. The FCC acknowledged that since 1974 the European Court had been developing law for the protection of fundamental rights, with declarations on rights and democracy also made by the European institutions. During this time all EU member states had acceded to the ECHR. Hence, it was no longer necessary to control the application of European secondary law in every case as long as the Community, and in particular its Court of Justice, ensured the effective protection of fundamental rights (2 BvR 197/83 Wünsche Handelsgesellschaft, 1986). This development illustrates how important judicial dialogue between the European Court and national courts has been for the development of European law.

Completing the internal market

One of the areas where the Court exercised the greatest influence in strengthening and extending EU policy competence in the

1970s and 1980s was the internal market. Its rulings allowed the European Commission to act in areas where its competence was otherwise poor. In the *Dassonville* ruling of 1974 (8/74), the Court argued that all trading rules enacted by member states that were capable of (directly or indirectly, actually or potentially) hindering intra-Community trade were to be considered as measures having an effect equivalent to quantitative restrictions. Here we see the beginning of jurisprudence aimed at removing hidden barriers to trade and fighting national protectionism (see also Chapter 8).

Cassis de Dijon in 1979 (120/78) can be considered a further means of removing trade restrictions, in line with the *Dassonville* ruling. Through the *Cassis de Dijon* case, the Court obliged member states to legally recognize goods produced in other member states. Harmonization of national legislation was not a prerequisite for the free movement of goods, but would rather be used to overcome remaining barriers created by trade restrictions, and to ensure essential standards where there was a risk of a race to the bottom (use of the lower standards that are effective in some member states).

The *Cassis* ruling concerned the establishment of the so-called principle of *mutual recognition*. The down-to-earth question in this case concerned alcohol percentages. According to German law, products sold as fruit liqueur had to contain no less than 25 per cent alcohol by volume. As *crème de cassis* (blackcurrant liqueur) only contains 15–20 per cent alcohol, the German alcohol authorities (*Bundesmonopolverwaltung für Branntwein*) did not allow the German importer Rewe to import *Cassis de Dijon* into Germany, nor to market it as a fruit liqueur. The Court held that German legislation was in breach of article 30 of the EEC Treaty (now art. 34 TFEU). More precisely, fixing a minimum alcohol content for alcoholic beverages had to be considered as a 'measure having an effect equivalent to quantitative restrictions on imports', which was prohibited by this treaty provision.

From the internal market to equal treatment and social policy

The *Defrenne* case (43/75) illustrates how the Court's attempt to establish the embryonic elements of a European social policy was made possible by the preliminary rulings system. Gabrielle Defrenne, a Belgian flight attendant for the airline Sabena, was paid less than her male colleagues who did the same work. Ms Defrenne complained that this violated her right to equal pay on grounds of gender under article 119 EEC (now art. 157 TFEU). The Court held that the principle of equal pay for equal work was binding not only upon member states but also, directly, upon private employers. In other words, an individual could rely on treaty articles to enforce her rights against another individual in the national courts. Direct and overt discrimination could be determined according to the criteria set out under article 119 on equal pay for equal work, whereas indirect and covert discrimination could be determined by referring to the more explicit implementing provisions of a Community or national law. Here we see that the direct effect of treaty provisions, stemming from the *Van Gend en Loos* ruling, could be invoked in national courts to protect individual rights.

The constitutional role of the European treaties

The *Van Gend en Loos* and *Costa vs. ENEL* rulings in the 1960s, as well as the development of the general principles of EU law, signalled the Court's *penchant* for thinking in constitutional terms. In the mid-1980s, the Court made it clear that it considered the treaties as a quasi-constitution. Two cases were groundbreaking in this respect. In the case of *'Les Verts'* (294/83) in 1986, the Treaty of Rome was referred to as 'the basic constitutional charter' of the Community. The member states accepted the ruling without any opposition, thus further contributing to an understanding of the EU as a quasi-state (Schmidt, 2006).

In the *Francovich vs. Italy* ruling (C–6/90), the CJEU established that EU member states could be liable to pay compensation to individuals that suffered a financial loss owing to a member state's failure to transpose a EU directive into national law (that is, to give force to a directive by passing appropriate measures at national level). The ruling is also known as the principle of state liability in EU law. Under the Insolvency Protection Directive 80/987 (now 2008/94/EC), EU member states were expected to enact provisions in their national law to give a minimum level of insurance for employees with unpaid wages if their employers went bankrupt. One man, Mr Francovich, who had worked in Venice for CDN Elettronica SnC, was owed 6 million lira, while another, Mr Bonifaci, and 33 of his colleagues, were together owed 253 million lira after their company, Gaia Confezioni Srl, had gone bankrupt. The directive was meant to be implemented by 1983, but five years later nobody had been paid a thing; the company's liquidators informed them that there was no money left. The men brought a claim against the

Italian state, arguing that it should pay damages to compensate for their losses on account of the failure to implement the directive. The CJEU held in its ruling that, indeed, the Italian government had breached its obligations and was liable to compensate the workers' loss resulting from the breach. The Court further held that it should be possible to claim damages for such breaches in national courts. It asserted that to establish state liability on the basis of the failure to implement a directive, claimants must prove that the directive conferred specific rights on them:

> It should be borne in mind at the outset that the EEC Treaty has created its own legal system, which is integrated into the legal systems of the Member States and which their courts are bound to apply. The subjects of that legal system are not only the Member States but also their nationals. Just as it imposes burdens on individuals, Community law is also intended to give rise to rights which become part of their legal patrimony. Those rights arise not only where they are expressly granted by the Treaty but also by virtue of obligations which the Treaty imposes in a clearly defined manner both on individuals and on the Member States and the Community institutions.

To summarize, in the 1970s and 1980s the Court established a number of landmark rulings where it not only ruled on the case but effectively also 'wrote' the law (see Chapter 7). We can distinguish three types of cases (Maduro & Azoulai, 2010, pp. xv–xvi):

- Cases that created the basis for a legal order that is federal in nature. Such cases distinguished the European legal order from both international and national legal orders. They established and guaranteed the authority of the European legal order, its incorporation in national law and its direct link to individuals (*Van Gend en Loos, Costa vs. ENEL, Internationale Handelsgesellschaft, Simmenthal, 'Les Verts', Factortame*).
- Cases that legitimized the authority of the European legal order through the progressive development of a system of values, which not only includes the protection of human rights (*Internationale Handelsgesellschaft, Nold*), but also those values specific to the legal order itself, including those related to the internal market (*Dassonville, Van Duyn, Rutili, Cassis*). Such cases also brought elements of social justice into the internal market (*Defrenne*).

- Cases where the Court defined the borders of European law: between national and EU competences and between national and EU jurisdictions (*Van Gend en Loos, Costa vs. ENEL, Van Duyn, Simmenthal, Ratti, 'Les Verts', Factortame*).

It is important to note, however, that these cases did more than just establish a legal doctrine that would be applied automatically to other cases brought before the court. As underlined in Chapter 1, we can only truly understand the Court's action as a whole if we consider three factors: the legal implications of the decision (or the *legal frame* as we have called it in Chapter 1); the actors who brought the cases before the Court; and the interaction of the Court with other European institutions, member states and national courts (strategic actions and interactions).

Domestic courts' responses to the Court's activism

The period from the 1960s to the 1980s is generally regarded as the heyday of the Court. Despite the politics of the 'empty chair' crisis and the subsequent Luxembourg Compromise, which gave member states the right to veto decisions they could not agree on – or, as some argue, precisely because of these events – the Court managed to play a crucial role in European integration by way of its legal rulings (Cappelletti, Seccombe & Weiler, 1986; Burley & Mattli, 1993). Its judges contributed to the development of a 'legal epistemic and discursive community' (Maduro & Azoulai, 2010, p. xvii; see also Chapter 3). In other words, they fostered a network of professionals with recognized expertise and competence in the domain of European law, and made an authoritative claim on policy-relevant knowledge within that domain (Haas, 1992). In so doing, they shared a cognitive/legal frame, however conflict-ridden internally, when interpreting the law.

This does not mean, however, that the Court's activism went unchallenged, as we have seen in the field of fundamental rights. Most national judges gave a warm welcome to the Court's jurisprudence. Indeed, ensuring compliance with EU law implied rewards for domestic courts. EU law increased the powers of domestic courts with respect to other domestic actors, in particular the legislature. In cases such as the UK, where courts are denied the right to review primary legislation, the courts were more ready to challenge orthodoxy and subject legislation to greater scrutiny (Dehousse, 1998).

A number of times, however, more powerful national constitutional courts and high courts questioned the European Court's rulings. The French *Conseil d'État* (the French highest administrative court) and the German FCC are specific examples in this context (Chapter 5). The *Conseil d'État* began contesting the Court in the 1960s. It refused to recognize the primacy of EU law over national law in its *Syndicat national des fabricants de semoules* ruling of 1968, later denying the principle of direct effect (*Cohn-Bendit* ruling of 1978). It took time for the *Conseil d'État* to end its inflexible position vis-à-vis the Court. In 1989, however, the *Conseil d'État*'s *Nicolo* ruling finally accepted the *primacy* principle and opened a period of dialogue with the European Court (Mangenot, 2005). It also steadily drew closer to the Court's position on the direct effect of directives, with the *Dame Perreux* ruling (1999) the final stage of this process.

In Germany the FCC opposed the Court's principle of supremacy on democratic grounds, as we have shown above, demanding limits to the erosion of national constitutional sovereignty. A fundamental pillar of post-war German identity was the integrity of its constitutional order. When the European Court started rendering constitutional rulings linked to economic rights of the European Community, the FCC showed resistance (B. Davies, 2012a, 2015; Everson, 2015). In its famous *Solange I* ruling of 1974, the German Court insisted on the fact that the European political system did not guarantee the protection of fundamental rights in the same way as the German federal system did. In *Solange II* (1986), however, the FCC relaxed its jurisdictional hold on basic rights. It held that the protection of human rights by the Court was in line with the protection enshrined in the Basic Law. Thus, 'as long as' a high level of protection was secured by the Court, the FCC would only exercise its jurisdiction on European secondary law unless there was a decrease in the level of protection ensured by the European Court.

A very similar judgement was delivered by the FCC in its *Maastricht* decision (1993), which reaffirmed the position it adopted in *Solange II* on the protection of basic rights. At the same time, however, the FCC ruled that it would 'examine whether legal acts of the European institutions and organs are within or exceed the sovereign powers transferred to them'. In other words, the FCC, not the European Court, would decide where the limits to European power lay. Furthermore, the FCC stated that any legal acts of the EU exceeding the competences outlined in the Treaty on European

Union (Maastricht Treaty), as interpreted by the German Court, would not be legally binding in Germany (Bloom, 1995).

Retreat from activism? (1992–)

The end of the 1980s saw an active Court actually increasing the number of rulings (Figures 2.1 and 2.2) and placing further pressure on the Council to establish a Court of First Instance (now General Court) in 1988 (see Chapter 3). Nonetheless, scholars are divided as to whether the Court's activities could be considered less audacious in terms of the legal implications of its rulings – an attitude defined as 'self-restraint' – or whether the Court's rulings were as groundbreaking as in earlier times.

Defining and explaining the 'retreat from activism'

Arguments in favour of judicial self-restraint lay in the number of rulings where the Court has shown a high degree of deference to member states' positions and/or produced technical decisions that did not strike legal scholars as particularly audacious in terms of pushing the interpretation of European law to its limits. From this perspective, the pre-Maastricht period was one of great activism, with the Court mostly giving interpretations that effectively 'created' the law, not just 'spoke' the law. The post-Maastricht period, on the contrary, is then one of self-restraint, with the Court in most cases giving literal interpretations of the treaties instead of showing a more creative and ambitious flair to its law-making (see Chapter 7).

It is very difficult to determine whether the Court has retreated from activism or not. To do so, one could make a longitudinal study of the Court's case law in order to see whether the proportion of 'activist' rulings has decreased over time (Saurugger & Terpan, 2015). Yet rather than a systematic analysis of its jurisprudence, scholars have tended to study a limited number of cases deemed to be of most significance.

For example, the Court has displayed utmost caution when confronted with sensitive issues, such as the UK's claim that the Council had exceeded its powers under article 118a EC when deciding the Working Time Directive (2003/88/EC). In this case, the Council opposed UK legislation favouring work on Sunday but the Court steered a middle path, declaring that while the Council had

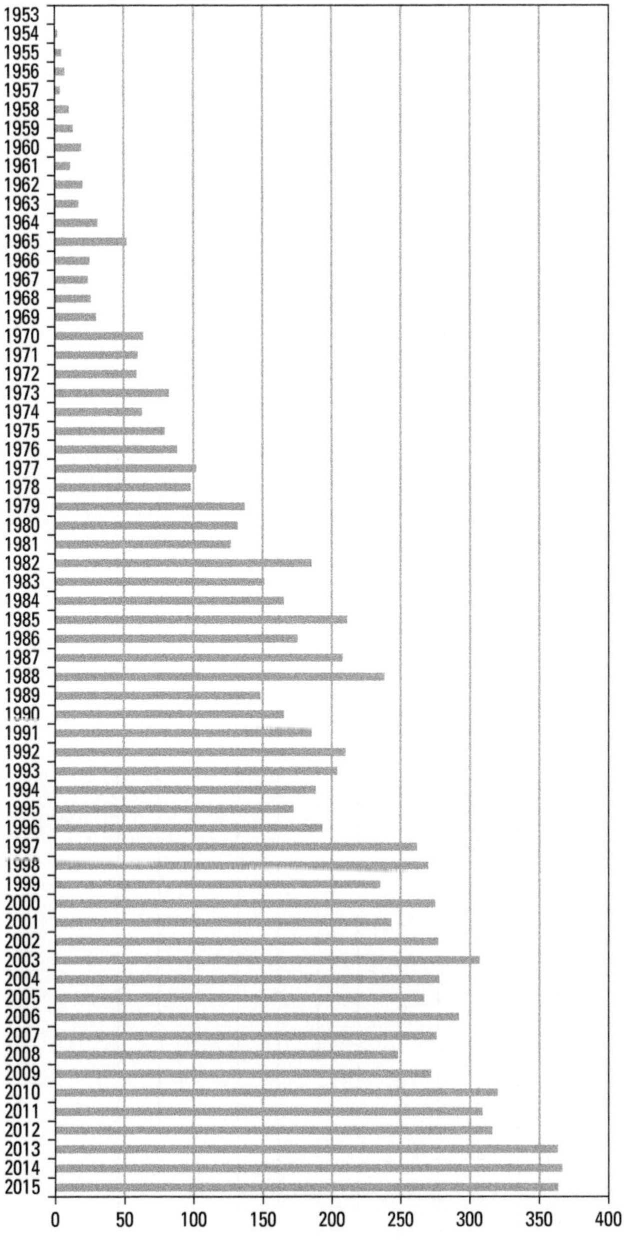

FIGURE 2.1 *Number of completed cases/year*

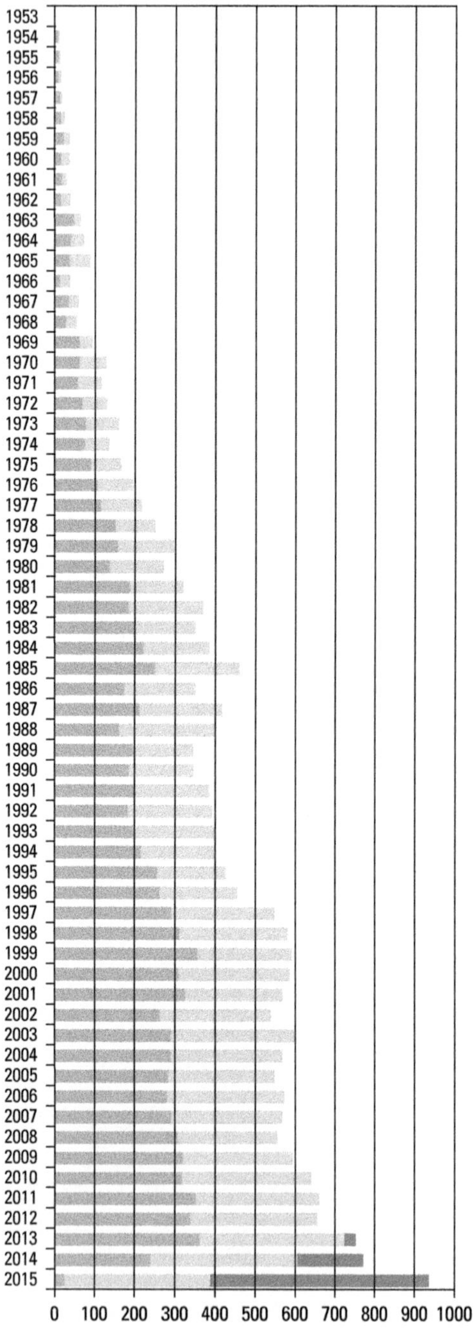

FIGURE 2.2 *Number of new cases/number of completed cases/ number of pending cases*

stayed within the margin of article 118a, it had failed to explain 'why Sunday is more closely connected with the health and safety of workers than any other day of the week' (*United Kingdom vs. Council* C–84/94).

Four explanations for the argument of a 'retreat from activism' are generally put forward (Saurugger & Terpan, 2014). First, there was the dramatic reform of the European Community via the Single European Act in 1986 and the Maastricht Treaty in 1992. On the one hand, the general availability of QMV in the Council of Ministers increased the possibility for member states to overrule the Court's decisions through new regulations and directives (Garrett, Kelemen & Schulz, 1998; Garrett & Tsebelis, 2001). Thus, the Court became more cautious in its rulings, knowing that member states could dismiss rulings they disagreed with by introducing new legislation.

The second explanation is related to the first and refers to increased public scrutiny of the Court's rulings. Member states' administrations traditionally knew of the rulings, but the media and citizens were showing more interest in the activities of the Court. This is a specific illustration of a more general phenomenon, known as the end of the 'permissive consensus' (the unquestioned and assumed support for European integration). Empirically, this can be illustrated through two parallel phenomena. On the one hand the fact that crucial CJEU rulings – whether they are linked to fundamental rights (*Kadi and Al Barakaat International Foundation vs. Council and Commission* C-402/05 P and C-415/05) or the introduction of macroeconomic governance provisions (*Commission vs. ECB* C–11/00; *Commission vs. Council* C–27/04) – are often commented upon extensively in the national media. On the other hand, a number of reform initiatives were launched at the European level as a result of public scrutiny to respond to criticism over the inflexibility and coerciveness of EU regulations and, therein, the role of the Court. In 1996 the Santer Commission launched a first regulatory simplification initiative (SLIM), to 'do less in order to do it better' (Commission, 1996). In 2002 the Commission reinforced this idea by launching a second regulatory reform action plan, 'Simplifying and Improving the Regulatory Environment', considered crucial to enhance the competitiveness of the European economy (Commission, 2002). This was then followed in 2005 by a high-profile 'better regulation' initiative, promising to simplify EU regulation (Commission, 2005). One of the first decisions of Jean-Claude Juncker, acting as the new President of the Commission, was to limit the regulation agenda of the EU to a small number of 'important' initiatives. In this context, it is sometimes argued that the Court, in parallel with the Commission and its quest for more 'constrained' regulation, has tried to refrain from issuing ambitious or far-reaching rulings.

A third explanation establishes a correlation between the social background of the judges sitting on the Court and the Court's presumed retreat from activism. Contrary to the Court's composition until the 1990s, nearly all judges now have a legal background (see Chapter 3). Legal training is, however, said to make the judges increasingly aware of the complexities of domestic law and may help to explain the Court's approach not to confront individual member governments with rulings that are too audacious, and which would put them in a difficult position politically, and potentially jeopardize their re-election to the Court. However, finding evidence to support this argument remains quite difficult, if not impossible (Saurugger & Terpan, 2016d).

Finally, the Maastricht Treaty introduced 'new modes of governance', which were further developed in the so-called Lisbon Strategy in 2000. This has led to an increased number of soft law rules 'escaping' the Court's scrutiny in areas such as employment and social and environmental policies (Terpan, 2015). These rules refer to framework directives, soft law, co-regulation, self-regulation, voluntary agreements, economic instruments and the 'open method of coordination' more generally. They foster flexible and informal governance characterized by a greater degree of deliberation among public and private actors, and the coordination of multiple levels of government. The introduction of new modes of governance has thus limited the influence of the Court, which exerts no control over soft law rules.

Challenging the 'retreat from activism'

Contrary to these explanations of the Court's retreat from activism, some scholars have argued strongly that the judicialization of the EU is enabling the Court to adopt a more activist stance, even if the degree of renewed activity varies across policy areas.

The continuing judicialization of the EU

A number of publications since the late 1990s have focused on the continued judicialization of the EU (Kagan, 1997, 2007; Maduro

& Azoulal, 2010; Schmidt, 2012; Grimmel, 2012). Kelemen, for example, argues that 'across policy areas ranging from employment discrimination to consumer protection to securities regulation to the free movement rights of workers, students, and even medical patients, we can observe more coercive legal enforcement, more rights claims, and a growing judicial role in shaping policy' (Kelemen, 2011, p. 5). This can be observed more generally in the fields of social policy, equal rights and environment (see Chapters 7 and 8).

We can observe two mechanisms at play here. First, the process of deregulation and judicial reregulation in the context of the creation of the European Single Market. This has led to a situation where the arrival of new policy players, such as interest groups, companies, NGOs and newly created regulatory authorities, has upset the traditional cooperative and informal arrangements that long characterized the policy-making process.

The second mechanism is the EU's fragmented institutional structure. A weak administrative apparatus has led to the establishment of a powerful judicial system (also Grimmel, 2012). Fragmentation between the European and the national level, as well as among EU institutions, has generated principal-agent problems, encouraging the establishment of strict, judicially enforceable goals based on transparent and accountable procedures. Drawing on a sociology of law approach (Black, 1976), Kelemen (2011) argues that the higher the distrust between regulators and regulated actors in liberalized markets, the more formally transparent and legalistic the laws and regulatory processes become, and thus, the more important the judicial apparatus. In fragmented systems, policy-makers have an increasingly difficult job to create majorities to pass their new legislation (Skowronek, 1982; Garrett, Kelemen & Schulz, 1998; Pollack, 2003). In other words, the fragmentation of power helps to protect the judiciary from being overruled too easily, as well as from other forms of political backlash.

Areas of remaining activism

Some argue that the Court's activism remains uneven across policy areas (De Witte, Muir & Dawson, 2013). One of the most striking and significant indications of the Court's continued activism is its role in the enforcement of individual rights, which are a category of economic, social and political rights. As stated above, in the 1970s the Court declared for the first time that it would uphold fundamental rights, in line with the collective constitutional traditions of the member states, and drawing on the ECHR. From the 1990s 'the language of rights' (De Búrca, 1995) gained prominence in many areas of EU case law. Existing statutory rights, and more particularly anti-discriminatory or social rights, were extended through successive Court rulings (Stone Sweet, 2004; De Búrca, De Witte & Ogertschnig, 2005; Conant, 2006, 2007; Cichowski, 2007; Micklitz, 2009).

Another example is given by Court rulings whereby national courts are obliged to ensure the full and effective protection of EU rights by altering national rules of administrative procedure and remedies, where necessary, to ensure the protection of individuals. The Court has restricted or outlawed national rules that limited the availability of judicial review of administrative acts (*Johnston* C–222/84); the time available for instituting judicial proceedings (*Emmott* C–208/90; *Levez* C–326/96); interim relief for plaintiffs (*Factortame* C–213/89); and state liability (*Francovich* C–9/90) (Kelemen, 2011, p. 54).

The Court's extension of one of the few administrative legal provisions explicitly mentioned in the EU treaties – the 'giving-reasons requirement' – provides another good example of the Court's remaining activism. The EU institutions are required to give reasons for their rule-making decisions. The Court has concentrated in particular on the Commission and rejected those decisions deemed inadequate (Shapiro, 2001). This requirement was furthermore extended to the domestic level: national courts were called upon by the Court to assess whether an administrative measure that imposed a burden on the individual was suitable, necessary and proportional to the objective sought (Craig & De Búrca, 2008).

This growing importance of fundamental rights litigation in the jurisprudence of the Court is also arguably linked to the 'constitutionalization' of fundamental rights in the EU (Schimmelfennig, 2006) and the Charter of Fundamental Rights of the EU. The drafting of the Charter has allowed the Court to gain more influence in this area, and to do so within a complex multi-level institutional system. In 1999 the member states established a European Convention, with the aim of drafting a Charter of Fundamental Rights for the EU. A list of EU rights, including civil liberties, as well as social, economic and political rights, was included in a Charter attached to the Treaty of Nice in 2001. At that time, the Charter was not recognized as enforceable law, but rather as a set of legal principles that the EU institutions had to take into account. However, the Treaty of Lisbon (2009) finally included the Charter in primary law, stating that it 'shall have the same legal value as the Treaties'. As such, the Court is not limited to applying the general principles of EU law, inspired by national constitutions and the ECHR, but can also reply on a whole set of EU principles within primary law.

Conclusion

Seen from a historical perspective, the Court is an impressive example of institution-building. It has gained power both through member state delegation and through its activism and a number of bold legal rulings. In the 25 years since the Maastricht Treaty, we have seen the increased judicialization of the European political system. The crucial role of law in the EU has placed tremendous pressure on the rule of law in the EU, as well as the CJEU. With an ever-growing body of European law and an increasingly diverse network of national courts – since 2004 some 13 additional member states, with their many national and regional courts – the CJEU now faces greater challenges than ever before in simply maintaining the coherence of the EU's legal order (Lenaerts, 2007; Rasmussen, 2010; Kelemen, 2011, p. 252).

However, the influence of the European Court has also led to increased criticism, with new rules and policies resulting from litigation achieving less impact (due to resistance at national level) and opening up questions of accountability. Judicial activism, sometimes seen as 'government by judges', has led to unease, raising the question of how far unelected judges are substituting their own will for that of elected representatives (Dehousse, 1998 – a question we will deal with specifically in Chapters 7 and 8).

It is difficult to judge from a historical perspective what impact the various recent crises – the rejection of the Constitutional Treaty, the difficult ratification of the Treaty of Lisbon and the economic and financial turmoil of the Eurozone since 2008 – have had on the role of the Court and the politics of law in the EU. Has the Court chosen to put an end to its own ambitions in the field of constitutional law? Will the member states reinforce hard law, such as through the Treaty on Stability, Coordination and Governance (TSCG) signed in 2012, in the field of economic and monetary policies (Saurugger & Terpan, 2016b; Saurugger, 2016)? Will we see stronger rules put in place, with the EU adopting an automatic procedure for imposing penalties in case of breaches of either public deficit or public debt rules? Or, on the contrary, will we see soft law mechanisms reinforced as a means for the member states to circumvent the Court?

In the chapters that follow we try to make sense of these questions by examining how the Court works in detail, when and where it intervenes, and what its relations are with the member states, national courts and civil society. The Court is but one element of the European political and legal system, and it is only in the context of this broader system that we can truly understand its role and its evolution.

Chapter 3

The Membership and Organization of the Court

In order to understand the Court of Justice of the European Union's (CJEU's) role in the EU's political system, we first need a clear sense of how it is composed and organized. This chapter provides a sociological perspective, focusing on the social characteristics of its judges, as well as an institutionalist perspective that looks closely at the structures of the CJEU. The former approach sees the judges as individuals socially embedded in the European Court, and assumes that judicial output also depends on people acting as judges. The latter approach is based on the idea that the content of case law is partially derived from the way in which the Court is structured.

Since its establishment in 1952, the Court's internal structure and functioning have adapted in response to several factors: external pressures, an increasing workload, a strengthening institutional role and EU enlargements that increased the number of judges from 7 to 28 – in, specifically and strictly speaking, the Court of Justice, excluding the General Court and the Civil Service Tribunal. These organizational transformations have had a deep impact on the Court. While in the 1957 version of the Treaty of Rome, there was only one self-sufficient Court of Justice (see Chapter 2), today it is made up of several courts (Box 3.1). The growth of the Court's workload caused major delays in its rulings in the 1970s and 1980s (see Figures 2.1 and 2.2). This increasing pressure led to the establishment of two other 'courts'; in 1988 the Court of First Instance (CFI) was created by the Council decision 88/591 and in 2004 the Civil Service Tribunal (CST) was established to deal with disputes between the Union and its staff. Until 2016, the CJEU was thus made up of the Court of Justice (the 'original' Court), the General Court (the former CFI, renamed by the Treaty of Lisbon) and the CST. In December 2015, the Council, together with the Parliament, adopted a reform of the General Court in order to tackle the challenge of an increasing caseload. It was decided to merge the CST with the General Court in December 2016.

Another European court, the Unified Patent Court, should be created, provided that the 2013 agreement (JOEU C175/01) is ratified by the member states. It will not be part of the CJEU and will be subject to the same obligations under Union law as any national court of the member states, and will thus be obliged to make preliminary references.

Box 3.1 The changing structure of the Court

Dates	Structure
1952–58	Court of Justice of the European Coal and Steel Community
1958–88	Court of Justice of the European Communities
1988–2004	Court of Justice of the European Communities – including a Court of First Instance (attached to the Court of Justice)
2004–09	Court of Justice of the European Communities – including a Court of First Instance (attached to the Court of Justice) – including a Civil Service Tribunal (attached to the Court of First Instance)
2009–16	Court of Justice of the European Union, composed of: – the Court of Justice – the General Court (formerly the Court of First Instance) – the Civil Service Tribunal
2016–	Court of Justice of the European Union, composed of: – the Court of Justice – the General Court (formerly the Court of First Instance)

This chapter presents the members of the courts, with a focus on their social and professional background (sociological perspective), and the organizational structures of the three courts (institutionalist perspective). The composition and functioning of the General Court is similar to that of the Court of Justice (until the end of 2016). The CST, however, was distinctive in that it oversaw a very different type of jurisdiction due to its highly specialized nature. However, any examination of each of the different components of the CJEU raises similar questions related to the effectiveness and legitimacy of the European judiciary.

The members of the Court

The role of the CJEU in the wider EU political system cannot be properly analysed without a clear view of its structure, the principles governing this structure and the sociological profile of the judges and advocates-general. Until recently, only a limited number of studies had concentrated on this question. However, we now have a better grasp of its make-up thanks to historical and socio-historical research (Kenney, 1998; Cohen, 2008, 2012; B. Davies, 2012a; M. Rasmussen, 2012; de Witte & Vauchez, 2013; Bobek, 2015; Chalmers, 2015).

Composition of the Court

Number of judges

The Court of Justice currently consists of one judge per member state, appointed for a six-year renewable term. The number of judges has increased over time as a consequence of successive enlargements. In the 1990s, when the legal doctrine anticipated the accession of the Central and Eastern European countries and the large increase in the number of judges, serious concerns were voiced as to whether or not the Court's deliberative process would remain efficient. Two main scenarios were foreseen: either maintaining the principle of 'one judge per member state' or finding a way to limit the number of judges by no longer maintaining a correlation with the number of member states.

Looking to the future, the Court of justice itself (and not the Commission) explored the opportunities and pitfalls of the increase in the number of judges (Arnull, 2006). As for the pitfalls, the Court argued that an increase in the number of judges would lead to a situation whereby the Court functions more and more as a deliberative assembly rather than a collegiate tribunal. This development would then affect its efficiency. To avoid this risk, one idea was for the use of chambers composed of a limited number of judges (3, 5 or 15) to become the standard, with the number of cases where the Court sat in full Court drastically decreased. However, as these (reduced) chambers would then hear the majority of cases, there were fears that this might pose a threat to the consistency of the EU's case law.

At the same time, the Court of Justice identified three advantages of an increase in the number of judges.

- First, the presence of judges from all the member states might help take account of the diversity of the national legal systems, which might be of crucial importance in particular for the new member states. While the independence of the judiciary constitutes an essential element of dispute settlement mechanisms in democratic political systems, the EU is based on 28 different legal systems and, thus, is in need of know-how and expertise from these national levels. The CJEU, as a legal jurisdiction in its own right, has to take into account the laws of the member states in its day-to-day work.
- Second, the principle of 'one judge per member state' might help enhance the legitimacy of the courts and that of the Union as whole. Indeed, judicial decisions at the EU level could potentially be more easily accepted at the national level if all the member states were represented in the courts.
- Third, it was deemed important to have a large number of judges in order to cope with the increasing volume of cases brought before the Court.

Not surprisingly, the EU member states decided in the Treaty of Nice (2001) that each member state should retain its own judge at the Court of Justice, despite the considerable size of the anticipated enlargement. In the EU, as in other international organizations, national governments consider that they should have one 'representative' in each institution. Since the Treaty of Nice (2001), the Council is also able to increase the number of judges by unanimous vote, in order to ease the Court's workload, should it receive such a request from the Court. This could lead to a Court made up of more members than the number of member states.

In the General Court there has to be 'at least' one judge for each member state (Statute of the CJEU). In practice, the number of judges was equal in both the General Court and the Court of Justice until 2016 (28 judges per Court). By contrast, the CST was composed of only seven judges, which reflected the more limited scope of the CST's jurisdiction. The 2015 reform of the General Court allows the member states to nominate two members of the General Court instead of one. The increase in the number of judges at the General Court is taking place progressively including, in September 2016, the transfer of the seven posts of judges at the CST to the General Court. At the end of this process (September 2019), the General Court will be made up of 56 judges.

Number of advocates-general

The 28 judges in the Court of Justice are assisted by eleven advocates-general, a post that takes inspiration from the French '*rapporteur public*' within the *Conseil d'État*. Advocates-general, such as *rapporteurs publics*, are charged with the task of making reasoned submissions on cases brought before them, depending on their appointed jurisdiction. The advocates-general have the same status and receive the same salary as the judges. The Statute of the CJEU allows for the General Court to be assisted by advocates-general, but this has not been the case so far. Instead, each judge at the General Court is allowed to perform the function of an advocate-general in difficult cases, which happens very rarely.

The number of advocates-general may be increased if the Council unanimously decides that the caseload justifies such an increase. This can be decided at the request of the Court of Justice. Each of the larger member states has managed to have one of their nationals performing the functions of advocate-general. At present, six posts are allocated to France, Germany, Italy, Poland, Spain and the United Kingdom, while the remaining posts rotate between the other member states. Poland has joined the group of 'privileged' member states quite recently. A declaration annexed to the Treaties (Declaration no 38 on art. 252 TFUE) allowed Poland to have a permanent post when the number of advocates-general increases by three (from eight to eleven).

Principles governing the composition of the courts

The composition of the CJEU reflects three main principles, which, at first sight, seem to be at odds with one another: representativeness, independence and accountability. These principles are not explicitly stated, but have been deduced from the treaties by legal doctrine. First, the judges must remain connected with member states' societies, mainly for functional reasons – EU law and national laws are deeply interconnected and the impact of the CJEU's jurisprudence depends on its relations with national courts. The Court being a supranational jurisdiction needs to be anchored in the national legal systems. Second, the judges must be independent from political parties or any other interests, in particular from those of their national governments. This separation of powers, and hence, the Court's independence, is a requirement of the EU's legal system as it is in all democratic legal systems in respect of the rule of law. Doubts about the independence of the judges weaken their authority and legitimacy. Third, and despite this independence, the judges are nevertheless accountable to the member states to some extent, as is consistent with the appointment procedure. The principle of accountability must therefore be reconciled with the principle of independence.

Representativeness

The first principle is that the judges in the Court of Justice and the General Court shall remain connected to national societies. The Treaty on the Functioning of the European Union (TFEU) states that judges must be appointed 'by common accord of the governments of the member states' for a term of six years (art. 253 TFEU). As such, this article does not actually specify whether all member states have to have a judge in the two courts. The lack of explicit requirements regarding nationality could even lead to the appointment of judges from non-member states. In practice, however, and contrary to the spirit of the rule, each member state is charged with the task of proposing one judge among its nationals, which the Council then approves by unanimity. Usually, the choice of each national government is not questioned. This unwritten rule ensures that all member states are present in the two courts, and in so doing helps to maintain neutrality with regard to the nationality of the parties.

Since the accession of Austria, Finland and Sweden in 1995, the member states have been placed on an equal footing when it comes to the appointment of the judges. In the past, the 'big' member states (France, Germany, Italy, Spain and the United Kingdom) used to benefit from having an extra judge. They still possess an advantage given the nine advocates-general of the Court of Justice (and, until the end of 2016, seven judges of the CST appointed by the Council for a period of six years). The practice remains that the 'big' member states have an advocate-general (or a judge at the CST until the end of 2016), while the other posts rotate among the smaller member states.

Every three years, 14 of the 28 judges are replaced or re-appointed under the conditions laid down in the Statute of the CJEU. A partial rather than total replacement of judges helps to ensure continuity within the Court of Justice. Four advocates-general are replaced every three years (as were three to four judges of the CST until the end of 2016). The terms of the judges and advocates-general can be renewed without any limitation; they usually hold office for two terms, which also helps in ensuring continuity in the institution.

Contrary to the appointment rules applying to judges and advocates-general, the choice as to the president of the Court of Justice (see the section on the President of the CJEU below) is not controlled by the member states. The judges themselves elect their president for a period of three years following the partial renewal of the Court.

Independence

According to the TFEU, the members of the Court of Justice are chosen from persons whose independence is beyond doubt and who possess the qualifications required for appointment to the highest judicial offices in their respective countries or who are 'jurisconsults' of recognized competence. These requirements are very similar to those applying to the judges at the International Court of Justice (art. 2 of the Statute of the International Court of Justice adopted in 1945 as part of the United Nations Charter). The reference to jurisconsults of recognized competence allows the Court of Justice to bring in academics and civil service lawyers, as well as lawyers with professional qualifications that are not otherwise sufficiently qualified to be appointed to the highest judicial offices in their country. The members of the General Court, as well as those of the CST, are chosen from persons whose independence is beyond doubt and who possess the ability required for appointment to high judicial office. Advocates-general must have legal qualifications stemming from experiences in the civil service, the national judiciary, the Bar or academia.

Under the European Coal and Steel Community (ECSC) Treaty, no legal qualification was required to be a member of the European Court. Individuals such as the Dutch labour leader Joseph Serrarens or the French economist Jacques Rueff were thus appointed. Another example is Adrianus Van Kleffens, a senior civil servant at the Dutch ministry of economy before his appointment to the Court of Justice in 1952. However, unlike the two judges mentioned above, he did have legal experience as he had sat as a judge at the Court of Amsterdam. The 1957 Treaty of Rome put an end to this situation and required legal qualifications in order to prevent the member states from appointing judges on political grounds.

Appointments decided by national governments were never disputed at the European level until the Treaty of Lisbon, which provided for the consultation of a panel of experts known as 'the 255 panel' based on article 255 TFEU. This expert panel comprises seven individuals chosen from among former members of the Court of Justice and the General Court, members of national supreme courts and lawyers of recognized competence, one of whom is proposed by the European Parliament. The Council now adopts a decision establishing the panel's operating rules and a decision appointing its members. Acting on the initiative of the president of the Court of Justice, the panel provides an opinion on candidates' suitability to perform the duties of judge and advocate-general of the Court of Justice and the General Court. This occurs once a member state has nominated a candidate but before the governments of the member states collectively make the appointments referred to in articles 253 and 254 TFEU. The idea is that the panel should make the member states more demanding in the choice of the judges.

In its first four years, excluding the renewal of appointments of existing members of the courts, the '255 panel' examined 32 applicants. Of these 'first timers', they issued a negative opinion with respect to seven candidates (255 Panel, 2014, pp. 8–9). Although non-binding, these negative opinions have always been followed by the member states. Overruling these opinions is very difficult as it requires unanimity, and it might not be deemed suitable in terms of member states' legitimacy (Sauvé, 2013; Bobek, 2014b, 2015).

There is, however, a limit to the influence of the panel, given that only one name is ever put forward by the member states. Another option would be for the member states to propose a list of three people from which the panel would then choose one. This option offers a better guarantee of the independence and competence of the judges, while respecting the interests of the member states (Arnull, 2006, p. 23).

The Statute of the CJEU guarantees the independence of the judges during their mandate. For that purpose, they are immune from legal proceedings, unless the Court of Justice, sitting as a full Court, waives this immunity. The judges cannot engage in any activity that is seen to be incompatible with their functions; they must 'perform their duties impartially and conscientiously', and 'preserve the secrecy of the deliberations of the Court', which is supposed to free them from the influence of the member states, as well as private actors (see art. 2 and 3 of the Statute of the Court of Justice of the European Union, Protocol 3). It is highly likely that secret deliberations give the judges a certain freedom of manoeuvre but it is also highly difficult to prove.

The fact that the judges' mandate is short (and renewable) is an important limit to their independence, as it makes them more aware of national preferences. Some argue that, even if the members of the Court have no real guarantee, their mandate can be renewed without any limitation, and is often renewed, in practice. The fact that judges often serve for more than one term, instead of being systematically replaced following their first mandate, does not prove that they are actually independent, since it is still possible for national governments to make the renewal of the term conditional upon the judges' proper behaviour in the Court. And replacements, albeit infrequent, sometimes happen; judge Zuleeg, whose rulings displeased both Chancellor Kohl and the German Constitutional Court in the early 1990s, did not see his appointment renewed by the German government in 1994 (Dehousse, 1998, p. 12).

The temptation to use career considerations to influence the judiciary exists, but it is extremely difficult to prove as the Court's rulings are discussed in secrecy. The Court issues only per curiam rulings, which means rulings decided collectively with no dissenting votes or opinions. Hence even if, as occasionally happens, the specific positions of judges are known, no systematic research establishing correlations (beyond pure speculation) seems possible (Pollack, 2013). The situation could change by modifying the rules and opting for one long, non-renewable term of around 12 years, as in many national constitutional courts. The CJEU has supported the idea (Court of Justice, 1996, quoted in Craig, 2001) but the member states are not convinced of the need to adopt new rules in this field. One might infer from this that member states influence – or are eager to maintain the means to influence – the judges.

Few scholars have supported the idea that the CJEU is responsive to the preference of national governments, especially the most powerful ones (Garrett, 1992; Garrett & Weingast, 1993; Carrubba, Gabel & Hankla, 2008, 2012). Most scholars argue that the CJEU enjoys a remarkable amount of discretion in comparison with national courts, despite less favourable rules of appointment (Burley & Mattli, 1993; Alter, 1998, 2008; Pollack, 2003, p. 166). As we have pointed out above, we know very little about how judges are chosen by the member states. Only the names of the successful candidates are made public (Arnull, 2006, p. 23). Yet, in spite of the example of judge Zuleeg's non-renewal, many scholars agree that the member states refrain from seeking to control the Court by selecting docile judges or by refusing to renew 'uncontrollable' judges. French president de Gaulle even appointed Robert Lecourt, who had resigned from the French government in protest at the anti-Community stance that it had taken (Rasmussen, 2008). There is also no evidence of 'political' appointments being made in the same way as nominations to the Supreme Court of the United States. The reasons for this self-restraint remain unclear. Are national leaders satisfied with the Court's jurisprudence, or do they anticipate a socializing effect of the Court on the judges, which would make any attempt to control them totally useless?

Several factors might explain the high level of judicial independence of the Court (Pollack, 2003, pp. 167–8); none of them is specific to the European case, as a brief comparison with other courts, and especially the US Supreme Court, shows (Ferejohn, 1998; Ferejohn & Kramer, 2002). The first one is not specific to the CJEU. Courts, generally speaking, are said to exert a strong socializing effect upon their members. They help judges to perceive themselves as servants of the law and/or to present themselves as non-political actors. Members of the courts must use the 'language of reasoned interpretation, logical deduction, systemic and temporal coherence' in order to secure legitimacy (Mattli & Slaughter, 1998, p. 197). Alter goes even further by underlining that 'Courtroom politics take place in an environment highly constrained by law and legal procedure, where judges have a privileged position because they get to ask the questions, decide what is and is not relevant, and determine the outcome' (Alter, 2008, p. 47).

A second reason is linked with decision-making; the threat of the Court's interpretations being overruled with new primary or secondary law is relatively weak within the EU, because the threshold for such an overruling is very high (see Chapters 5, 8 and 9). For this precise reason, and because of the complicity of national courts, scholars such as Burley and Mattli (1993), Beach (2001), Stone Sweet (2004) and Alter (2009) argue that the CJEU does not hesitate to rule against the preferences of the member states.

Third, according to article 35 of the Statute of the CJEU, 'the deliberations of the Court of Justice shall be and shall remain secret', which means that the publication of dissenting opinions is not allowed. Hence, judgements of the courts are issued collectively by consensus or on a simple majority vote. This is similar to the French and Italian constitutional courts and contrary to the US Supreme Court. The fact that appointments are made individually by the member states explains why the Council cannot collectively and consistently frame the composition of the CJEU. At most, a member state may nominate a judge with a nationalist or an ideological bias. But it is very unlikely that a member state will succeed in exerting influence over the Court as a whole by one judge alone.

To some extent, the member states could use the judges who have been designated by the president of the Court to act as *rapporteurs*. Indeed, the judge *rapporteur* is in a position of influence due to the main tasks for which he or she is responsible: presenting a report, once all the pleadings have been received, that summarizes the arguments of the parties; preparing draft judgements that will be used as a basis for the deliberations. The judge *rapporteur* is sometimes supported by one or more assistant *rapporteurs*. Assistant *rapporteurs* are appointed by the European Parliament and the Council in accordance with the ordinary legislative procedure (formally known as the co-decision procedure) and at the request of the Court of Justice. They may be required to participate in preparatory inquiries in cases pending before the Court and to cooperate with the judge rapporteur. The rules attempt to prevent the judge *rapporteur* from being in a position where he or she might defend the position of her or his country of origin; a non-written rule states that a case coming from a member state shall not be given to a judge from the same country. Furthermore, preliminary references from a specific member state are given to a judge from another country.

Accountability

As a result of the appointment procedure, the judges are accountable to the member states only, provided that their independence is not threatened. A difficult balance must be found between accountability to national institutions and judicial independence. The main requirements of judicial independence are that judges are personally and professionally equipped to resolve legal disputes impartially. The key questions concerning judicial accountability are: accountability for what, and to whom? In the EU, as in other democratic political systems, judicial accountability is essentially 'explanatory' accountability (Bogdanor, 2007), whereby the judiciary gives an account of those matters for which they are responsible, that is, it makes clear the legal reasoning on which the decision is based.

More specifically, accountability applies first at the individual level of judges and advocates-general. Judges must satisfy the requirements of the TFEU in order to be appointed, and comply with the provisions of the Statute of the CJEU. Secondly, accountability applies to the CJEU as a whole, with different rules ensuring that it works as a jurisdiction. In the Court of Justice we see a numbers of provisions: the allocation of chambers must be carried out according to objective rules established previously; hearings must take place in public; judgements and opinions of advocates-generals must be read in open court; judgements must state the reasons on which they are based and contain the names of the judges who took part in the deliberations; and judgements are to be published on the Court's website.

The appointment of the judges does not need to be approved by the European Parliament, contrary to the United States where nominees at the Supreme Court need to be endorsed by the Senate after public hearings, a procedure which focuses the attention of the media. On that basis, it could be concluded that the CJEU suffers from a lack of democratic accountability. The European Parliament itself favours giving assent on all appointments to the Court, be it for judges or advocates-general, but this is not the case today. This would require a procedure of 'confirmation hearings', replicating the US model. However, the CJEU believes that such hearings would endanger the independence of the judges. This line of argument defends the idea of appointments being made behind closed doors on the basis of the rule of law and, accordingly, on the basis of democracy.

Who are the judges and advocates-general?

Contrary to appointments to the US Supreme Court, we know comparatively little about the individual judges sitting on the CJEU. The appointments are not based on public hearings or lengthy negotiations, commented upon in the press. And the courts' rulings are collegial. Hence, the composition of the courts is neither a subject of importance in the media nor receives much scholarly attention (for an exception, see Vauchez, 2008).

Looking close up at the detail, one sees that the members of, specifically and strictly speaking, the Court of Justice (without taking into account the members of the General Court) have a very similar sociological profile when it comes to their age and gender. At the time of writing (early 2016), most judges were over 50 when appointed by the member states (24 out of 28); the average age is 58 years. There are few female judges (5 out of 28). The ratio is similar for advocates-general with only two being women. The legal qualification requirement (see the section on Independence above) also brings a certain degree of homogeneity to the Court. It does not, however, result in complete uniformity, as former judges, academics and high-ranking civil servants as well as private-practice lawyers can all be called to serve at the Court.

Academia vs. judiciary?

The member states started to appoint former university professors at the end of the 1950s (Cohen, 2012). In 1958, Andreas Donner, a Dutch professor of administrative and constitutional law, was the first president of the Court. His professional experience was based solely on an academic career. In the 1960s, academics became the largest group in the CJEU despite them having no judicial experience prior to their appointment (Dehousse, 1998). This is often considered as one factor behind the considerable level of judicial activism. Given that the careers of former professors do not depend on national authorities, they benefited from a large room for manoeuvre and were said to be more inclined than former judges at the national level to develop far-reaching case law.

From the 1990s onwards, however, academics were gradually outnumbered by practitioners, most being former members of the judiciary. When examining the last position of each judge of the Court of Justice prior to their appointment to the CJEU (Table 3.1), we see that only four were academics in the full sense (most of them

TABLE 3.1 *The professional origin of the judges at the Court of Justice (May 2014)*

NAME OF THE JUDGE	LAST POSITION BEFORE NOMINATION TO THE CJEU	NAME OF THE JUDGE	LAST POSITION BEFORE NOMINATION TO THE CJEU	NAME OF THE JUDGE	LAST POSITION BEFORE NOMINATION TO THE CJEU	NAME OF THE JUDGE	LAST POSITION BEFORE NOMINATION TO THE CJEU
Koen Lenaerts (president) Belgium	Member of the Brussels Bar	**Anthony Borg Barthet U.O.M.** Malta	Member of the Board of Governors of the Malta Arbitration Centre	**Thomas von Danwitz** Germany	Professor of German public law and European law (University of Cologne)	**Egidijus Jarašiūnas** Lithuania	Dean of the Law Faculty of Mykolas Romeris University (Lithuania)
Michail Vilaras Greece	Lecturer at the National School for the Judiciary and Member of the '255' Panel	**Marko Ilešič** Slovenia	President of the Arbitration Chamber of the Ljubljana Stock Exchange	**Alexander Arabadjiev** Bulgaria	Member of the Bulgarian National Assembly	**Carl Gustav Fernlund** Sweden	President of the Administrative Court of Appeal
Antonio Tizzano Italy	Member of the independent group of experts appointed to examine the finances of the European Commission	**Jiří Malenovský** Czech Republic	Judge at the Constitutional Court	**Camelia Toader** Romania	Judge at the High Court of Cassation and Justice (Romania)	**José Luís da Cruz Vilaça** Portugal	Lawyer at the Lisbon bar

Allan Rosas Finland	Deputy Director-General of the European Commission Legal Service	**Egils Levits** Latvia	Judge at the European Court of Human Rights	**Marek Safjan** Poland	President of the Polish Constitutional Court	**Christopher Vajda** UK	Barrister
Rosario Silva de Lapuerta Spain	Professor of Community Law at the Diplomatic School, Madrid	**Eugene Regan** Ireland	Senior Counsel (Ireland)	**Daniel Šváby** Slovakia	Judge at the Court of First Instance	**Sinisa Rodin** Croatia	Professor at University of Zagreb
Endre Juhász Hungary	Minister for the coordination of matters of European integration	**Lars Bay Larsen** Denmark	Judge at the Højesteret (Danish Supreme Court)	**Maria Berger** Austria	Member of the European Parliament	**François Biltgen** Luxembourg	Minister for Justice (Luxembourg)
Constan-tinos Lycourgos Cyprus	Agent of the Cypriot Government before the Courts of the European Union	**Jean-Claude Bonichot** France	Judge at the Council of State	**Alexandra (Sacha) Prechal** Netherlands	Professor of European Law at the University of Utrecht	**Küllike Jürimäe** Estonia	Judge, Tallinn Court of Appeal (Estonia)

giving lectures at universities in addition to professional activity), while 15 were lawyers or held a position in the judiciary before their appointment. Among the nine remaining EU judges, five held high-level positions in national or EU institutions, four were engaged in political activities (governmental and/or parliamentary) and most had a background of some sort in the national judiciary.

Does this evolution towards a less academic-oriented CJEU help support the argument that the Court has 'retreated from activism' since the 1990s? The answer is clearly no, for three main reasons. First, we have seen (Chapter 2) that there is still activism in the CJEU even if it is uneven across different legal fields. Second, the number of academics is far from the only factor accounting for the activist position of the CJEU. Third, other factors, linked to the organization of the CJEU (see the section on the Organization of the Court, below), and the political environment in which they take decisions (see Chapters 4, 5 and 6), also need taking into account (Saurugger & Terpan, 2016d).

Politicians and officials controlled by the member states?

The requirement that judges and advocates-general have legal qualifications does not preclude the member states from appointing politicians or high officials. Indeed, some members of the courts may have worked in legal departments of national ministries, or may have even been ministers in charge of justice. At first sight, these types of administrative or political careers do not give the same guarantee of independence as legal careers. This might suggest that the member states, and particular the larger ones, are able to maintain control of the Court (Garrett, 1995; Garrett, Kelemen & Schulz, 1998), though there is insufficient evidence to back up this argument.

Several members have had a political career prior to their nomination, be it as a member of the national government or parliament. In March 2016, there were six judges in this category: the Austrian judge, Maria Berger (member of the European Parliament in 1996–2007 and 2008–09, Minister for Justice in 2007–08); the Bulgarian judge, Alexander Arabadjiev (member of the National Assembly in 2001–06); the Hungarian judge, Endre Juhász (Minister for European Affairs in 2003–04); the Latvian judge, Egils Levits (Vice Prime Minister and Minister for Justice, acting Minister for Foreign Affairs in 1993–94); the Luxembourg judge, François Biltgen (member of the Government in 1999–2013); and the Portuguese judge, José Luís da Cruz Vilaça (member of the Government in 1980–83).

Very often, judges with a political background at national level have also been legal practitioners. Robert Lecourt, the fourth president of the Court of Justice between 1967 and 1976, was a well-known politician of the Christian-Democrat MRP (*Mouvement républicain populaire*) and a former Minister of Justice when he was first appointed as a judge at the Court of Justice in 1962. He also held a PhD in private law and had been a lawyer in Paris and Rouen for fifteen years before the Second World War (Pescatore, 2005).

The advocate-general Melchior Wathelet provides another interesting example of a career combining governmental and judicial responsibilities. He was Belgium's Minister for Justice in 1988–95 before serving at the Court between 1995 and 2003. The legal profession in his country protested against his appointment on the basis that it might undermine the authority of the Court of Justice (Dehousse, 1998, p. 8). In 2009 the same story was repeated: Melchior Wathelet was a Minister of State when he was appointed advocate-general to the Court of Justice.

Again, the fact that some member states appoint politicians does not seem to have a huge impact on the Court's case law. It could be argued that 'political' appointments are intended as a way of controlling the judges' behaviour. However, four arguments counter this hypothesis. First, some member states, such as the UK and Ireland, have a tradition of appointing 'political opponents' to important administrative, diplomatic and judicial positions, in order to strike a balance between the different political parties. Second, the possibility of one judge being controlled individually by a member state does not mean that the entire Court is controlled by the member states. Third, it is not clear whether a judge with a 'political' background can be more easily influenced than a judge with a background in the judiciary. Fourth, it has been often said that the judges and advocates-general have a pro-integration bias, due to sociological or other reasons (see the following section); were this true, it would counter the argument that they are controlled by the states.

Do judges at the Court of Justice have a pro-integration agenda?

It is often argued that the judges and advocates-general have adopted a pro-integration stance since the landmark rulings of the early 1960s (see, for example, Vauchez, 2008, 2012). The argument is arrived at by looking at both the jurisprudence of the CJEU and the sociological profile of the judges. Empirically, however, the correlation is rather difficult to prove.

As far as the jurisprudence is concerned, scholars arguing in favour of a pro-integration bias of the judges assume that the CJEU has systematically favoured pro-integration through its main rulings. In this book, Chapter 2 has offered a general overview and discussed the idea of judicial activism. Chapters 7 and 8 provide a more precise study of the constitutional and policy-making role of the CJEU, helping to assess its influence on the European integration process. Even if the idea of activism cannot be rejected, other scholars argue in favour of a more nuanced position, asserting that the judges have sometimes refrained from activism, especially though not exclusively in the period following the Maastricht Treaty. However, even here we still find many legal arguments to justify the pro-integration ruling (Alter, 1996; Kelemen, 2011).

The sociology of the judges would also explain the pro-integration bias of the judges. Four main ideas are put forward in support of this idea. First, most of the members of the courts have specialized in national rather than international law (Cohen, 2010). This would explain the tendency to transform EU law into something that somehow resembles national law, with values and principles of a constitutional nature, and principles such as *direct effect*, *primacy* and so on. The argument is quite convincing but remains extremely difficult to prove empirically. A counter-argument would be that judges are more likely to preserve national sovereignty precisely because their areas of expertise and professional origin are linked with national law. As such, a French judge coming from the *Conseil d'État* is not necessarily inclined to defend supranational positions (see Chapter 5).

Second, a more institutionalist argument is that the judges and advocates-general defend pro-integration positions because they have been socialized in a pro-European environment (Nowak et al., 2011; Mayoral, Jaremba & Nowak, 2014). The argument goes that while they may not have necessarily held a pro-EU bias when they were appointed as judges, they quite soon learned the legal reasoning of the European Court and became accustomed with a European legal way of thinking. This original argument needs more extensive empirical research, implying that the precise working habits (the so-called 'standard operating procedures') of all CJEU's staff, not only those of judges, would require detailed analysis.

The third argument, also arrived at from an institutionalist perspective, asserts that the EU judges, as agents of the Court, have fought to reinforce the Court's position in order to strengthen their own position. Several factors suggest that this might be the case. In the 1950s and early 1960s, the first Court of Justice had to struggle to strengthen its own position in the political and judicial system of the European Communities (Chapter 2). Moreover, the CJEU has rarely restricted itself to controlling national breaches of EU law. Many rulings have benefited the supranational institutions, such as the Commission and the Parliament, to the detriment of intergovernmental institutions such as the Council (see Chapter 4). This can be explained by a search for allies within the EU institutional framework – the Court's collaboration with the Commission and the Parliament is a means to reinforce supranationalism in general, and its own position in the EU system in particular.

A fourth idea, close to the second and third (at least at first sight), is more sociological in nature. It assumes that the legalization of European integration is not only explained by the pro-integration bias of the judges, but can also result from the activist behaviour of lawyers, both in the EU institutions and the member states, who succeed in advancing the cause of EU law (Vauchez, 2012). As such, these lawyers reflected core principles of European law, such as *primacy* and *direct effect*, in their day-to-day practice. This argument is striking, as it recognizes links between different institutions (for example the CJEU and the Commission) and different professional arenas (for example the judiciary and academia), all driven by the same rationale. However, when trying to show that the Court has never been the unitary actor that lawyers and political scientists considered it to be (Pollack, 2013), the argument overestimates the degree of unity among lawyers, and tends to depict European integration as a kind of plot driven by lawyers against 'the people'.

More generally, the argument supporting the notion of a pro-European agenda must be placed in a wider context. As we have underlined in Chapter 1, judges do not take judicial decisions in a legal and political vacuum. Their sociological profile is one factor among others explaining the Court's choices over the years (Saurugger & Terpan, 2016d). Among them are the objectives of the treaties, in particular the promise of an 'ever closer Union', as enshrined in the preamble of the Treaty of Rome (Schepel & Blankenburg, 2001; Craig, 2003), and the organization and functioning of the Court (see below) as well as its interactions with other actors (Pollack, 2013) (Chapters 4, 5 and 6).

The organization of the Court

The CJEU does not decide alone on how it is organized. The member states control the procedures for revising the organizational rules of the courts (see also Chapter 5). These rules can be found in the Treaties (Treaty on European Union and TFEU), the Statute of the CJEU (which is, according to a protocol annexed to the Treaties, part of the Treaties), and the rules of procedure that are established by each Court with the approval of the Council. They define the formations of judgement, the powers of the president, judges *rapporteurs* and advocates-general, as well as the way in which cases are heard.

Different formations of judgement

The Court of Justice sits in full Court (28 judges) or, more commonly, in Chambers or in a Grand Chamber, in accordance with the rules laid down for that purpose in the Statute of the CJEU. The same rules apply to the General Court. Until its merger with the GC, the CST sits in full Court, or in chambers of three or five judges. More precisely, the ordinary formation of the CST is the chamber of three judges. A case may be referred to the full Court or to the chamber sitting with five judges only in special circumstances: when there is difficulty over the legal questions raised, or when the importance of the case or special circumstances justify it. On the contrary, when the case is deemed to be of limited importance and there is no difficulty with regard to the questions of law or facts raised, it is possible for a single judge to give a ruling on actions brought by private parties (but this seldom happens).

The Statute of the Court of Justice specifies the cases that must be dealt with by a particular formation, be it the full Court, the Grand Chamber of 13 judges, chambers of three or five judges. In general, the more difficult or important the case, the larger the formation to which the case is assigned (Arnull, 2006, p. 8). In particular, there are four possibilities for the Court of Justice to sit as a full Court: (1) the dismissal of the European ombudsman (who, created by the treaty of Maastricht can investigate any EU institution on the grounds of maladministration); (2) compulsory retirement of a member of the Commission or deprivation of his or her pension rights or other benefits; (3) removal from office of a member of the Court of Auditors or suspension/withdrawal of his or her pension or other benefits; and (4) if the Court of Justice, after hearing the advocate-general, considers that a case brought before it is of exceptional importance. In practice, recourse to the full Court is extremely rare, however (one case out of 406 cases judged in 2012).

The Grand Chamber is composed of 13 judges, presided over by the president of the Court and including the vice president, three presidents of five-judge chambers who are designated on the basis of a rotation mechanism and ten judges who are designated, also on the basis of a rotation mechanism, from among the other judges. This occurs: (1) when a member state or an institution of the Union that is party to the proceedings so requests; and (2) when the case is particularly important or difficult. The creation of the Grand Chamber was decided by the Treaty of Nice (2001) in order to reduce the need for recourse to the full Court, especially in the context of EU enlargement. In 2012, some 9 per cent of cases were judged by the Grand Chamber (CJEU, 2013, p. 11).

Most frequently, however, the Court of Justice sits in chambers of three or five judges. In 2012, some 34 per cent of cases were judged by three-judge chambers, and 54 per cent by five-judge chambers (CJEU, 2013, p. 11). There are four chambers of three judges and four chambers of five judges. Judges elect the presidents of the chambers from among their number. The presidents of the chambers of three judges are elected every year while the presidents of the chambers of five judges are elected for three years and can be re-elected once. Although the five-judge formation is often considered the most effective since its small size helps it to be decisive, in some cases it is up to the Grand Chamber to decide, because of its greater legitimacy. The same criterion of legitimacy explains why the five-judge chambers take precedence over three-judge chambers.

Due to the existence of several group formations, the work of the Court of Justice is more and more fragmented and specialized, which increases the influence of individual judges. The smaller the formation of judgement, the greater the importance of individual judges in the rulings. Another consequence of the division of the Court into different formations is that the president of the Court has gained importance over time, insofar as she/he establishes the case list, distributes cases to the chambers, and decides which cases each judge will consider.

However, there is no situation whereby the presence of all judges is required. Even when the Court of Justice sits in full Court, decisions are valid if 15 judges are in attendance. Arguably, this signals that the judges do not necessarily represent their own member state.

Similarly, the decisions of the Grand Chamber are valid provided that nine judges (out of the 13) are present. Finally, decisions of the five-judge chamber are valid if they are taken by at least three judges.

Special roles in the courts

The functioning of the Court of Justice also depends on the role played by the advocates-general in helping the judges making their decisions, as well as on the special duties taken up by the judges (president, vice president, *rapporteur*). Judges and advocates-general receive the support of a sizeable staff, among which the *référendaires* (legal assistants) are particularly valuable.

Advocates-general in support of the judges

The Court designates a first advocate-general for a period of one year, who is in charge of assigning each case to one of the nine advocates-general of the Court of Justice. The duty of the advocates-general is to make reasoned submissions on cases requiring her/his involvement. The Treaty of Nice ended the previous system that required the opinion of the advocate-general for each case. They now only give opinions in important cases, where the judges come up against a particular legal difficulty or a factual complexity.

Advocates-general present opinions to the Court in between the submissions by the parties (oral hearings where lawyers from both sides put their case to the judges and advocate-general, who can question them) and the start of the judges' deliberations (which do not include the advocates-general). Advocates-general must be independent and impartial, and provide recommendations to the judges on how to decide the case. Advocates-general benefit from a large degree of autonomy: they give opinions on questions of both fact and law, make a thorough examination of all the points involved in the case, are free to choose the applicable texts, to invoke precedents, and can take radical positions, while the judges have to seek compromise. Deliberations being secret, as we know, it is difficult to gauge whether the opinion of the advocate-general is influential or not. At least, there are some indications of how the judges use the opinions of the advocate-general, thanks to a new practice of the judges who now make direct references to the opinions. And it has often been argued that advocates-general played an important role in building European law, even though it must be balanced with the influence of other institutions (the legal service of the Commission) and the member states (Stein, 1981). An illustration can be found in a recent collective volume dedicated to the 'legacy' of Francis Jacobs, advocate-general at the Court of Justice for 18 years (Moser & Sawyer, 2008), who many scholars recognize as having made a huge contribution in fields such as fundamental rights, citizenship, international market, competition law, external relations and intellectual property.

The president of the CJEU

The judges of the three courts elect the president of the whole CJEU from among their own, and for a renewable term of three years. Since 2012 they also elect a vice president whose role is to assist the president in the performance of her/his duties and to take the president's place when the latter is prevented from attending, or when the office of president is vacant.

The president directs the judicial business of the CJEU by setting the timetable of the Court and Grand Chamber, assigning cases to the chambers for examination, as well as to the judge *rapporteurs*. He or she presides over general meetings of the members of the Court of Justice and at hearings before, as well at the deliberations of the full Court and the Grand Chamber (meaning that he or she does not preside over hearings and deliberations of smaller formations of the Court of Justice and the General Court, nor at CST meetings). The administrative task of ensuring the proper functioning of the Court is also given to the president as well as the more symbolic task of representing the Court externally. In addition, the president is entitled to adopt interim measures, meaning that he or she may order the suspension of a contested act and prescribe measures aimed at preventing the applicant from suffering irreparable harm.

Judges acting as rapporteurs

The president of the CJEU assigns cases to judges who act as *rapporteurs*. The judge *rapporteur*, with the support of assistant *rapporteurs* appointed by the Council, manages the progress of the case through the Court. He or she writes a report that summarizes the facts and the arguments of the parties concerned, in order to help the chamber decide on the case. The content of this report may be in contradiction with the opinion given by the advocate-general. If the chamber prefers the approach of the judge *rapporteur*, the opinion of the advocate-general may be put aside. Conversely, the

Box 3.2 List of the presidents of the CJEU

TERM	PRESIDENT	MEMBER STATE OF ORIGIN
1952–58	Massimo Pilotti	Italy
1958–64	Andreas Matthias Donner	Netherlands
1964–67	Charles Léon Hammes	Luxembourg
1967–76	Robert Lecourt	France
1976–80	Hans Kutscher	Germany
1980–84	Josse Mertens de Wilmars	Belgium
1984–88	Ole Due	Denmark
1988–94	John Mackenzie-Stuart	United Kingdom
1994–2003	Gil Carlos Rodríguez Iglesias	Spain
2003–15	Vassilios Skouris	Greece
2015–	Koen Lenaerts	Belgium

report by the judge *rapporteur* may be rejected, and a majority of judges may request that the opinion of the advocate-general be followed. Again, due to the secrecy of the deliberations (see the section on Secret deliberations, below), we know very little about these issues (Solanke, 2011, p. 769).

The staff of the Court

The CJEU employs a staff of around 1,500 in permanent posts and 450 in temporary posts, engaged in administrative and linguistic duties. Each judge and advocate-general is assisted by three and four *référendaires*, who play a role similar to those of the law clerk attached to a Justice at the US Supreme Court. This staff is given tasks such as performing research on points of law, and drafting opinions and judgements. Hence, the CJEU is not only a judicial institution composed of judges and advocates-general but also an administration headed by the registrar of the Court, similar to the role of an organization's secretary-general. The registrar is appointed for six years by the Court and is in charge of its records. She or he is also responsible for the administration and financial management of the Court.

Main features of the Court procedures

Written and oral stages

As a general rule, cases submitted to the Court of Justice and the General Court are processed in two stages: a written stage and an oral stage. There are very few exceptions, such as the simplified preliminary ruling procedure, where no oral phase is necessary.

During the written stage, the parties send a statement to the judge in charge of the case (judge *rapporteur*). When the written part of the procedure is finished, the president fixes a date on which the judge *rapporteur* can present his/her preliminary report to the general meeting of the Court. The preliminary report contains proposals for: particular measures of organizational procedure, measures of inquiry, and (where appropriate) requests to the referring court for clarification.

The second stage concerns the public hearing. Having heard the position of the advocate-general, and on the proposal of the judge *rapporteur*, the Court may decide not to hold a hearing if it considers to have received insufficient information to give a ruling, that is, when the written pleadings or observations lodged during the written part of the procedure are inadequate. At the hearing, lawyers from both sides put their case to the judges and the advocate-general, which can in turn question them.

The advocate-general then gives his or her opinion (only in cases before the Court of Justice), which is not necessarily followed by the Court. Thereafter the judges discuss the case together and give their judgement. The Court's judgements are majority decisions and are read out at public hearings.

Most cases take one to three years to judge (Figure 3.1). Many acknowledge the danger of excessive delays in the administration of justice, particularly concerning the respect of the rule of law. The creation of both the General Court and the CST was aimed at relieving the workload of the Court of Justice, and thus reducing the duration of cases. The same was intended with the internal organization of the courts, where small formations of judgements became normal practice. In 2012, the duration of cases averaged

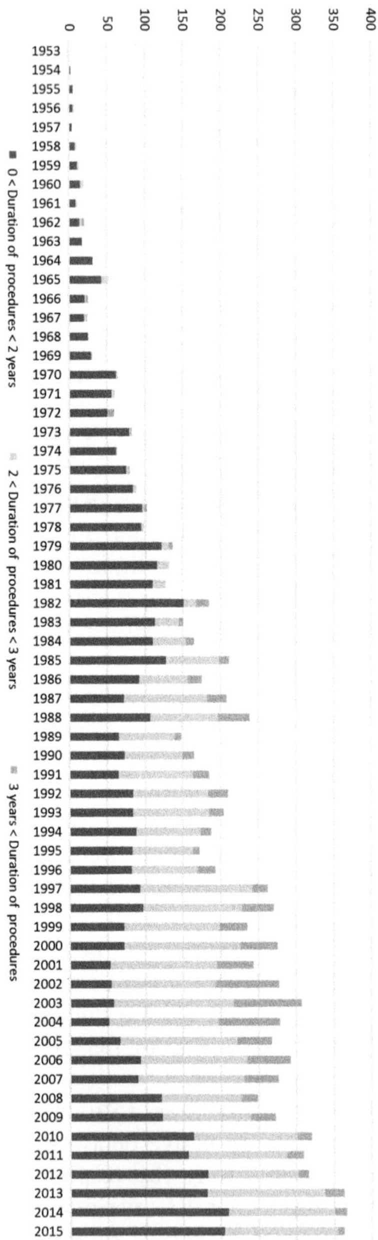

FIGURE 3.1 *Number of completed cases/duration of procedures/year*

24.8 months, which was 1.9 months shorter than in 2011 (CJEU, 2013). Compared to the average domestic court procedure, the length of a procedure at the EU level remains considerably longer.

Secret deliberations

When the Court of Justice was created in the early 1950s, the source of inspiration was the French legal system. In France the courts are considered to be merely the mouthpiece of the law, as advocated by the eighteenth-century philosopher Montesquieu. This understanding of law tends to shroud the diversity that actually exists among judges, and suggests that there is only one possible interpretation of the law when in fact there are several. Just as in the French system, judgements of the Court of Justice are based on secret deliberations. Current as well as former judges never reveal the views expressed by individual members. We know that the judge acting as *rapporteur* circulates a draft judgement on which other judges can disagree. But differences of opinion must be kept secret. There are no dissenting opinions in the Court of Justice, contrary to the ECtHR and the International Court of Justice, or a federal court such as the US Supreme Court. Each judge states his or her opinion but a consensus has to be found. In the absence of consensus, the opinion of the majority prevails. Hence, rulings are ultimately decided collegially, without publishing the dissenting judgements. Judges swear an oath to preserve the secrecy of the vote.

As secrecy applies to judicial decision-making, it is rather difficult to open the 'black box' of the CJEU. Differing interpretations can only be found in the legal doctrine (comments made by legal experts) as well as in advocates-general's opinions, which are published in advance (before the judgement) so that the Court of Justice has time to consider it. When the Court does not share an opinion, this if often because it reflects the position of a minority of judges.

There are two main criticisms of the secret and consensual nature of Court deliberations. The first is that rulings lack clarity and coherence. The fact that the Court of Justice issues a single judgement based on a compromise arguably has a negative effect on the quality of its reasoning. Some might argue that its reasoning loses coherence because of the need to make concessions to minority opinions. Conversely, the coherence and clarity of the judgements might be increased were dissenting opinions actually allowed. As the legal scholar Joseph H. H. Weiler advocates: 'One of the virtues of separate and dissenting opinions is that they force the majority opinion to be reasoned in an altogether more profound and communicative fashion' (1999, p. 13).

One way to enhance the coherence and clarity of the rulings, without allowing for dissident opinions, would be to ensure that the drafting of the judgements were left to those members who share the majority opinion (Arnull, 2006, p. 12). Thus, the author of the draft ruling would not necessarily act as the judge *rapporteur*. Moreover, to maintain the secrecy of the deliberations, the name of the judge *rapporteur* would not be given.

A second point of criticism is related to the alleged lack of democratic basis of the procedure (Lasser, 2009). In this regard, democracy requires the maximum transparency of institutions possible, including of legal institutions. Some see the lack of transparency in the Court's decision-making as a means for the real justifications of Court case law to be hidden from citizens.

How can we justify the rejection of dissenting opinions in the EU legal system? First, one might argue that the authority of the Court would be undermined, were the conflicting views among judges publicized. The fact that decisions were collegial in nature was important in the early years of European integration, because the European Court needed to gain legitimacy. This remains important as the EU experiences a crisis of legitimacy.

Second, we might consider the way judges are appointed. As we have seen above, the mandate of the judges is relatively short, but renewable. Judges must remain totally independent from the government that nominated them. They should not be tempted to defend positions that support the potential renewal of their mandate. As discussed earlier in this chapter, the decision of the German government not to renew the mandate of German judge Zuleeg on account of his critical views on a German government position is an illustration of this particular point.

The legal style of the CJEU

It has often been noted that the CJEU has a specific legal style (Beck, 2012; Conway, 2014), which is rather cryptic and 'Cartesian' (based on the logic of the legal reasoning and the inevitability of the results). The analysis of the issues and of previous case law is rather brief, compared to common law standards.

There are two alternative explanations for this. First, it is primarily the French judicial system that has shaped the CJEU (Chapter 2). This can be explained on account of the role France played during the first years of European integration, in a European Community composed of six members where French was the official language in three member states. While French may not necessarily be the language of the case under review, deliberations take place in French, and judgements are drafted in French before being translated into the language of the case. The rules of procedures stipulate the languages that can be used for cases before the courts. As for direct actions, the language is usually chosen by the applicant. In referrals for preliminary rulings, the Court uses the language of the national court that made the referral. But since the 1950s, French has been the sole internal working language of the CJEU.

The second explanation, on the other hand, focuses on diversity. The legal style of the CJEU is the result of a compromise between different legal traditions and reflects 'the deep diversity of languages and legal cultures which the working language – French – can hardly surmount'. This 'creates a strong culture of consensus that does not favour a more discursive style of legal argument in the Court's opinions' (Schönberger, 2015, p. 505).

Weiler recommended that the Court of Justice abandon this 'cryptic' style, and opt for a more 'conversational' and 'discursive' style associated with common law. He argued that such a change would help the Court better explain its judgements, and in so doing help overcome the perceived legitimacy deficit (Weiler, 2001, p. 225).

Conclusion

Knowledge of the structure and staffing of the Court of Justice of the European Union is essential for any understanding of the Court's case law from the 1950s and 1960s to the present day. The member states may have established the rules outlining the appointment of the judges with a view to controlling them. Yet several factors suggest, on the contrary, that the CJEU is quite independent from national governments owing to the status of the judges and advocates-general; the lack of cohesion among the member states; unique operational rules, including secrecy in deliberations; and the sociological profile of the judges. These factors help explain how the CJEU has succeeded in developing its bold jurisprudence, challenging the sovereignty of the member states. While perfectly valid, these factors do not explain the variation in the Court's case law (activism vs. self-restraint); and other than for the appointment procedure, they do not situate the CJEU in the wider institutional and political context. What they do is help us understand the way in which decisions are made, by making clear the standard operating procedures in place and capturing the dynamics of interaction between the *référendaires*, the judges and advocates-general in preparing the Court's rulings. To understand the Court's overall role, we need to place the CJEU and its judges in the broader environment of the EU's political system.

The following chapters therefore focus on the interactions between the CJEU on the one hand, and the EU institutions (Chapter 4), the member states (Chapter 5) and civil society (Chapter 6) on the other. They provide more comprehensive and rounded insight into the Court's role and the institutional context in which it operates today.

Chapter 4

The Role of the Court in the EU Political System

The duty of the Court of Justice, as defined in article 19 of the Treaty on European Union (TEU), is to ensure that 'in the interpretation and application of the treaties, the law is observed'. In other words, it ensures that the institutions and member states of the EU correctly interpret and apply EU law. In doing so, however, the Court does not act in a political vacuum, but is embedded in a dense network of actors. This chapter aims to explain the interconnectedness of these political and judicial institutions. It first studies how the Court reviews the legality of European acts such as regulations, directives and decisions, how it ensures that the member states comply with obligations under the various treaties, and how it interprets EU law at the request of national courts and tribunals. Two different types of review are examined, the first aimed at the EU institutions (actions for annulment, actions for failure to act, direct actions), and the second concerning EU member states (actions for failure to fulfil an obligation, requests for a preliminary ruling). However, this chapter goes a step further to show that the Court is an embedded actor, and as such, we need to study its powers in relation to the larger political system.

The judicial powers of the Court

Article 19-3 TEU classifies the functions and powers of the Court by distinguishing between direct and indirect actions. Direct actions are brought directly before the Court by a member state, an EU institution, or a natural or legal person. Indirect actions arise through preliminary references, which are questions of legal clarification stemming from national courts (Arnull & Chalmers, 2015). This section distinguishes between direct actions against European institutions, preliminary references, and direct actions against the member states.

Direct actions against EU institutions

TABLE 4.1 *Main actions against EU institutions*

Type of action	Legal Basis	Content
Actions for annulment	263 TFEU	Annulment of a measure adopted by an institution, body, office and agency of the European Union.
Actions for failure to act	265 TFEU	Control the legality of an institution, body, office and agency inaction.
Plea of illegality	241 TFEU	Action allows parties in proceedings against a measure to plead the illegality of its parent measure.
Actions for damages	268, 340 TFEU	Action may be brought by individuals. Enables compensation for damages caused by the institutions, body, office and agencies of the European Union. The EU's Contractual and Non-Contractual Liability can be engaged.
Action brought by officials	270 TFEU	CJEU has jurisdiction to give judgement in any dispute between the Union and its servants.
Responsibility of a member of the institutions	245 TFEU	CJEU may rule that the member of an institution be compulsorily retired or deprived of his right to a pension or other benefits having if he or she breaks his obligations under the treaties.

Source: Curia.europa.eu

Actions for annulment

Under article 263 TFEU, the European Court can review the legality of certain EU acts. The proceedings must be instituted within two months of the publication of the measure, or of its notification to the plaintiff; or in the absence thereof, of the day on which it came to the knowledge of the latter. If the Court considers that an action for annulment is founded, it declares the acts concerned to be void (art. 264-1 TFEU), and the Union is henceforth 'required to take the necessary measures to comply with the judgment' (art. 266 TFEU).

Which acts can be challenged in judicial review proceedings? According to article 263 TFEU, the Court is entitled to review all legislative acts adopted by the Council and the Parliament. Judicial review also concerns the non-legislative acts of all Union institutions with exception of the Court of Auditors and the European Court, as well as all EU bodies, offices or agencies, provided that these acts produce legal effects *vis-à-vis* third parties. Recommendations and opinions cannot be reviewed as they have no binding force; nor can purely preparatory acts of the Commission and Council, which are considered 'internal' acts. In *International Business Machines Corporation vs. Commission* (60/81), for example, IBM sought the annulment of a Commission letter notifying it that competition proceedings had been opened against it and requiring a reply to be sent before a specified time. The action failed; the Court considered the letter to be a preparatory act, not a final decision, and therefore was unchallengeable.

For what reasons can EU acts be challenged? There are four different grounds for review under article 263 TFEU. Three of them are formal. First, the EU institution may lack the competence to adopt an act, because the latter should have been adopted by another institution or by the member states. Second, the adoption may infringe an essential procedural requirement (when the Union leaves out an institution that should have been involved according to the treaties; and when the act is adopted under a wrong voting arrangement in one institution). In *Roquettes frères vs. Council (Isoglucose)* (138/79), for example, the Council failed to consult the Parliament on an act where consultation was required.

Third, a misuse of powers may also justify judicial review, that is, a situation where an EU institution uses its powers for ends other than those provided for by European law. In 2002, for example, the directive on the manufacture, presentation and sale of tobacco products was challenged on the basis that it aimed at defending public health, which was not a European competence at that time, rather then improving the conditions of the functioning of the internal market. The Court of Justice in this case (C-491/01) stated that, indeed, it was not established that the directive had been adopted with the sole or at least the main purpose of achieving the internal market.

The fourth ground is not formal but substantive; an EU act may be challenged on the basis that it infringes the treaties or any rule of law relating to their application, including international agreements to which the Union is a party, as in *Netherlands vs. Commission and Parliament* (C–377/98).

In a way, a fifth ground can also be found in article 5-4 TEU, which states that 'the content and form of Union action shall not exceed what is necessary to achieve the objectives of the Treaties'. This principle of *proportionality* began as an unwritten principle before being codified in the EU Treaty. For instance, in the *Kadi* case (*Yassin Abdullah Kadi, Al Barakaat International Foundation* C–402 and 415/05), the Court considered that a regulation freezing the assets of people suspected to be associated with Al-Qaeda restricted the right to property of the applicant in a disproportionate manner.

Who can challenge the acts? Article 263 TFEU distinguishes between three categories of applicants. 'Privileged applicants' (the member states, Commission, Council and Parliament) can always bring an action for judicial review (Arnull, 2001). 'Semi-privileged' applicants (the Courts of Auditors, European Central Bank and Committee of the Regions) may only bring actions for the purpose of protecting their prerogatives. The European Parliament was a semi-privileged applicant until the Treaty of Nice signed in 2000, which allowed it to become a fully privileged applicant. The European Council is not a claimant under article 263 TFEU, which is surprising since it is entitled to seek judicial review under article 265 TFEU (failure to act). Natural and legal persons compose the third category; they are 'non-privileged' applicants who must demonstrate that a Union act affects them specifically. Their situation has, however, changed since the Treaty of Lisbon (see Chapter 6).

Before Lisbon, the Rome Treaty establishing the EC gave private parties three possibilities to challenge EU acts (art. 230-4 TEC, now art. 263 TFEU). They could institute proceedings against a decision addressed to them; against a decision addressed to another person but who was of direct and individual concern to them; or against a regulation which was of direct and individual concern to them. In the first case, the concern was presumed whereas in the second and third cases it had to be proven. The third case was heavily disputed. In *Codorniu vs. Council* (C–309/89), the Court stated that 'although it is true that ... the contested provision is, by nature and by virtue of its sphere of application, of a legislative nature in that it applies to the traders concerned in general, that does not prevent it from being of individual concern to some of them'. Thus, it became clear that it was not only possible to challenge executive acts but also legislative ones. The other contribution of the Court concerned the meaning of 'direct and individual concern'. In the *Plaumann* case (25/62), the Court said that to prove individual concern it is not sufficient to rely on the effects that the act has on the private parties; instead the private parties must show that the effects are peculiar to them. This restrictive interpretation limits the individual's right to judicial review.

The Treaty of Lisbon has brought about two major changes in article 263-4 TFEU (formerly art. 230-4 EC), with regard to general acts. The new provision specifies that private parties may challenge 'a regulatory act which is of direct concern to them and does not entail legislative measures'. The consequences of this new formulation are unclear. The difference with the *Plaumann* ruling is evident, as only direct (and not individual) concern has to be proven. This should encourage greater access to the Court for private parties. However, the term 'regulatory act' has not yet been defined and can be seen either as all general applicable acts (which would liberalize the standing of private applicants significantly), or non-legislative acts (which would reduce the standing of private applicants significantly).

The CJEU has been given several opportunities to broaden the admissibility of direct actions. For example, in *Unión de Pequeños Agricultores* (C–50/00), the claimant, an association of Spanish farmers, requested that in the absence of adequate national legal remedies, the CJEU could hear a direct action for annulment, even if the applicant does not meet the requirements for admissibility. The Court refused this request on the grounds that it might be seen as a *contra legem* interpretation (against the law).

The Kadi case (*Yassin Abdullah Kadi, Al Barakaat International Foundation* C–402 and 415/05) provides a good example of the annulment procedure. In 2002, the Council adopted Regulation

TABLE 4.2 *Categories of litigants/action for annulment*

	Before the Treaty of Nice (< 2000)	*After the Treaty of Nice (> 2000)*	*Since the Treaty of Lisbon (> 2009)*
Member States	**'Privileged applicants':**	**'Privileged applicants'**	**'Privileged applicants'**
Commission	Can always bring an action for judicial review.		
Council			
Parliament	**'Semi-privileged':**		
Courts of Auditors	May only bring actions for the purpose of protecting their prerogatives.	**'Semi-privileged'**	**'Semi-privileged'**
European Central Bank			
Committee of the regions			
Natural persons	**'Non-privileged':** Must demonstrate that the Union act affects them specifically. Private parties could institute proceedings: – against a decision addressed to them; – against a decision addressed to another person but who was of direct and individual concern to them; – against a regulation who was of direct and individual concern to them (C–309/89: executive acts could be challenged but also legislative ones, 25/62: the private parties must show that the effects are peculiar to them).	**'Non-privileged'**	**'Non-privileged':** Private parties may challenge 'a regulatory act which is of direct concern to them and does not entail legislative measures' (art. 263-4 TFEU).
Legal persons			

881/2002, which provides for the freezing of the funds and other economic resources of several individuals and entities. The Sanctions Committee of the United Nations had designated these individuals and entities as being associated with Al-Qaeda or the Taliban, and they appeared in a list annexed to the regulation. Regulation 881/2002 implemented UN Security Council resolutions aimed at fighting terrorism. Mr Kadi, a Saudi resident, with the Al Barakaat International Foundation established in Sweden, brought actions for annulment before the Court of First Instance (CFI) (now General Court). They were directly and individually concerned by the regulation because their names appeared in the list, and therefore they had standing before the CFI. The regulation was clearly among those acts that were subject to review.

With regard the grounds for review, the claimants argued that the Council was not competent to adopt the regulation and that it had breached several of their fundamental rights, in particular the right to property and the rights of the defence. In its judgements of 21 September 2005 (C–306/01), the CFI dismissed these actions, taking the view that the member states were required to comply with the Security Council resolutions. Hence, the CFI refused to review the legality of the regulation.

On appeal, the Court of Justice confirmed the relevance of the regulation's legal bases, and therefore confirmed the competence of the Council. However, it also concluded that the CFI erred in law by refusing to review the legality of the regulation. In its own ruling, the CJ stated that the appellants' rights of defence were not respected. This breach also resulted in an infringement of the right to judicial review, since the appellants were not able to defend their rights before the CFI. With regard to the restriction of the right to property, the CJ found that the contested regulation was adopted without furnishing any guarantee enabling Mr Kadi to put his case before the competent authorities.

In the light of these breaches, the Court of Justice annulled Regulation 881/2002 insofar as it concerned Mr Kadi and Al Barakaat. However, the Court took into account the fact that the immediate annulment of the regulation would seriously and irreversibly prejudice the effectiveness of the restrictive measures. Furthermore, the Court recognized that imposing such measures on Mr Kadi and Al Barakaat could be justified. For this reason, the ruling maintained the effects of the regulation for a period of three months in order to allow the Council to correct the infringements found in the regulation.

Actions for failure to act

Actions for failure to act are governed by article 265 TFEU. Even though this type of action is quite the opposite of an action for annulment, and therefore very close to article 263 TFEU (which reviews the legality of certain acts), there are a few differences between the two procedures. The scope of article 265 is at the same time both wider and narrower than the scope of article 263. It is wider, because actions for failure to act, contrary to actions for annulment, can be brought in relation to preparatory acts (*Parliament vs. Council* 377/87). Hence, proceedings for failure to act may be brought against the European Parliament, European Council, Council, Commission, European Central Bank, as well as EU bodies, offices or agencies. It is also narrower because the Court requires the action to be an *obligation* on, and not merely a *right* of, the institution concerned. There cannot be a general obligation to develop a policy (such as a general framework for the common transport policy) but merely a legal obligation to adopt specific measures (*Parliament vs. Council* 13/83).

Like infringement actions against member states, the procedure is divided into an administrative and a judicial stage. First, the relevant institution must have been called upon to act. If, within a period of two months, it has not defined its position, then a second period of two months begins during which an action may be brought.

In *Asia Motor France and Others vs. Commission* (T–28/90), a group of applicants considering themselves to be the victims of an unlawful cartel operated by five importers of Japanese cars into France (namely Sidat Toyota France, Mazda France Motors, Honda France, Mitsubishi Sonauto and Richard Nissan SA), lodged a complaint with the Commission on 18 November 1985, followed by another complaint on 29 November 1988. The Commission failed to reply to the applicants and they therefore sent a letter on 24 November 1989 requesting the Commission adopt a position on the complaints. When it failed to reply, the applicants brought an action for failure to act. As they were directly and individually concerned by the situation, they had legal standing to bring the case before the CFI (now General Court). The CFI held that the applicants could bring an action for failure to act because, although required to give an answer by art. 6 of Regulation 99/63, the Commission did not inform the applicants of the reasons why it had declined to pursue a complaint. Action for failure to act, in this case, was very instrumental insofar as it forced the Commission to make a decision that could be reviewable under article 263 TFEU. This example shows how action for failure to act is complementary to action for annulment.

The plea of illegality

The plea of illegality, as defined in article 277 TFEU, allows parties in proceedings against a measure to plead the illegality of its parent measure, notwithstanding the expiry of the period laid down in article 263 TFEU, that is, after the two-month period during which parties can bring an action for annulment before the Court. The plea for illegality is often seen as a 'parasitic procedure' (Chalmers, Davies & Monti, 2014, p. 457). It cannot be brought as an independent action but needs to be invoked in the context of proceedings brought under another procedure. For example, parties can challenge a decision under article 263 TFEU within the two-month period, and plead for the illegality of the regulation on which the decision was based, on the grounds that the Court has not been given the opportunity to declare it illegal (because no direct action was brought before it within the two-month period).

Invoking the inapplicability of parent measures is particularly important in the field of delegated or implementing acts. In a way, article 277 TFEU compensates for the strict time limit of article 263 TFEU. However, parties cannot raise a plea of illegality if they have had an earlier opportunity to challenge the parent measure and not used it. This is the case of privileged applicants under article 263 who can bring an action before the Court without having to prove that they are directly or indirectly concerned. In *Spain vs. Council* (C–442/04), the Court has ended this restriction; applicants can invoke article 277 TFEU even if they had the opportunity to contest the measure in due time under article 263 TFEU and did not use it.

Simmenthal I (92/78) provides a good example of a plea of illegality. The applicant sought to annul a Commission decision concerning the minimum selling prices for frozen beef. For this, he pleaded the illegality of the regulations and notices that formed the legal basis of the contested decision. In this case, the Court held that there was no doubt that the applicant could indirectly challenge the concerned regulations. However, it was questionable whether the same applied to the 'notices of invitation to tender' as they were not mentioned explicitly in the Treaty provision dealing with the plea of illegality. Such notices, said the Court, are general acts, which determine in advance and objectively the rights and obligations of the traders who wish to participate in the invitation to tender and, therefore, they produce the same legal effects as regulations. Moreover, as private parties could not challenge the notices under the annulment action, the Court allowed the applicant to challenge them indirectly through the plea of illegality.

Damages actions: contractual and non-contractual liability

Article 268 TFEU acknowledges an action for damages, as specified in article 340 TFEU. This provision distinguishes between *contractual liability*, governed by national law, and *non-contractual liability*, governed by European law.

The action for damages – or liability action – used to be a dependent action, meaning that it had to be preceded by a (successful) annulment action (*Plaumann* 25/62). This changed with Lütticke (*Lütticke et al. vs. Commission* 31 & 33/62), which established article 340 TFEU as an independent action. The action can be brought against all damages caused by EU institutions and servants. There are no limitations on potential applicants. Unlike annulment actions, which are only possible within two months after the publication or notification of the act, the liability action can be brought within a five-year period. As far as the procedure is concerned, it is rather liberal. The substantive conditions, however, are more restrictive.

Two periods must be distinguished. During the first period ending in the early 2000s, a difference is made between administrative acts and legislative action involving measures of economic policy. Though the Union can be liable for administrative actions or inactions that have caused damages, it does not incur any liability for legislative actions involving measures of economic policy 'unless a sufficiently flagrant violation of a superior rule of law for the protection of the individual has occurred' (*Schöppenstedt vs. Council* 5/71). During the second period, starting with Bergadem in 2000 (*Bergadem et al. vs. Commission* C–352/98P), the distinction between administrative and legislative acts comes to an end, and the restrictive conditions for legislative actions are softened. Henceforth, three conditions have to be met: the rule of law infringed must intend to confer rights on individuals; the breach

TABLE 4.3 *Formal and substantive conditions for damages actions*

Category of conditions	Conditions
Formal conditions	Independent action (since *Lütticke et al. vs. Commission* 31 & 33/62).
	Against all action or inaction that is claimed to have caused damages.
	No limitations on applicants.
	Five-year period to claim (art. 46 of the CJEU Statute).
Substantive conditions	Existence of the damage.
	Sufficiently serious breach of a rule of law protecting the rights of the individuals.
	Direct causal link between the damage and the breach of the obligation.

must be sufficiently serious; there must be a direct causal link between the breach of the obligation resting on the state and the damage sustained by the injured parties.

The *Arcelor* case (T–16/04) exemplifies actions for damages in the post-*Bergadem* period. The claimant sought damages for loss caused by a 2003 directive establishing the European Emissions Trading Scheme (ETS). Prior to this directive, Arcelor had enjoyed almost unrestricted carbon emissions in its operations. The ETS system introduced a significant change to the legal and economic conditions under which the investments of the company had been made. One of the legal arguments Arcelor used was that the ETS amounted to discriminatory treatment of its operations because the scope of the directive had excluded the chemicals and non-ferrous metals sectors (Miles, 2011, p. 275). The CFI (now General Court) held that it was for the claimant to demonstrate the actual breach. Reiterating the test from the *Bergadem* ruling, it emphasized the breadth of European discretionary power in this field, stating that EU legislature was required to evaluate 'ecologic, scientific, technical and economic changes of a complex and uncertain nature' and balance 'the various objectives, principles and interests' set out in the Treaty provision dealing with environment (Craig & De Búrca, 2011, p. 563). According to the General Court, Arcelor had not shown that the directive was a sufficiently serious breach of (1) the right of property; (2) the freedom to pursue an economic activity; (3) the principle of proportionality; (4) the principle of equal treatment; (5) freedom of establishment; or (6) the principle of legal certainty, to give rise to non-contractual liability on the part of the EU. In particular, it stated that the directive did not infringe the principle of equal treatment, since the difference in treatment brought about by the exclusion of the chemicals and non-ferrous metals sectors from the scope of the directive was justified by objective criteria. For these reasons, Arcelor's application for damages was rejected.

Preliminary rulings

The preliminary rulings procedure is generally presented as 'the cornerstone of the Union's judicial federalism' (Schütze, 2012, p. 152) compared to those actions presented above. The term 'judicial' or 'collaborative federalism' means that, in the case of preliminary rulings, the European Court and national courts collaborate in the adjudication of a single case. National courts ask for interpretative help from the European Court, with a view to ensure national compliance with EU law.

The obligation to comply with EU law derives from the primacy principle as well as the principle of *sincere cooperation*, the implications of which are explained by article 4-3 TEU: 'The member states shall take any appropriate measure, general or particular, to ensure fulfilment of the obligations arising out of the Treaties or resulting from the acts of the institutions of the Union. The member states shall facilitate the achievement of the Union's tasks and refrain from any measure which could jeopardize the attainment of the Union's objectives.'

The Treaties establish a dual enforcement mechanism for European law, relying on European courts at a centralized level and national courts at a decentralized level. Because EU law is part of each member state's legal order, the rights and obligations emanating from the EU are enforced in national courts rather than before the CJEU. All national courts are entitled, and obliged, to apply EU law to disputes brought before them. In a way, this decentralized application of EU law transforms national courts into 'European' courts. State courts are not hierarchically subordinated to the CJEU: their relationship with the CJEU is based on voluntary cooperation. The former, however, are not totally free when enforcing European law. By providing a link between national courts and the CJEU, the preliminary reference helps ensure that EU law is uniformly applied in the member states. Indeed, according to article 267 TFEU, the CJEU gives preliminary rulings in order to guarantee the uniform interpretation and application of EU law. Most EU rules have *direct effect*, which implies that national courts are primary enforcers of Union law. The fact that direct effect applies to both Treaty provisions and EU directives, combined with the existence of indirect review through preliminary rulings, means that preliminary reference represents a kind of infringement procedure for those citizens wishing to see EU law enforced at national level, thanks to the indirect support of the European Court (Prete & Smulders, 2010).

The European Treaties have recognized procedural autonomy in the national enforcement of European law. Were the interpretation of Union law left to national courts, it would be difficult to ensure uniformity: each court could opt for a specific interpretation, consistent with its national legal context, traditions and method of interpretation. For this reason, the CJEU has jurisdiction to give preliminary rulings on: first, the interpretation and validity of EU secondary legislation; and second, the interpretation of EU primary law (the validity of the Treaties cannot be questioned before the Court). This mechanism to provide interpretative assistance to national courts has existed since the 1950s (Alter, 2000; Hornuf & Voigt, 2014).

In the case of preliminary references, an action is first brought before a national court. If the case rests on a legal basis within EU law, then the national court can, or may have to, make a referral to the Court of Justice (referral cannot be made before the GC and the CST). It is important to note, however, that it is for the national court, and not the parties to the case, to decide whether a reference should be made. The CJ has accepted referrals from a large variety of tribunals and courts, including arbitration panels or administrative tribunals (like in *Van Gend en Loos* 26/62). Giving a wide interpretation to the notion of 'referring court' has been one way to increase the number of preliminary rulings and, in so doing, strengthen the interpretative power of the Court of Justice.

Article 267-2 TFEU states that any court or tribunal 'may, if it considers that a decision on the question is necessary to enable it to give judgement, request the Court of Justice to give a ruling thereon'. The CJ has interpreted this to mean that the Court is not bound to make a reference to the European Court (*Simmenthal* 92/78). An exception is provided by article 267-3 TFEU: national courts or tribunals 'against whose decisions there is no judicial remedy in national law ... shall bring the matter before the Court of Justice'. This means that any court from which there is no appeal *must* make a referral to the Court of Justice. High courts are among these courts of last resort, which have an obligation to refer. Lower courts usually have discretion to refer questions of interpretation of EU law. Questions of validity, however, must be referred to the Court of Justice, which is granted the exclusive power to invalidate European law.

In practice, lower courts have widely used their authority to make references. According to Karen Alter, this has allowed them to gain powers with regard to high courts. Using the Court of Justice 'allowed lower courts to circumvent the restrictive jurisprudence of high courts, and to re-open legal debates which had been closed, and thus to try for legal outcomes of their preference for policy or legal reasons' (Alter, 1996, p. 466). The Court of Justice's backing of a lower-court decision results in it being less likely to be overturned by a high court at national level. Attempts by high courts to limit the power of lower courts to refer preliminary questions was opposed by the European Court, which held that: 'a rule of national law whereby a court is bound on points of law by the rulings of a superior court cannot deprive the inferior courts of their power to refer to the Court questions of interpretation of (Union) law involving such rulings' (*Rheinmühlen-Düsseldorf* 166/73).

On the other hand, high courts sometimes escape their obligation to ask preliminary questions, based on the principle of *acte clair* imported by the CJEU from French law into the European legal order. This doctrine means that, when it is clear how to act, a national court need not ask a preliminary question (*Da Costa* 28 and 30/62; *C.I.L.F.I.T.* 283/81). In addition, the principle concerns situations where previous decisions of the Court already dealt with the point of law in question. The way that high courts make use of this principle is a very sensitive issue. Indeed, the principle can be used as an instrument of sovereignty, allowing national courts to resist the Court of Justice. The French *Conseil d'État* widely used the principle until the 1990s. Since the mid-1990s, however, the French court has shown greater readiness to acknowledge the supremacy of the CJEU's interpretations (Mangenot, 2005), and thus the reference to '*acte clair*' has decreased.

Once the Court of Justice has given its interpretation of EU law or declared the validity or invalidity of EU secondary legislation, the referring national court (and not the parties in the national dispute) is bound by the preliminary ruling. The national court has no choice but to apply the ruling to the case brought before it. However, the Court of Justice cannot exceed its power and decide on the case itself, nor can it interpret rules pertaining to national law and decide whether or not a national law violates the Treaties. The fine line between the interpretation and application of European law to a specific case is rather blurred. Preliminary rulings have effects that go beyond the national referring court. The interpretation they give to European law generally binds all national courts (Trabucchi, 1974, p. 56). Hence, preliminary rulings are an indirect means to ensure compliance with EU law, in addition to the direct actions that can be brought before the CJEU against the member states.

While preliminary rulings feature amongst major landmark decisions such as *Van Gend en Loos* 26/62, *Simmenthal* 92/78, or *C.I.L.F.I.T.* 283/81 in which national courts' referrals played a crucial role in opening up the possibility for a broad interpretation of EU law, the relationships between the CJEU and domestic lower courts can be rather conflictual. *Arsenal Football Club vs. Matthew Reed* (C–206/01) illustrates such a difficult relationship. Matthew Reed had been selling football merchandise articles bearing the registered trademarks of Arsenal FC from stalls near Highbury Stadium for around 30 years. Arsenal FC started proceedings against Reed in January 1999 at the British High Court of Justice. They alleged that Reed infringed certain of their registered trademarks. The case turned upon the effect of an EU Directive on trademarks, and that issue was referred to the Court of Justice by the High Court. The CJ made it clear that there was an infringement, but the High Court refused to follow the ruling because it thought the European Court had exceeded its jurisdiction by making findings of facts which were inconsistent with those made by the High Court prior to the reference. In the end, the High Court's ruling was later overturned by the British Court of Appeal (Wyatt et al., 2011, p. 217).

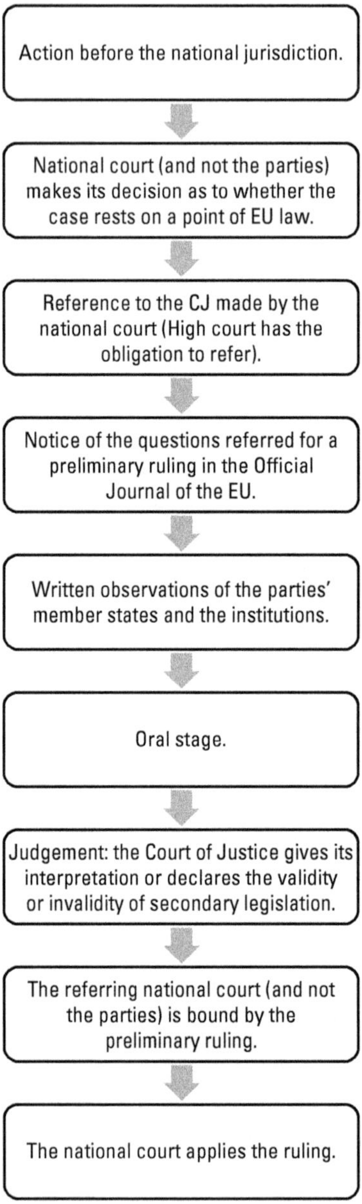

FIGURE 4.1 *Proceedings for preliminary rulings*

To avoid these kinds of problems, the Court of Justice often remains prudent in the wording of its rulings, giving the layman the impression of being particularly obscure. National courts, on the other hand, when confronted with a preliminary ruling that they perceive as a misinterpretation of the facts, are supposed to make a further reference, instead of ignoring the reference (Vink et al., 2009). Very often, the European Court and national courts are cautious and find a way to avoid any direct conflict. In some cases, however, the European Court goes a little further than simply giving an interpretation of the EU rule. Similarly, national courts have room for manoeuvre in the way they apply the CJEU ruling, and sometimes take distance from the ruling without directly confronting it (G. Davies, 2012).

Enforcement actions against member states

Apart from enforcement at national level, the CJEU establishes breaches of the law following a procedural action against the member states, in what is known as the infringement procedure. The preliminary rulings and the infringement procedure are, according to the Court, not mutually exclusive but complementary (*Van Gend en Loos* 26/62). The former is placed in the hands of the national judge, to whom citizens must have access, and the latter in the hands of the Commission (with additional possible actions from the members states). Article 258 TFEU provides for actions by the Commission, while article 259 TFEU gives one member state the possibility to act against another member state. This section concentrates on proceedings brought by the Commission, as member states rarely bring actions against another member state, for fear of retaliation.

TABLE 4.4 *Types of action against the member states*

Type of action	Legal Basis	Content
Action for a declaration of failure to fulfil an obligation	258, 260 TFEU	On the initiative of the Commission.
Action for a declaration of failure to fulfil an obligation	259, 260 TFEU	On the initiative of a member state.

The European Court has given a very extensive definition of what can be considered national breaches of European law. A breach is either an act of a member state or a failure to act, to implement EU legislation; to remove a piece of legislation that is in conflict with existing European legislation; to implement a directive incorrectly, be it inadvertently or on purpose; or to comply with a previous judgement of the Court. The breach may concern the Treaties as well as secondary legislation, EU international agreements, CJEU decisions or general principles of EU law. The breach may arise from any part of the state, not only governmental actions or inactions, including legislative, regional, local or judicial authorities. Besides, the Court interprets very restrictively the reasons that might justify breaches of EU law. It has refused to accept several arguments put forward by third parties: breaches of EU law by other member states (*Commission vs. Luxembourg and Belgium* 90 and 91/63; *Commission vs. France* 232/78), internal constitutional problems (*Commission vs. Ireland* C–39/88), and budgetary restraints (*Commission vs. Italy* 30/72). Similarly, the Court has rejected the argument put forward by the member states that a national law must not be considered as contradictory to EU law as long as it is not used domestically (*Commission vs. France* 167/73). Only *force majeure* in an emergency situation has been accepted by the Court as a legal justification for violating European law.

The Commission investigates possible breaches of EU law. In 2013, the Commission launched some 1,023 investigations on its own initiative. Breaches can also be reported by other member states, other EU institutions, or concerned individuals, businesses and NGOs. Some 3,505 potential breaches were reported to the Commission in 2013 (Commission, 2014a). The Commission usually welcomes complaints coming from outside but has no obligation to act on them. If the Commission is convinced that the state is in breach of an obligation, it gives the state an opportunity to answer the allegation or to correct its action or inaction before any formal procedure begins.

The procedure under article 258 TFEU comprises two main stages: administrative and judicial. The administrative stage starts with a letter of formal notice sent by the Commission to the member state. By way of the letter, the Commission seeks a reply from the member state on a particular point, and the member state can do so while submitting its observations. If the Commission is not convinced by the arguments provided, then a 'reasoned opinion' can be delivered. While the sending of a letter of formal notice is not mentioned in the TFEU, article 258 makes the reasoned opinion compulsory.

The reasoned opinion records the factual and legal reasons as to why the Commission considers the member state has failed to fulfil its obligations under EU law. A further time limit (normally two months) is given to the state to resolve the infringement. Many complaints are settled at this stage. If the Commission is still not convinced, the case can be referred to the CJEU. Referral to the Court is a matter of discretion for the Commission. Roughly 10 per cent of new procedures are brought to the Court by the Commission, whose decisions to pursue the action or to close proceedings are often published in the Official Journal.

The Commission's decision to bring a matter before the Court opens up the litigation stage of the procedure. If member states comply before the judgement, the case can be withdrawn. However, if the member state has only complied with the reasoned opinion beyond the deadline, the Court can proceed to judgement (*Commission vs. Greece* 24/86), which is important as it can help to establish exactly what the law is, and to set a precedent to control other member states' behaviour. It may also be the basis on which the liability of a state is determined. Only around 5 per cent of cases reach a final judgement.

The only possibility for a member state to prevent being found guilty is to prove that there has not been a breach, something it often cannot manage to do – the Commission success rate is between 90 and 99 per cent of the cases brought to the Court (Foster, 2013, p. 202; Panke, 2010). The CJEU has rejected other defence arguments, often acceptable in international law.

One of the main problems with the procedure of article 258 TFEU is its length. It takes on average 17 months to reach a judgement, if you consider the judicial phase only, and even more if you take into account the informal stage. In order to prevent the irreparable harm that a contested act might cause, the CJEU can order the suspension of this act (art. 278 TFEU) or may prescribe interim measures (art. 279 TFEU). Interim measures must be requested before the final judgement and applied only in urgent circumstances.

The European Court only goes as far as to declare that the national law or national practice violates EU law. It is up to the state 'to take the necessary measures to comply with the judgment of the Court', which is an obligation under article 260 TFEU (see Kilbey, 2010; Smith, 2010b). However, if the state does not comply with the Court's judgement, the Commission may apply for a lump sum or penalty payment, or both (the Court has held that article 265 TFEU allows to impose a lump and a penalty at the same time) (*Commission vs. France 'French Fisheries II'* C–304/02). However, for violations to be sanctioned there must be another case brought before the Court by the Commission. There is only one exception for the requirement of a second judgement, which is related to the transposition of directives. If a member state fails 'to notify measures transposing directives adopted under a legislative procedure' (art. 260-3 TFEU), the Commission may apply for a financial sanction in the first enforcement action. The Commission has adopted a communication explaining how this provision should be implemented (Commission, 2011). In 2013, nine member states were implicated in 14 decisions imposing sanctions for the late transposition of directives, mainly in the field of energy policy: Belgium, Bulgaria, Estonia, Romania, the United Kingdom (two cases each) and Austria, Cyprus, Poland and Portugal (one each). The proposed daily penalty ranged from 4,224 euros to 148,177.92 euros. The Commission has not yet pushed for the Court to establish fixed amounts to be paid (Commission, 2014b).

Thus, the Court's rulings can be seen as important tools in the context of the debate on compliance and Europeanization. Diana Panke presents them as 'a prominent compliance instrument', arguing that 'ECJ judgments create publicity and differentially empower societal compliance proponents vis-à-vis opponents. In a second step, societal proponents can push their governments into compliance via shaming and reframing strategies' (Panke, 2007, p. 848).

The number of open infringement cases has fallen continuously in recent years, from nearly 2,100 cases in 2010 to 1,775 cases in 2011 and 1,343 cases in 2012 (Commission, 2013). This might be due to the efficiency of the 'EU Pilot', a coordination instrument the Commission introduced in 2008, which uses a database and an online communication tool with the aim of improving cooperation between member states and the Commission on issues concerning the conformity of national law with EU law, and the correct application of EU law. EU Pilot discussions allow member states to remedy potential EU law infringements by complying voluntarily with the Commission's position. However, even if infringement cases have decreased, actions against the member states for failure to

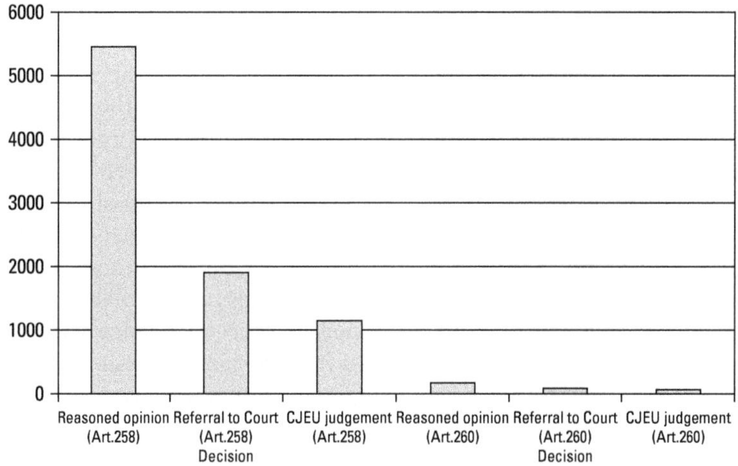

FIGURE 4.2 *Number of infringement proceedings at different stages of the procedure (from 01/01/2002 to 01/05/2015)*

Reasoned opinion (art. 258): 5,434
Referral to Court – Decision (art. 258): 1,907
CJEU Judgement (art. 258): 1,146

Reasoned opinion (art. 260): 132
Referral to Court – Decision (art. 260): 54
CJEU judgement (art. 260): 26

Source: Court of Justice of the European Union, Annual Reports 2003–2015.

fulfil their European obligations remain central to ensuring national compliance with EU law.

A legal case pertaining to fishing provides an interesting example of an infringement procedure that ended with a financial penalty. In a series of regulations adopted in 1982, 1987 and 1993, the Council established certain control measures for fishing activities undertaken by vessels of the member states. One of these measures concerned the minimum mesh size for nets, justified as a measure to protect fishery resources.

In the judgement of 11 June 1991 in Case C–64/88 *Commission vs. France*, the Court of Justice upheld five complaints against France, including inadequate controls in relation to the minimum mesh size for nets. By letter of 8 November 1991, the Commission requested the French authorities to inform it of the measures taken to comply with this judgement. On 22 January 1992, the French authorities replied that they intended to do their utmost to comply with the Regulations' provisions. In the course of a number of visits to French ports, the Commission inspectors found that the situation had improved, but noted that the French authorities' controls were inadequate in several respects. After requesting the French Republic to submit its observations, on 17 April 1996 the Commission issued a reasoned opinion in which it stated that the judgement in Case C–64/88 had not been complied with. The Commission set a time limit of two months for the French authorities to take all the measures necessary. Through an exchange of correspondence with the French authorities, Commission staff were kept informed of the measures taken. At the same time, inspection visits were made to French ports.

Taking the view that France had still not complied with the judgement of June 1991, the Commission brought an action before the Court. In its judgement of 12 July 2005 (C–304/02), the Court ordered the French Republic to pay the Commission (into the account 'European Community own resources') a lump sum of 20 million euros as well as a penalty payment of almost 60 million euros for each six-month period from delivery of the judgement in Case C–64/88.

The judicial powers of the Court in its political context

While it is crucial to understand the legal bases and proceedings that make the Court's rulings possible, as we have done above, to be properly understood and thoroughly analysed, the judicial powers of the European Court must be placed in the wider context of the EU political system (Saurugger & Terpan, 2014). The Court's powers are passive and active at the same time, yet both dimensions relate to the political system. On the one hand, the Court has actively extended its powers through its own case law, opening up the debate on 'judicial activism'. The Court's activism has had a strong impact on the institutional balance within the EU, each institution being affected by judicial decisions. On the other hand, the CJEU remains a rather passive power insofar as it relies on other actors seizing it in order for it to exert its influence.

This section presents how the CJEU interacts with three central EU institutions: Commission, Parliament and Council (relations between the CJEU and the member states, as members of the

Council, are explored in more detail in Chapter 5). We argue that the Court has benefited from these institutional relations, which have also helped increased its influence within the overall system. It is thus fair to describe the institutional structure of the EU as a kind of institutional four-party system (*'quadripartisme institutionnel'*) (Pescatore, 1978). By contrast, the Court has been somewhat left out in several areas where the member states have not wanted judicial 'interference'. The fact that the treaties do not allow EU decisions to be legally controlled in all areas has meant the Court's powers are limited. Nonetheless, it is fair to see the European Court as the high court of a quasi-federal politico-legal system.

How the Court interacts with the other institutions

The CJEU, while exerting its treaty-based powers, interacts with the main EU institutions. Each of these interactions can be studied individually: starting with the Commission, which has empowered the Court by acting as the guardian of the treaties; continuing with the Parliament, which has used the Court as a means to increase its own prerogatives; and finishing with the Council, which ultimately has not opposed the Court's activism. In this section we examine the degree of influence and independence of these actors, dealing with both the legal basis that defines their relationships and the political issues arising in these contexts.

The Court and the Commission

The Commission, acting in the general interest of the Union, can be seen as the 'conscience' of the EU. By referring to the CJEU, the Commission acts within its mandate to ensure the application of the treaties and to oversee the application of EU law (art. 17 TEU). In its role as guardian, the Commission is granted significant powers to act as 'police' and 'prosecutor' of the Union. The Commission has the power to monitor and investigate infringements of EU law, and potentially bring the matter before the Court. This power may be directed against both the member states (infringement procedure under art. 258 TFEU) and EU institutions (enforcement actions under arts. 263 and 265 TFEU). Other provisions of the TFEU allow the Commission to take actions in respect of infringement of state aids provisions (art. 108-2 TFEU), derogations from the internal market (art. 114-9 TFEU), and emergency security measures (arts. 346 to 348 TFEU). Even when it is not acting as the claimant, as with preliminary references, the Commission weighs in with observations carefully drafted by its legal service. Thus, the Commission is particularly central to the EU system of governance in ensuring that the member states give effect to EU law. The development of the abovementioned EU Pilot initiative of the Commission is an indication of the intense activity of the Commission in this field. In 2013, some 1,502 cases were brought before the Commission with regard to the non-compliance of EU law.

The Commission has played a great role in strengthening the Court's position in the EU's institutional system by using its powers extensively. The Court would not be as influential today had the Commission not brought the Council or the member states before it in the 1960s. To date the Commission has been consistent in the use of its power to refer cases to the Court. The infringement procedure, in particular, has created a permanent link between the two institutions. In 2013, for example, the Commission launched 761 new infringement proceedings and sent 217 reasoned opinions to member states, while the Court delivered 52 judgements under article 258 TFEU (Commission, 2013). Very few proceedings actually resulted in Court judgements. This is not a sign of the weakness of the Court, but quite to the contrary shows that the Court has a huge impact in helping ensure compliance with EU law before the judicial phase of the procedure. The shadow of a Court's judgement helps the Commission convince the member states to comply with EU law during the administrative phase. The Commission also reinforces the Court's powers when monitoring the member states' compliance with its judgements. Indeed, the Commission may bring to Court those member states it considers to have failed to comply, often leading to fines, as in the example of the fishery case in 2005 (C–304/02). In 2013 the Commission referred nine cases for a second time to the Court, in order to enforce compliance with a first ruling.

On the other hand, the Commission is also a defendant before the Court in annulment proceedings, and has a record of losing many of these cases. In particular, the Commission is placed under tight judicial control in the field of competition, where the CJEU has often ruled against its decisions since the 1990s. After a period where fines imposed on EU competition law infringers were relatively low, the Commission has increased the level of fines since the 1980s. The lack of transparency in the Commission's methods for calculating fines, combined with the fact that the General Court often seems prepared to reduce the amount of the fines imposed by the Commission, has generated a massive amount of litigation against the Commission (Geradin, 2005).

More generally, being the guardian of the treaties does not mean that the Commission never infringes European law, nor that it can escape the control of the CJEU. The Council and the member states as well as Parliament and private litigants often use the Court in order to ensure the Commission's compliance with EU rules.

The Court and the Parliament

Contrary to the Commission, the Treaty of Rome did not grant the Parliament legal standing before the European Court, meaning that it could neither refer cases to the Court nor be brought before the Court by other applicants. However, its legal status has improved tremendously as a result of important Court rulings, as well as successive treaty revisions.

In the early 1980s, the European Court argued in the case '*Les Verts*' (294/83) that the European Parliament (EP) could be taken to the Court by a party seeking to annul a legal act or asking the Court to sanction a failure to act. This meant the Parliament could hypothetically find itself a defendant before the Court, but with no right itself to bring actions before the Court. As only the Council and Commission were specified as potential litigants in the Treaty of Rome, the Court considered that this excluded the EP ('*Isoglucose*' 138-79; '*Les Verts*' 294/83; '*Comitology*' 302/87). It was conceivable that the Parliament would need to defend its 'legislative right'. However, one could also argue that the Commission, which enjoyed an unlimited right to bring actions for annulment, could defend the Parliament's rights. The Court chose to follow the letter of the treaty and excluded the Parliament from the category of litigants.

In '*Isoglucose*' (138-79), a private litigant, the firm Roquette Frères SA, filed a lawsuit against the Council for annulment of the contested legislation on the grounds of a lack of consultation with the Parliament. However, the Parliament did not have the legal capacity to defend itself before the Court. The Court merely established that the Parliament might act as intervener in legal proceedings, instead of accepting it as litigant.

The Court eventually granted the EP a limited standing to bring actions for annulment if it could show that its prerogatives were affected ('*Chernobyl*' 70-88). In '*Chernobyl*', the Parliament's conflict was with the Commission, which did not respect Parliament's right to be consulted. This led the Court to conclude that the Commission could not always be considered an effective safeguard of Parliament's rights.

The admissibility of lawsuits from the EP has remained quite controversial – it was not until 1992 that the EP brought its first action, the admissibility of which was not challenged by a member state or the Council (McCown, 2003, p. 977). At the same time, the Maastricht Treaty codified the CJEU's case law, even repeating the language of the rulings, stating that the Court shall review 'actions brought by the European Parliament ... for the purpose of protecting its prerogatives' (now art. 173-3 TEU).

Finally, the Treaty of Nice extended the legal standing of the EP. The Parliament now enjoys unlimited powers to challenge the acts of other EU institutions, as well as their failures to act when required to do so. Subsequently, parliamentary litigation has changed in the last decade. Initially, the EP set out to secure institutional powers for itself. In so doing, it hoped to exert the greatest influence possible in the legislative process, and challenge procedures from which it was excluded. The litigation powers of the Parliament have evolved. They now have a more general objective to challenge those acts that cannot be vetoed in the legislative process (McCown, 2003). For example, the Parliament recently challenged the agreement between the European Community and the United States allowing American authorities access to the passenger records of those airlines flying to and from the United States (*Parliament vs. Commission* C–317 and 318/04).

In a way, the relationship between the Court and the Parliament can be seen as an objective alliance between supranational institutions, whose common interest is to strengthen themselves in the face of the Council and the member states. Contrary to the Commission, the Parliament has had to empower itself, as it had no litigation prerogatives from the outset. Thus, the European Court's rulings have helped the Parliament enhance its position in the institutional system; and in so doing they have enlarged the number of possible litigants and consequently increased the Court's own propensity to be called upon to give rulings. While the Parliament has brought cases 'with the intent of triggering institutional change and increasing its influence in the legislative process' (McCown, 2003, 976), the Council and the member states have opposed these developments, rather unsuccessfully as we see in the next section.

The Court and the Council

In the framework of article 263 TFEU (actions for annulment), the Council is a privileged litigant, meaning that it can bring actions before the Court without any limitation to its prerogatives. It has widely pursued this option against supranational institutions such as the Commission and Parliament. This is consistent with the *raison d'être* of the Court in the 1950s, which was to ensure that the High Authority of the European Coal and Steel Community (that is, the Commission) did not go beyond the limits of its prerogatives.

The Court has not systematically defended the Commission and Parliament in cases where it has been opposed to the Council. The principle of institutional balance has sometimes led to rulings favourable to the Council. However, while the Council has often acted as a claimant, it has increasingly been the subject of litigation strategies developed by the supranational institutions. In a large number of rulings, the Court, contrary to arguments put forward by Garrett (1995), has not ruled in favour of the biggest member states. The latter have, however, not been able or willing to override the European Court in a EU-level legislative procedure. At the domestic level, the situation is different, as we will see in Chapter 5, with the member states managing to circumvent Court rulings in certain cases (Martinsen, 2015).

The attribution of litigation powers to the Parliament is a good case in point. The European Court has allowed the legislature to defend its prerogatives against the Council and successfully strengthen its position in the European system of governance. The Council and the member states have tried to stop this evolution, without success. For example, they advocated a narrow interpretation of the 'Chernobyl' rule: the EP should be granted litigation powers to protect its prerogative only in cases where its position differed from the Commission (as the UK alleged in C–295/90); in other cases, this was not seen as necessary, since the Commission was responsible for defending the rights of the Parliament through the infringement procedure. The Court, however, has opted for a wider interpretation (the EP can bring actions for annulment to defend its prerogatives). In the 1990s, the member states changed their minds and codified the Court's interpretation in the Maastricht Treaty; they even enlarged it in the Treaty of Nice, allowing the Parliament to act as litigant in cases where its prerogatives are not at stake. Hence, claims of inadmissibility for legal cases brought by the EP have declined as intergovernmental actors have adjusted to the new judge-made rules (McCown, 2003, 985).

As for the EP's litigation powers, as in other cases, the Council and the member states have not sought to censure the Court (see Chapter 5). Where they have disagreed with past CJEU judgements, instead of overruling the Court through Treaty revisions or new legislation, they have presented legal arguments to the Court, in an effort to win on an individual case-by-case basis (McCown, 2003, pp. 978, 981).

Court curbing

In any legal system, political powers may use 'court curbing' mechanisms to counter jurisdictions that have overstepped the boundaries (Vanberg, 2008; see Chapter 5). As we show in the following chapter, in the EU a number of institutional features actually 'insulate (the *CJEU*) from threats of legislative override and other forms of reprisal by member state governments' (Kelemen, 2012). Legislating and revising treaties require large majorities or even unanimous decisions, which enhance the independence of the Court. Decision-making is made more difficult by the need to reach consensus among 28 member states with very different preferences (Stone Sweet, 2000; Alter, 2001; Pollack, 2003). Resource punishment through budget cuts or decreasing the pay of judges is very unlikely. Public opinion is a more controversial issue. Following Gibson and Caldeira (1995, 1998), we might claim that public opinion is a Court-curbing mechanism. For Kelemen, on the contrary, it provides a solid base of 'diffuse support' for the Court. Kelemen's argument is based on the premise that levels of diffuse public support 'can only be gauged in relative terms. In an environment where public institutions are widely despised, those that are even moderately respected may be in a position of strength relative to other political institutions that might attack them' (Kelemen, 2012, p. 47).

Another reason for not using Court-curbing mechanisms may be the unwillingness of the member states to do so. This kind of explanation has been insufficiently explored. The member states may not be willing to pay the (substantial) costs of overruling the Court (Stacey & Rittberger, 2003, p. 876). There may also be a change in the preferences of intergovernmental actors, who have finally been moving in a more integrative direction, as we examine in more detail in Chapter 5.

Policy areas excluded from the Court's control

Intergovernmental actors have not overruled the Court in areas where judicial control was set out in the treaties. They have rarely revised the treaties or legislated with the purpose of opposing the Court's rulings. Neither have they used 'jurisdiction stripping', which involves removing particular areas of law from the Court's jurisdiction. Yet, they have chosen to exclude new policy areas from judicial control when new areas were included in successive treaty revisions, in so doing preventing possible conflict with the judges. This is the case for the former intergovernmental pillars of the Maastricht Treaty (common foreign and security policy as 'pillar two', and justice and home affairs as 'pillar three') as well as the so-called 'new modes of governance' (Graziano & Halpern, 2016) including the open method of coordination (OMC). In a nutshell, the CJEU's powers do not apply to the whole spectrum of EU competences, but are limited to those areas relying on the Community method. The development of less integrative ways of functioning in new areas of competences has led to the European Court being circumvented.

This is not to say that the Court has lost powers in all areas of European integration. On the contrary, arguably the Court's position has been strengthened in several other policy areas, starting with the Charter of Fundamental Rights, which has become enforceable and will open new fields of rights litigation, leading the Court into even more sensitive terrain (Kelemen, 2011, p. 43; see Chapter 2). Yet this trend towards positively reinforcing the Court is not exclusive of the trend of circumventing the Court. Circumvention takes two forms: implicit or explicit. Implicit circumvention applies to competences governed by new modes of governance in fields such as economic coordination, social and employment coordination, culture, research or education. In these fields, soft law tend to be more prevalent, and EU institutions do not give rise to secondary law. In the absence of legally binding acts, the Court cannot exert control over EU normative activities. Explicit circumvention derives from treaty provisions that specify the Court's limitations in two fields: justice and home affairs, and foreign and security policy.

Following the entry into force of the Maastricht Treaty, justice and home affairs (the third pillar of the EU) was left out of the reach of the European Court. With the Treaty of Amsterdam, most of the third pillar was 'communautarized', meaning that in this field it was now possible to adopt secondary law placed under the Court's control. Exceptions remain, in particular according to article 276 TFEU, where the European Court has no jurisdiction to review the *validity* or *proportionality* of the operations carried out by the police or other law-enforcement services of a member state; nor does it have a jurisdiction to control the exercise of responsibilities incumbent upon member states with regard to the maintenance of law and order and the safeguarding of internal security.

Regarding CFSP, article 275 TFEU states that the CJEU has no jurisdiction with respect to the provisions relating to foreign and security policies, nor to acts adopted on the basis of those provisions. There are two exceptions: First, the Court is allowed to review acts adopted under CFSP in situations where they should have been adopted within one of the Union's TFEU external policies. This possibility exists in order to avoid the use of CFSP as a means to escape from applying supranational decision-making to external policies. Second, since the Treaty of Lisbon, a CFSP decision can be reviewed if it is claimed to restrict the rights of a natural or legal person. This might be a first step towards the 'progressive judicialisation' of CFSP (Hillion, 2015; Wessel, 2015).

Is the CJEU the high court of a (quasi-)federal system?

Now that we have considered the extent of, and limits to, the powers of the European Court, we can turn to the question of its legal and political nature. A comparative analysis allows us to distinguish the rulings and role of the Court from those of other national (Cappelletti et al., 1986, 1987) and international courts. Has the European Court been transformed into a kind of Supreme Court? Or is it closer to an international court? We would argue that the treaties have given the Court powers that go beyond the usual prerogatives of an international court, and that the Court itself has managed to increase the scope and impact of these powers.

The CJEU is not only part of an enforceable legal framework, but is also the highest court in the EU's judicial system. National courts are vested with wide authority to resolve European legal issues, but they rely on the CJEU for: first, the interpretation of the treaties; and second, the validity and interpretation of acts of the institutions, bodies, offices or agencies of the Union (art. 267 TFEU). Moreover, national courts' decisions can be brought before the European Court for failure to fulfil an obligation under the treaties (art. 263 TFEU). The judgements of the CJEU are binding for the member states, which include political as well as judicial institutions.

The CJEU performs much the same function as the US Supreme Court with respect to issues regarding the vertical and horizontal division of powers. The European Court is not (yet) clearly established as the authoritative constitutional interpreter of the legal system (even if it engages in extensive constitutional review), and as such it is in a very similar position to that of the US Supreme Court. Thus, the argument still holds that the Court is a kind of federal tribunal (Rosenfeld, 2006, p. 622).

The jurisdiction of the European Court is compulsory while that of the International Court of Justice (ICJ) is not. The ICJ is competent to settle a dispute only if the states concerned have accepted its jurisdiction. Moreover, individual litigants can bring actions before the European Court, whereas only states may be parties to contentious cases before the ICJ. The European Court has clarified that breaches of EU law by one member state cannot justify breaches by another member state, thus differentiating European law from international law. By rejecting the interpretation of European treaties as international law, the European Court has applied EU law in a similar way to a national court in its application of domestic law. With the exception of the ECtHR, the CJEU is the only international court that possesses such extensive supranational features.

The CJEU is different from national courts in a number of ways. The European Court cannot repeal national laws that violate European law. Its judgement is simply a declaration that a violation of EU law has taken place. It remains within the competence of the member states to remove national laws or practices that are incompatible with EU law. As Rosenfeld put it, 'whereas the US federal government was able to send federal marshals to force resisting state officials to implement Supreme Court desegregation decisions, nothing comparable exists within the EU to back up the ECJ (CJEU), if needed' (Rosenfeld, 2006, p. 628). Both the US Supreme Court and the European Court give binding decisions, but the CJEU does not have as many tools at its disposal as its US counterpart when it comes to enforcing decisions. EU judicial mechanisms are still inspired by the logic of international law. Yet, the Commission can ask the Court to decide on financial sanctions in cases where its rulings are not complied with, and this makes the Court's decisions more coercive than in the past. In the EU, the authority of the European Court's rulings mainly derives from the attitude of national courts, which have not brought any serious challenges, instead opting for judicial cooperation.

Another difference between the CJEU and national high courts, or at least some of them, is that individuals are excluded from enforcing their rights under the infringement procedure. They can use European law before national courts but cannot bring actions against national authorities before the European Court. In the US system, individuals have access to the Supreme Court. In states with courts specialized in constitutional matters, individual access is frequent but not always provided.

At a more political level, it can be argued that supreme courts or top courts at national level are not influenced by the same kind of actors as the CJEU. While supreme and high courts are dependent on the behaviour of executive and legislative powers, and the attitudes of public opinion, the European Court is mainly influenced by sovereign entities within the EU, that is, the member states and their constitutional courts. As such, the Court has a legitimacy problem that stems from the fact that the supremacy of EU law has not been enshrined in the treaties, contrary to the US constitution which establishes federal law as paramount. The European Court itself has ruled that EU law prevails over national law. The *supremacy* principle is judicially grounded, instead of being treaty-based (apart from a declaration annexed to the treaties making a reference to the Court's case law on supremacy). As we will see in the next chapter in more detail, there is also no means to deal with conflicts between EU law and national constitutions. The co-existence of two kinds of supreme rules (EU treaties and national constitutions) is often depicted by the legal doctrine as one of 'constitutional pluralism' (Walker, 2002; Avbelj & Komárek, 2012; Jaklic, 2014), a concept that captures the lack of consensus over the hierarchy of norms. The legitimacy problem is mitigated by the efforts of both the European Court and national constitutional courts to prevent conflict (Leron, 2014).

Conclusion

This chapter has shown how the CJEU interacts with the other main institutions in the political system of the EU. The Court managed to strengthen its position with the support of supranational institutions and the consent of intergovernmental institutions. The Commission has widely used its power as the guardian of the treaties, in particular through the extensive use of the infringement procedure. The Parliament has progressively gained access to the Court, thanks firstly to Court rulings, and secondly to treaty revisions. By making use of its rights as a litigant, the Parliament has largely contributed to the empowerment of the European Court. The Court has often supported the views expressed by both the Commission and the Parliament, although it has by no means been systematic in this support. The Council and the member states have also managed to convince the Court to align with their positions in a number of important cases. Conversely, they have refrained from (or not succeeded in) overruling the Court when faced with an unfavourable decision (see Chapter 5).

There are normative limits to the review powers of the Court, in order to keep it outside of sensitive policy areas such foreign and security policy. In policy areas where new modes of governance have been used, the Court has not played a significant role, because these areas rely on soft rather than hard law (Terpan, 2015a). However, in spite of these attempts to limit the normative scope of judicial control, the European Court has still managed to keep a grip on a vast array of EU activities, hence Daniel Kelemen's argument that EU integration is still driven by Eurolegalism (Kelemen, 2011). Moreover, the CJEU can be seen as the high court of a quasi-federal judicial system. Not surprisingly, there are similarities between the CJEU and national courts, even federal ones such as the US Supreme Court. The main difference in the EU is that national sovereignty, although significantly curtailed in recent years, compared to the situation of the European states in the early 1950s, still can play an important role, as we explain in Chapter 5.

Chapter 5

The Court, EU Law and the Member States

One of the most intriguing questions for a social scientist is how the law becomes a constraining force. While this is a crucial issue in all political systems, it is even more relevant in the EU. Scholars have observed the transformation of EU law from international treaty to autonomous legal order based on the CJEU's 'constitutional doctrine', which is itself virtually impossible to reverse (Stone Sweet, 2010). They refer to EU law as a quasi-federal legal order and recognize the active way in which the CJEU exercises its legal and judicial power (Weiler & Haltern, 1998; Stone Sweet, 2004) as 'perpetual momentum' (Kelemen & Schmidt, 2012). This raises the question as to why the member states have accepted the constraints of European law and the continued interpretations of the Court.

As Chapter 4 has shown, contrary to federal supreme courts, the European Court cannot repeal national laws that violate European law. Contrary to the US Supreme Court it cannot send federal marshals to go face to face with state officials who refuse to comply with the law. The CJEU's judicial mechanisms, although deeply integrated, remain partially inspired by international law, and hence the acceptance of its jurisprudence is dependent on national courts.

Nonetheless, even a cursory study of the CJEU's jurisprudence leads to the surprising conclusion that it has been capable of playing a much more important role than that played by the majority of international courts at national level. The CJEU has been able to create and implement a constitutional structure (see Chapter 7), which is even more impressive when we consider that it possessed relatively weak legal foundations at the outset; using the meagre resources of the Treaty of Rome (Chapter 2), 'the Court was able to construct its jurisprudential edifice, assuming to itself a role as innovator unparalleled in national supreme courts – not to mention international political fora' (Dehousse, 1998, p. 118).

The aim of this chapter is to analyse why the Court's rulings, both audacious and day to day, have not encountered greater resistance from its principal interlocutors, the member states.

The impact of the Court depends on the way its decisions are implemented at national level by the judiciary (Slaughter, Tulumello & Wood, 1998; Adam, 2016), parliaments, governments and their administrations (Garrett, Kelemen & Schulz, 1998; Versluis, 2007; Panke, 2010; Alter, 2012). While the majority of the judiciary has been eager to implement the Court's rulings, a minority has been reluctant to accept key doctrines such as *primacy* or *direct effect*, because they have been anxious to protect national laws. But most resistance has progressively disappeared. The remaining exception is the question of the primacy of EU law over national constitutions, which remains a controversial issue for constitutional courts in countries such as France, Italy, the Czech Republic and, in particular, Germany. National governments in the early 1960s tried to resist the development of the Court's doctrine of *primacy* and *direct effect*, but since then, they have never seriously attempted to put a brake on judicial integration.

This chapter addresses these issues as follows. A first historical section presents the national higher courts' initial opposition to CJEU's rulings. While some resistance remains, most of the courts have come to accept the CJEU. A second section analyses the institutional reasons for the widespread acceptance of the Court's jurisprudence by national governments. In a third section, we then turn to more sociological explanations for member state compliance with the Court's rulings, concentrating on the role of networks of lawyers and judges.

Conflicts between national high courts and the CJEU

The relations between national high courts and the CJEU must be understood in the context of the legal principle of state sovereignty. A legal order is sovereign when no external legal norm is superior to the fundamental norm of that legal order (an understanding developed through Hans Kelsen's famous '*Grundnorm*' in 1934).

With the landmark case of *van Gend en Loos* (26/62) and *Costa vs. ENEL* (6/64), the CJEU created an external legal order distinct from both international law and national legal orders (see the section on Germany below). At the same time, however, no hierarchy governs the relationship between national constitutional courts and the CJEU. In other words, there is no structural hierarchy whereby a court could overturn the legal decisions of another court. Theoretically, it is very difficult to determine which fundamental norms sit at the top of the legal hierarchy – is it the national constitution, as domestic constitutional courts says, or the EU treaties, as the CJEU argues?

This difficulty of fully articulating EU law with national constitutional law was for a long time viewed merely as a theoretical matter. Legal scholars argued that no clear principle within the field of law could tackle the problematic issue of how EU law and constitutional law interact. In the legal literature, this situation of paradigmatic stalemate (or paradigmatic *aporia*) led to an unsatisfying term of 'normative disorder'.

While most constitutional courts pragmatically recognized the primacy of the CJEU's rulings and therefore left this paradigmatic *aporia* in its theoretical realm, domestic constitutional and high courts of three member states in particular – the German *Bundesverfassungsgericht* (BVGh) or Federal Constitutional Court (FCC), the French *Conseil constitutionnel* and *Conseil d'État*, and the Italian Constitutional Court (*Corte constituzionale*) – have questioned the CJEU's primacy. More recently, the Czech Constitutional Court has shown itself to be equally sceptical, similar to the Nordic countries where fewer courts refer cases to the CJEU.

Germany

When the European Court rendered its first ground-breaking judgements in *Van Gend en Loos* (26/62) and *Costa vs. ENEL* (6/64) in the early 1960s, it ruled that the EC Treaty was establishing an autonomous legal order, which took precedence over those of the member states and could have (in part) direct effect on them (see Chapter 2). The German FCC agreed on this position by saying that the European Court was the jurisdiction of a *sui generis* community in the process of progressive integration, creating legal rules that were neither national nor international law. It founded Germany's legal basis to adopt the Court's positions in article 23 of the Basic Law (Germany's Constitution) dealing with Germany's participation in European integration. It argued that this article would not provide for any transfer of sovereignty but allow for the acknowledgement and implementation of the Court's legal acts. From the 1970s onwards, the FCC has had several occasions to clarify its position on the relationship between EU and German law. In a series of rulings, it has shown reluctance to accept the European Court's position on primacy, making it dependent on the strengthening of democracy and the rule of law at EU level.

The first conflict between the two courts occurred in 1974 (see Chapter 2, and for a detailed analysis, B. Davies, 2012) just a few years after *Internationale Handelsgesellschaft*, when the European Court reaffirmed the primacy principle. In *Solange I*, the FCC ruled in an export licence case, referred to it by a German administrative court, which considered that a European regulation was inapplicable because it was contrary to fundamental rights enshrined in German constitutional law. However, the European Court had previously confirmed the legality of the regulation. In its famous *Solange I* decision, the FCC reserved the right to review the compatibility of European and German law in each individual case 'as long as' (*solange*) the Community law had not received 'a catalogue of fundamental rights decided by the parliament and of confirmed validity'. Any German court could refer the case to the FCC if it 'concerns Community law and insofar it conflicts with one of the fundamental rights of the Basic Law' (BVerfGE 37, 271).

Twelve years later the *Solange II* decision in 1986 reversed this position, arguably because the European Court had meanwhile developed its jurisprudence on the protection of human rights. In a similar case, the FCC ruled that it would no longer review the Court's jurisprudence by the standard of fundamental rights contained in the German constitution and 'no longer exercise its jurisdiction to decide on the applicability of secondary Community legislation' as long as 'the European Communities, in particular European Court case law, generally ensure the effective protection of fundamental rights [...] and insofar as they generally safeguard the essential content of fundamental rights' (BVerfGE 73, 339). The FCC was essentially signalling that it would be willing to trust the Court's decisions as long as the latter continued to protect fundamental rights adequately.

However, a year after the member states signed the Maastricht Treaty, where several new competences were conferred upon the EU, particularly in the area of economic and monetary union, the FCC rendered another far-reaching decision on EU integration (BVerfGE 89, 155 12 October 1993, 2 BvR 2134, 2 BvR 2159/92). The decision made it clear that if European institutions were to adopt legislative instruments transgressing the rights conferred upon them by the treaties, it would not consider these instruments legally binding within the sphere of German sovereignty. According to the German court, the EU as a *Staatenbund* (association of states) had only been transferred a very limited amount of sovereignty, and as such, the FCC's right to review whether or not legal acts issued by the European Court remained within the scope of EU powers was preserved (Thym, 2009). As Grimm (2009) states, the FCC hereby ultimately moved itself into a situation of competition with the CJEU. Again, the FCC theoretically refused to recognize the primacy of Community law and the CJEU's prerogative to delimit the competences of the Community in a given case.

In 2009, the FCC returned to the stage with strong reservations with regard to the Treaty of Lisbon by spelling out the constitutional limits of the integration process and asserting a traditional view of sovereignty (BVerfGE 123, 267; see Thym, 2009), a view that was widely taken over by the Polish, Hungarian and Czech constitutional Courts (Beck, 2011). The German constitutional court thus asserts its own jurisdiction of last resort in relation to any issues involving potential clashes between EU and German constitutional law.

However, in its *Honeywell* decision in 2010 (BVerfGE, 2 BvR 2661/06; see Payandeh, 2011) the German court refined its own doctrine in a way that was reminiscent of its evolution from *Solange I* to *Solange II*. This decision illustrates the complex relationship between the CJEU and the German court based on judicial flexibility, political sensitivity and mutual forbearance (Beck, 2011). The decision is directly related to the CJEU's controversial *Mangold* ruling (C–144/04). The latter was based on a referral from the Labour Court in Munich, which concerned the compatibility of German law (the Employment Promotion Act of 1996) with EU law prohibiting discrimination on the grounds of age. In its judgement, the European Court held that Germany had to comply with the EU principle of non-discrimination on the grounds of age, irrespective of the implementation deadline of the 2000 Employment Equality Framework Directive (where this principle was stated) (see Chapter 8). In so doing, the Court recognized the prohibition of discrimination on the grounds of age as a general principle of EU law, regardless of the directive.

In 2005, the almost identical *Honeywell* case was referred to the FCC. A plaintiff had challenged the European Court's ruling in *Mangold* (C–144/04), arguing that it had created a new principle (prohibition of discrimination on grounds of age) that was not in the EU treaties. The community of legal scholars expected the FCC to accuse the CJEU of having exceeded its competence to interpret European law in *Mangold* (Bulman-Pozen & Gerken, 2009). Instead, the FCC argued that it would consider reviewing the compatibility of EU acts with German fundamental rights only if a breach of competences on the part of European bodies is sufficiently qualified, which was not the case in *Honeywell*. The German court used the case to clarify its position in the debate on *ultra vires* (beyond the limits of the treaties) vs. *intra vires* (within the limits of the treaties) actions of the European institutions. It accepted the presumption that the Union would generally act *intra vires*. However, it added that it could consider *ultra vires* a judicial review if there appeared to be a 'manifest' violation of the principle of conferral – upon which the EU only exerts the competences that were explicitly conferred by the EU treaties (Dyvre, 2011).

France

In France, the 1960s and 1970s were a period when the French supreme administrative court, the *Conseil d'État* (State Council), sought to oppose the CJEU's legal authority and the supremacy of European law. The refusal of the *Conseil d'État* vis-à-vis the CJEU's principle of EU legal primacy was arguably stubborn, and based purely on the idea of – and insistence on – the sovereignty of the French Parliament. The primacy principle was only accepted in conflicts between EU legislation and former national legislation, but rejected in conflicts between EU rules and subsequent national legislation in a number of cases: 1964 *Shell-Berre*, 1967 *Petitjean* and the 1968 *Syndicat général de fabricants de semoules de France* cases.

In the cases mentioned above, the *Conseil d'État* refused to transfer the cases to the CJEU, asserting that it could interpret European law on its own (*Acte Clair* doctrine, see Chapter 2). Interestingly enough, the CJEU endorsed the *Conseil d'État*'s *Acte Clair* doctrine, making the point that the courts of last instance could refrain from referring to the CJEU those questions they deemed irrelevant. In referring to article 267 TFEU, the Court added, however, that this exception to paragraph three of the article would only be possible if the correct application to EU law was 'so obvious as to leave no scope for any reasonable doubt as to the manner in which the questions raised is to be resolved'. In *C.I.L.F.I.T. vs. Ministry of Health* (238/81), it narrowly defined this obviousness in order to limit the cases of autonomous interpretations by national courts. This did not prevent the *Conseil d'État* from using the doctrine of *Acte clair* widely until the 1990s, which might be considered a form of resistance to EU integration.

Progressively, however, this resistance has decreased (Mangenot, 2005). With its *Synacomex* decision of 1970, it seemed that the *Conseil d'État* had started to accept the authority of the Court in interpreting European law, by sending its first preliminary case to the CJEU. However, any indication that the French court was opening up towards the CJEU was short-lived as other cases did not follow. Not only did the *Conseil d'État* continue to make large use of the doctrine of *Acte clair* in the 1970s and 1980s, but it refused to recognize the direct effect of European directives (*Cohn-Bendit*, 1978). The *Office national interprofessionnel des céréales* (ONIC) decision in 1985 provides another illustration of the French court's strong scepticism. In this case, the *Conseil d'État* refused to take into account the CJEU's preliminary rulings if and when it went beyond the specific question asked.

Only from the end of the 1980s onwards did the *Conseil d'État* start to soften its position, thanks to three key changes in legal direction. First, it eventually accepted the supremacy of EU law over subsequent national law with its decision *Nicolo* (1989), followed by *Boisdet* (1990) and *Rothmans* (1990). Secondly, with its *Alitalia* decision (1989) it repealed its principled refusal of the direct effect of European directives – but without formally abandoning its 1978 jurisprudence over *Cohn-Bendit*. Later, in its 2009 *Perreux* ruling, the *Conseil d'État* went against its previous ONIC decision (1985) and accepted the authority of the CJEU's preliminary rulings where they happened to exceed the scope of the preliminary question put by the national court; and thereafter, it withdrew its *Cohn-Bendit* decision. Thirdly, the *Conseil d'État* increased the number of preliminary references to the Court (Table 5.1), making a more limited use of the *Acte clair* doctrine.

However, one important remaining limitation on the part of the *Conseil d'État* was its refusal to allow European law to prevail over the French 1958 Constitution (*Sarran et Levacher*, 1998). This position is shared with the French Constitutional Court (*Conseil constitutionnel*), which also refused to accept the primacy of EU law over the French constitution. In its decision of 10 June 2004 (*Loi pour*

TABLE 5.1 *Preliminary referrals*

Member States	Jurisdictions	Number of referrals (1952–2014)
Germany	BVerfG	1
	Bundesverwaltungsgericht	117
	Other tribunals	2,098
Belgium	*Cour constitutionnelle*	32
	Cour de cassation	93
	Conseil d'État	76
	Other tribunals	593
France	*Conseil constitutionnel*	1
	Conseil d'État	99
	Cour de cassation	118
	Other tribunals	713
Italy	*Corte constituzionale*	2
	Consiglio di Stato	126
	Corte suprema di Cassazione	132
	Other tribunals	1,066
Luxembourg	*Cour constitutionnelle*	1
	Cour de cassation	27
	Cour administrative	27
	Other tribunals	35
The Netherlands	*Hoge Rad*	271
	Raad van State	107
	Other tribunals	571

Source: CJEU - Annual Report 2015 - Judicial activity http://curia.europa.eu/jcms/jcms/Jo2_7000/en/

la confiance dans l'économie numérique, the law for confidence in the digital economy), the *Conseil constitutionnel* exerted control over a French law transposing a European directive. It opposed the transposition, normally considered a constitutional obligation in French law (based on art. 88-1 of the Constitution dealing with French commitments towards the EU). In so doing it echoed the position of the German FCC by stating that the obligation could not prevent it from exerting constitutional control itself (*réserve de constitutionnalité*).

Italy

The Italian Constitutional Court (*Corte constituzionale*) (ICC) was also an early opponent of the European Court, refusing to accept the primacy of EU law – and hence the European Court's rulings – over national constitutional law (Bribosia, 1998; Bribosia et al., 2010). As highlighted earlier, we find the first example of such a refusal in its own *Costa vs. ENEL* ruling, which formed the basis of the CJEU's subsequent *Costa vs. ENEL* preliminary ruling (6/64) establishing the primacy of EU law. The ICC published its judgement in March 1964, ruling that while the ICC allowed for sovereignty to be limited in the case of international organizations such as the EEC, it did not affect the standard rule of statutory interpretation whereby, when two statutes are in conflict, the most recent prevails (*lex posterior derogat legi priori*). As a result, the Treaty of Rome, which was incorporated into Italian law in 1958, could not prevail over the domestic electricity nationalization law enacted in 1962.

In light of the ICC's decision, the Italian government's *amicus brief* (document submitted by a party to the European Court to suggest a legal rationale consistent with its own view), argued that the Italian lower court's request for a preliminary ruling was inadmissible on the grounds that the Italian court was not empowered to set aside the national law in question, and as such a preliminary ruling would not serve any valid purpose.

The CJEU ruled partly in favour of the government, arguing that the relevant Treaty of Rome rule on an undistorted market was one in which the Commission alone could challenge the Italian government. As an individual, Costa had no standing to challenge the decision because that Treaty provision had no direct effect. However, on the prior issue of Costa's right to raise a point of EC law against a national government in a legal proceeding before the national courts, the European Court disagreed with the Italian government. It ruled that EC law would not be effective were Costa not able to challenge national law on the basis of its alleged incompatibility with EC law.

As a consequence, the ICC developed its jurisprudence based on a dual understanding of the law: the primacy of European law only exists in international law. EU law in the domestic realm is equivalent to national law and hence, according to the *Corte costituzionale*, can be overthrown by national law. The Italian court started to revise this position for the first time in its 1973 *Frontini* decision, which recognized the principle of EU law *primacy*, re-qualifying the EU as *sui generis* structure. EU law is therefore neither international law, nor foreign law, nor internal law stemming from other EU member states. In its 1975 *I.C.I.C.* ruling, the *Corte constituzionale* further placed the right to rule on the applicability of EU law in the hands of the CJEU. However, similarly to the German Constitutional Court *Solange* rulings, the ICC questioned the constitutionality of EU fundamental norms, and argued that a conflict between domestic fundamental rights and European fundamental rights would lead to situations whereby domestic constitutional rights overruled European fundamental rights (*controlimiti*). Contrary to the German court, however, the Italian court argued that this conflict was highly improbable.

Northern, Central and Eastern European member states

As a series of studies has pointed out, it was not only the French, Italian and German constitutional courts that had difficulties accepting the supremacy of European law (Slaughter, Tulumello & Wood, 1998; Dyevre, 2012). As Marlene Wind has shown, the Nordic countries have no tradition of judicial review by courts and have generally been hesitant to make use of the preliminary ruling procedure in the EU. Nordic courts seem to prefer solving as many EU-related judicial disputes as possible without involving a supranational organ such as the CJEU. This is linked to the specific legal and democratic culture in these countries: majoritarian democracies express greater scepticism towards supranational judicial review than constitutional democracies such as the United Kingdom whose referral rate was very high (Wind, Martinsen & Rotger, 2009; Wind, 2010).

With regard to Central and Eastern European courts after their accession in 2004, the Czech and Polish Supreme Courts initially encouraged lower courts to refer cases to the CJEU under the preliminary reference procedure, arguing that they were not competent to deal with EU law (Bobek, 2008a). More recently, the Czech Constitutional Court's (CCC) attitude has changed, however, and has begun to resemble the FCC's. It declared a part of the CJEU's *Landtová* ruling (C–399/09) to be *ultra vires* (or 'beyond the powers' of the CJEU) under Czech constitutional law – a first in the EU. The ruling was, it transpires, an attempt to discipline the Supreme Administrative Court, which had referred the *Landtová* case to the CJEU in the first place (Bobek, 2014a).

Constitutional pluralism

The limits that these constitutional courts place on the supremacy of European law do not prevent them from cooperating with the CJEU, however. Such cooperation appears to have increased since the mid-1990s (Dehousse, 1998; Leron, 2014). While in the past the German, Italian and French constitutional courts were reluctant to transfer questions to the CJEU (Table 5.1), and more generally to cooperate, this has changed a little in recent years. As a means of comparison, we have added the data for Luxembourg, Belgium and the Netherlands, to illustrate the difference in the number of preliminary referrals among the constitutional courts of the EU's founding members. Table 5.1 also demonstrates that the highest number of preliminary references are made by the lower courts, which is consistent with the idea that the lower (rather than the higher) courts have been instrumental in advancing legal integration (Alter, 1996, 2009).

Legal scholars have begun to think about a new legal paradigm to enable us to explain this combination of theoretical contradiction and pragmatic cooperation between national courts and the CJEU. New theories abounded, such as 'network paradigm' (Ost & Van de Kerchove, 2002), 'ordinated pluralism' (Delmas-Marty, 2006) and 'constitutional pluralism' (Shaw, 1999; Avbelj & Komárek, 2012). These theories are not based on the vertical logic of the Kelsenian paradigm. Indeed, the Kelsenian hierarchy of norms and jurisdictions cannot successfully describe the current relationship between EU law and national law on the one hand, and the CJEU and national constitutional courts on the other. The non-hierarchical relationship between the EU and domestic courts is doomed to remain as long as national constitutional courts refuse to fully accept the principle of primacy. To find a way to describe this relationship, new theories are based on the idea of a horizontal logic and a de-centred legal and judicial power. In this understanding, constitutional courts and the CJEU are situated at the top of two intertwined legal structures, the national and European ones.

Members of supreme jurisdictions of the member states increasingly use these references as their cognitive frames in their own legal productions (Leron, 2014). Furthermore, they seem to perceive networking among higher jurisdictions as a way to address the problematic relationship between EU law and national constitutional law.

Institutional and legal factors explaining compliance

The German, French, Italian and Czech cases should not hide that the level of compliance with CJEU rulings in the member states is high. A recent study on the continued national disobedience of CJEU rulings only identified 13 verdicts delivered from second proceedings between 1 November 1993 and 1 November 2011. Second proceedings are cases in which a member state, already penalized by the CJEU for non-compliance with EU law, is referred back to the CJEU by the Commission and then judged for a second time (Falkner, 2016). This number of 13 second judgements ignores those proceedings that didn't go as far as requiring a Court verdict, but were solved before the Court's final decision. The second referrals concerned Greece in five cases, France in three, Portugal in two, and Germany, Italy and Spain each with one.

This high degree of compliance is surprising, given that the EU is not a state but a sort of international organization. The CJEU has been criticized for its continued activism, maybe more so than the supreme courts in national political systems. One might thus have expected more resistance from the member states. Instead, the European Court's rulings have been surprisingly influential. This is certainly one of the most fascinating puzzles in European studies, but also in the field of the politics of law more generally. Law does not become a constraining force because it is the law; judicial organs must be creative actors, and other bodies in their environment have to accept the rulings, even more so when they are tasked with applying texts of a general nature such as constitutions or treaties.

Three series of institutional and legal explanations help us to understand why the CJEU has come to play such an important role in the EU member states. Legal scholars are particularly fond of normative and legal reasoning; judges at the national and EU level have adapted to one another and managed to interpret law in a consistent manner. A second series of arguments can be found in the institutional and political constraints that limit the control of member states over the CJEU. A third series of hypotheses based on the principal-agent explanation defend the idea that the member states (in particular the most powerful ones) have had a vested interest in delegating to an independent judicial body the task of ensuring the fulfilment of EU commitments.

These series of arguments do not imply that there is no resistance by constitutional – and other – courts, or by national governments and administrations. Yet, resistance often takes more subtle forms such as attenuating the effects of unwelcome jurisprudence through legislative action (Granger, 2004; Micklitz, 2005; Nyikos, 2008; Mayoral, 2013; Martinsen, 2015a).

Normative and legal reasoning

Normative and legal arguments are particularly embedded in general historical and legal approaches to European integration. From such perspectives, the integration of European states into the EU constitutes one of the central post-war ideas in Western Europe. With support from the major political parties, and without outward contestation from citizens at the national level, the member states have tended to consider the European Court as a pure interpreter of European law. As such, when the Court has overstepped the existing legal bases, this has largely been considered legitimate to fill a political void (Dehousse, 1998). There are two types of academic reasoning to explain this phenomenon: positivist and constructivist.

Positivist legal reasoning sees courts as guarantors of neutrality. In modern Western societies, there is a general belief that calling on a jurisdiction offers the advantage of a neutral and legitimate decision. As such, judges are seen as simple interpreters of the law rather than law-makers, which offers an important guarantee for the litigants that their rights will be taken seriously. If the judges appear too strongly influenced by political considerations and/or if their impartiality is questioned, then their reputation suffers, placing their legal authority at risk (Shapiro, 1981; Delpeuch,

Dumoulin & de Galambert, 2014). Hence 'the respect accorded to judicial decisions does not stem solely from acceptance of its rule of law; it also reflects a fairly extensive acceptance of the social role fulfilled by judicial organs in taking under their wing the resolution of conflicts. This attitude has benefitted the CJEU just as its benefits its national counterparts' (Dehousse, 1998, 122).

The generally held perception of judicial neutrality is the cornerstone of the CJEU's own claim to be the sole interpreter of the rule of law. The Court's inherent legitimacy, difficult to contest politically (Stein, 1981; Weiler, 1981), is rooted in the Treaty of Rome, which tasks the Court with ensuring that the law is observed when interpreting and applying the treaties. Since its early jurisprudence of the 1960s, the Court has favoured a teleological interpretation of the treaties, in particular the Treaty of Rome (see Chapter 7 on the interpretation methods of the Court). The term 'teleological interpretation' refers to the Court using the treaty preambles and provisions relating to the objectives of the Union as a basis of its rulings. We find examples of this type of interpretation in many decisions. In *Van Gend en Loos* (26/62), for example, the Court refers to the objectives of the Treaty of Rome as laid out in its preamble. From the activities of European institutions, the Court makes out a desire on the part of the authors of the treaty to create a 'new legal order', and the need for an effective European legal system (*effet utile*) (Dehousse, 1998, 126). Although criticized as 'judicial activism', the CJEU's teleological interpretation is based on the successive EU treaties.

The judges put the Court's success down to its legal logic. Judge Pierre Pescatore argued that the CJEU's success is on account of it having created a coherent and authoritative body of community law based on the provisions of the Treaty of Rome and its use of 'constructive methods of interpretation', as well as in 'establishing a "complete architecture", coherent and well thought out, the lines of which, once firmly drawn, require to be extended' (Pescatore, 1974, p. 87). Judge Federico Mancini drew a logical relationship between *Van Gend en Loos* and *Costa vs. ENEL* (Chapter 2). For him, the primacy principle that came after the principle of direct effect 'was not only an indispensable development, it was also a logical development' (Mancini, 1989, p. 600).

The Court's rulings, even when considered to be path-breaking decisions, are in fact mostly solutions to technical problems, in particular in the field of economic integration. *Van Gend en Loos* was a problem of tariff classification; *Cassis de Dijon* (120/78) was a problem of free movement of goods; and *Costa vs. ENEL* (6/64) was a problem linked with the nationalization of the electricity sector. Yet, these cases also had a constitutional dimension as they dealt with the *direct effect* of EU law, its primacy over national law and the mutual recognition of national rules with regard to the free movement of goods.

Another illustration of this duality is the judgement in the case of *Commission vs. Council* ('*Titanium Dioxide*') (C–300/89). The case concerned a conflict between the Commission and the Council over a directive dealing with the reduction of pollution caused by waste from the titanium dioxide industry. The controversy around the case could have been contained, had there been a simple choice between economic priorities on the one hand, and environmental protection on the other. The Court decided otherwise, ruling in favour of the Commission, who argued that the directive in question should have been adopted on the basis of article 100a of the Treaty of Rome. The treaty foresees that, to achieve the internal market, a cooperation procedure should be used. In so doing, the Court shifted the institutional balance in favour of the supranational institutions.

A more constructivist legal approach takes us beyond the legal argument and posits that the 'variation in how judges understand their legal and political mandates creates cross-national and cross-issue variation in how courts deal with EU legal issues' (Alter, 2009, p. 200; see also Chalmers, 1997). The degree to which national courts participate in a dialogue with the CJEU also depends on their perception of it as a court in a similar vein to themselves. Such an understanding depends largely on what the national courts consider the constraints of judicial legitimacy. As such, the legal training specific to each member state, as well as the specific historic role of the court within a particular society, affects how the judges react to EU law (Bobek, 2008a; Cattelan, 2012).

Loschak (1992; Mangenot, 2000, 2008) argues that the background of a French *conseiller d'État* affects its jurisprudence on a number of issues. A French *conseiller d'État* specialized in French domestic law is less inclined to cooperate with the European Court than one who was mostly trained in European law, as was possible in French law faculties from the 1980s onwards (Bailleux, 2014). The same argument can be found in Germany, where Federal Tax Court judges, after having served several years in the tax administration, have a tendency to rule in favour of the tax administrations when issuing their rulings.

The difference between common law judges, who elaborate rules based on the doctrine of precedent, and civil law judges, whose source of authority stems from legal codes, is another illustration of how legal cultures influence the reasoning of judges. In this context, Paul Craig (1995) argues for instance that common law judges are pragmatic and *non-doctrinaire* (not constrained by the building of a consistent legal doctrine), characteristics that have allowed them to accept being part of the European legal order, with the CJEU as the legitimate court.

While the principle of direct effect was unproblematic for British courts, the principle of indirect effect posed challenges. It required them to ensure that national legislation conformed with an EU directive even if the national legislature had not yet implemented the directive. This was difficult to accept, because the legal reasoning was based on past decisions and not on a general legal doctrine (Craig, 1995; Jupille & Caporaso, 2009).

An altogether different and more macro-sociological way of looking at the question of how national legal culture and training influence judicial identity concerns the distinction between monism and dualism (Mattli & Slaughter, 1998, p. 203). Monism refers to a conceptualization of the national legal order as an integrated part of the international legal order. International law does not need to be translated into national law; it is incorporated and takes effect in national law as soon as it is ratified (for a treaty) or adopted (for an act adopted by international institutions).

The Netherlands has the strongest tradition of monism, leading the Dutch Supreme Court to declare in 1906 that treaties were directly applicable in Dutch law without 'transformation' or transposition into national statutes by the Dutch parliament. As such, the direct effect of *Van Gend en Loos* (26/62) was particularly easy to accept for Dutch judges because of their predisposition to the direct applicability of international law. The ICC, on the contrary, is embedded in a dualist tradition, which requires the translation of international law into national law. International law has to be translated into national law for it to have any legal status. This hampered the acceptance of EU law and CJEU rulings for decades, as we have seen above.

Legal and normative arguments thus explain part of the Court's influence with regard to member states' acceptance of its rulings.

However, several institutional and political variables also need to be taken into account if we are to understand why CJEU decisions cannot be easily curbed.

Institutional and political limits of Court curbing

The US literature on the politics of law and the Supreme Court has identified a series of court curbing mechanisms (Kelemen, 2012, p. 44): (1) legislative or constitutional override, referring to legislative or constitutional amendments that override court decisions; (2) resource punishment, whereby funding is withheld from the court or the judges; (3) jurisdiction stripping, referring to removing particular policy fields from the court's jurisdiction; and (4) court packing and judicial selection and reappointment, which is about expanding the size of the courts and filling them with judges that better reflect the preferences of political actors.

In the EU, member states' have several mechanisms at their disposal to control the CJEU, but there are considerable institutional and political limits. Legislative or treaty override, resource punishment, jurisdiction stripping or court packing imply treaty amendments or secondary legislation in the EU. The complex system of decision-making requires a high majority threshold and faces a complex set of veto players, which put limits on control mechanisms (Pollack, 2003).

Making treaty changes, in order to overthrow a CJEU decision, must be based on an intergovernmental conference with a unanimous decision by all member states, and ratification at the national level. When secondary law is needed to overthrow a ruling, the European Commission has to introduce the proposal, and the legislature (Council of Ministers and European Parliament) has to agree on it, through the ordinary legislative procedure or a special procedure.

Jurisdiction stripping, meaning that areas that have been formally conferred to the jurisdiction of the CJEU are removed from its jurisdiction, has never actually happened (Kelemen, 2012a, p. 46). Soft law procedures (through the Open Method of Coordination in particular) were introduced from the early 2000s (Scott & Trubek, 2002; Armstrong, 2010, 2013; Dawson, 2011; Korkea-aho, 2015). However, areas in which the Court had jurisdiction were not affected, at least from a legal point of view.

More fundamentally, a major difference in the political timeframes of member states and the EU helps to explain the relative independence of the CJEU from member states. The CJEU has played off – or taken advantage of – the shorter time horizons of domestic politicians and thus 'constructed the institutional building blocks of its own power and authority without provoking a political response' (Alter, 1998, p. 110). The fundamental differences in political systems have made it difficult for governments to overrule the CJEU's decisions. These timeframes at the domestic level determine when national governments seek re-election yet this has had no influence on the Court's rulings (Alter, 1998). While the relationship between politics and policies is strong in the US, where President and Congress decide on who the judges are that they put on the bench, this is not the case in the EU. The judges appointed to the CJEU are rarely sanctioned for their rulings, not least because it is impossible to know who has cast which vote; the decisions are entirely secret (see Chapter 3). One exception was the position taken by Manfred Zuleeg, the German judge, which became accidentally public. He was said to have contradicted the German government's position in a series of cases and, thereafter, he failed to be re-appointed in 1994 (Dehousse, 1998). Finally, appointing judges in order to control the Court is not a strategy currently used by member states.

The shadow of hierarchy

Fritz Scharpf's concept of EU decision-making as a 'joint decision trap' helps us to understand why there has only been a limited number of revisions of Court rulings by the member states (for an exception see *Barber* C–262/88) (Chapter 2). Decision-making in federal or quasi-federal systems very often leads to situations where the final decision taken reflects the smallest common denominator. Applying this insight from German federalism to the European system, Fritz Scharpf (1988) argues that in systems where member governments directly participate in unanimous decision-making, this process will systematically lead to suboptimal policy outcomes unless a problem-solving style of decision-making can be maintained. According to Scharpf, huge tensions (or 'joint decision-traps') are created in a federal system, and in the EU in particular. In the EU, European institutions identify problems and suggest solutions, which are then blocked by member states using their veto rights, on account of political conflict and disagreement among themselves over which course of action to take. The reason member states continue to participate in this system is largely because both disintegration and greater integration (centralization) are generally considered suboptimal outcomes.

Scharpf indicates three conditions under which a joint decision trap occurs: (1) when the decision rule requires (quasi) unanimous decision-taking; (2) when the decision style is bargaining; and (3) when the political preferences are fixed and divergent, and imported from the domestic level. This is due to the initial difficulties of agreement on a European policy between member states, but also because once in place European policies (or in this case CJEU rulings) are equally resistant to reform and constrain the independent action capacities of the constituent units, namely the member states. The outcomes are suboptimal; they are based on the smallest common denominator with quasi-unanimous decision-making very difficult to reform.

In a later, revisited version of the 'joint decision-trap', Scharpf (2006) added the role of the CJEU to his analysis. In cases where the Court is called upon, its decision must be applied to all member states, and no negotiation process is theoretically possible. In the field of legislative harmonization, this supranational, hierarchical governance system assumes that even the mere threat of Court action – the so-called 'shadow of hierarchy' or 'CJEU-driven Europeanisation' (Blauberger, 2014; see also Blauberger & Weiss, 2013; Schmidt, 2014, 2015) – greatly increases the willingness of all governments to accept the minimum harmonization directives proposed by the Commission (Scharpf, 2006, p. 853). Scharpf argues that attempts to avoid suboptimal outcomes encourage member states to continue their participation in a joint system, while acknowledging and accepting the Commission's monopoly of legislative initiative in most policy fields (see also Dehousse, 1998; Falkner, 2011).

Schmidt's analysis of electricity liberalization in the EU illustrates this particularly well (S.K. Schmidt, 2000). At the beginning of the 1990s, the Commission threatened member states with infringement procedures if they refused to agree on a directive allowing for the liberalization of the electricity market. Had the Council not agreed on a directive, the sector would have been liberalized in a piecemeal fashion through possible Court judgements. Blauberger and Weiss (2013) argue similarly that the adoption of a Military Procurement Directive in 2009 is based on an infringement procedure initiated by the Commission against Italy with reference to the procurement of military helicopters for civilian use in a non-competitive tender. Based on a 1999 judgement (*Commission vs.*

Spain C–414/97), the Court ruled that even in the field of defence procurement, competition law applies. Following this judgement, the member states agreed on a Military Defence Procurement directive in 2009, in a policy area where they had been reluctant to act for many years.

Principal-agent approaches

Principal-agent approaches seek to understand why national governments consent to abandon or at least share their sovereignty at the supranational level by creating supranational institutions such as the CJEU – a process known as 'pooling sovereignty' (for a detailed discussion, see Saurugger, 2013). The central assumption is that state actors rationally pursue their own interests while transferring competencies to institutions. States understand perfectly well that the *ex post* control of these institutions can be problematic. They nevertheless transfer competencies to the European level. Why? Because institutions help decrease the uncertainty that comes from the imperfect division of power between competing European actors. Furthermore, delegating powers to supranational institutions such as the Court helps to reduce transaction costs involved in the decision-making process. States agree to act by signing international agreements and in so doing benefit from the expertise of supranational actors.

In exchange for delegating competencies, these supranational bodies provide the states with control instruments to implement policies decided at European level. However, if the rules of implementation are not respected, the European Commission refers cases to the European Court. Thus, *principals*, meaning the states, accept being controlled by their *agents* – the Commission and the CJEU – to ensure that implementation is equally applied to all member states. Although European institutions generally behave as the agents of the member states, sometimes they are strongly independent. Principal-agent approaches explain on account of the fact that the mechanisms put in place by the states to control institutions are costly, which discourages their extensive use by national governments.

In studying the reasons for, and the conditions of, delegation by governments to supranational bodies, scholars have analysed why the CJEU succeeded in broadening its powers, thereby facilitating European integration and the creation of a European market

(Garrett, 1992, 1995; Garrett, Kelemen & Schulz, 1998; Garrett & Tsebelis, 2001; Kelemen, 2001; Stone Sweet & Brunel, 1998, 2012; Stone Sweet & McCown, 2004; Maher, Billiet & Hodson, 2009; Kelemen, 2012b).

The findings of these studies differ, however. While some scholars show that the Court remains independent from member state preferences, and thus consider the court to be a member state *trustee*, possessing a broader margin of manoeuvre than that of a tightly controlled agent (Stone Sweet & Brunel, 1998, 2012; Stone Sweet & McCown, 2004), others argue that the court is significantly influenced by member states. An example of this can be found in Carrubba and colleagues' (2008, 2012) large-scale study, in which the authors argue that the CJEU's rulings are based on both member state preferences as well as Commission observations across all policy areas. While the authors come to the same conclusion as Stone Sweet (2004) with regard to the influence of the Commission, their results are precisely the reverse when it comes to member state influence on CJEU rulings in the areas of free movement of goods and gender equality.

Pollack (2003) adopts a wider and overarching conceptualization of the principal-agent theory in EU studies in a number of qualitative case studies on the Commission and the Court. A first set of examples concerns cases regarding liberalization and the creation of the European market. By examining three cases involving the role of the European Commission in foreign trade (Blair House agreement), competition (De Havilland case) and the Court case law on the free movement of goods and services in the EU (*Cassis de Dijon* ruling), his research shows that supranational institutions influenced European integration and promoted the introduction of a single market when the control mechanisms set up by the governments were relatively weak.

A second set of examples concerns the case of the free movement of persons and social policy, focusing on CJEU rulings on equal pay for men and women (the *Defrenne* and *Barber* rulings, respectively 43/75 and 262/88) (for an in-depth historical discussion of these cases, see Dinan, 2004). Here, the supranational organizations fulfil their regulation and rule-making role, but their power and room for manoeuvre are closely controlled by national governments, which differs from the first set of rulings. This is because the major member states found the CJEU's discretional power to be excessive. They reacted by creating new control mechanisms or by limiting certain effects of the court's decisions in new treaties. An example of a Court override can be found in the limits set by the Maastricht Treaty with regard to the retroactive effect of the *Barber* ruling on the equalization of pension policies for men and women. The so-called '*Barber* protocol' was inserted into the Maastricht Treaty with the aim of limiting the impact of the *Barber* ruling (C–262/88), and in so doing, forcing the CJEU to go back to the previous state of law.

However, some argue that the revision of the Maastricht Treaty in dealing with the *Barber* ruling was merely an exception. Other than this example, it is hard to find cases where the Court is controlled. This may be because the CJEU uses the technique of prospective rulings in order to limit potential opposition from member states. It declares that its interpretations will be applicable in the future only, except in cases where plaintiffs have filed a suit. This strategy started with the *Defrenne* II case (43/75), as a response to fears voiced by governments claiming that the attribution of direct effect to the principle of equal pay contained in article 119 (now art. 157 TFEU) would have dramatic consequences for their economy. The same argument was used in the *Barber* case described above. The Court can exert influence and shape long-term action by political actors without preventing resistance in the short term.

Networking hypotheses

A more sociological set of arguments explaining why member states comply with CJEU rulings is linked to networking hypotheses. These posit that the power gained by the CJEU in the European system is due to cooperation between domestic lower courts, constitutional courts and lawyers' federations on the one hand, and CJEU judges on the other. These arguments seeking to account for the Court's capacity to ensure member states compliance recognize a vast network effect resulting from: (1) cooperation between lower courts and the CJEU (Burley & Mattli, 1993; Mattli & Slaughter, 1995; Alter, 1996; Ramos Romeu, 2002; Kelemen, 2011; Blauberger, 2012); (2) domestic lawyers' associations and the CJEU judges (Vauchez, 2007, 2010; Alter, 2010; Cohen, 2010; Bailleux, 2013); and (3) organized study visits by domestic constitutional judges to the CJEU, as well as the existence of trans-European databases (Leron, 2014).

Cooperation between lower courts and higher courts

One of the most prominent arguments explaining the influence the Court has acquired at domestic level pertains to the crucial role national judiciaries have played. This explanation is based both on a neo-functionalist framework (Burley & Mattli, 1993; Slaughter & Mattli, 1998) and a neo-institutionalist approach (Alter & Meunier-Aitsahalia, 1994; Golub, 1996; Alter, 2010).

Burley and Mattli, in their seminal 1993 article, as well as in a later text in which they revisit the Court (Slaughter & Mattli, 1998), argue that the Court has gained powers through the preliminary ruling procedure (art. 267 TFEU), and more precisely through the working relationship it has established with the lower courts. In practice, lower courts have leapfrogged the national judicial hierarchy and worked directly with the CJEU. Both the procedure and the Court's activism have provided a framework of links between the Court and subnational actors – private litigants, their lawyers and of course the lower national courts. Although the lower courts were able, though not obliged, to ask preliminary questions to the CJEU (since they did not have jurisdiction of last resort, see Chapter 4), they extensively used the opportunity to engage in a dialogue with the European Court through the preliminary rulings procedure.

For Burley and Mattli, the Court gained its influence by stimulating domestic groups, courts and governments to make new demands for organizational action. Hence 'when litigants did not appear to perceive the boon that had been granted to them, ... the Court set about educating them in the use of article 177 (now Art. 267 TFEU) procedure' (Burley & Matttli, 1993, p. 62), a procedure they call 'courting the national courts'. Litigants, were – and still are – crucial for the Court's rulings to be implemented (Conant, 2002, see Chapter 6).

The CJEU gave lower courts the possibility to circumvent opposition they had encountered at the domestic level (Alter, 1994, 1998; Dehousse, 1998). According to Alter, 'different courts have different interests vis-à-vis EU law ... national courts use EU law in bureaucratic struggles between levels of the judiciary and between the judiciary and political bodies, thereby inadvertently facilitating the process of legal integration' (1996, p. 21). To this vertical competition (between higher and lower courts within the different branches of the national court system), we must add horizontal competition, which takes place between courts and legislators, allowing national judges to invoke European law as a barrier to the enforcement of a particular legislative product (Mattli & Slaughter, 1998, p. 194).

Some lower courts were able to take up the CJEU's declaration on the primacy of EU law. British courts, for instance, went along with CJEU decisions. They have long claimed the introduction of interim injunctions, that is, orders suspending administrative action pending the decision of a court. Arrogating such a right to themselves would have been incompatible with the doctrine of precedent, a cornerstone of the British legal system. European litigation offered an opportunity for change. In *Factortame* (C–213/89), the CJEU confirmed the view that domestic law barring lower courts from granting interim injunctions had to be set aside if this was necessary to give effect to European law. The House of Lords went beyond the ruling; three years after *Factortame,* it ruled that interim relief was available even if no European law was involved (Harlow, 1995; Dehousse, 1998).

Thus, compliance with EU law has brought clear rewards for a large number of domestic courts. Instead of diminishing their room for manoeuvre, the CJEU has enabled them to increase their powers. The situation is different with regard to higher courts, and in particular constitutional courts, as we have seen in the first section of the chapter.

Besides, CJEU rulings have not always gone uncontested even when domestic courts have strongly favoured the outcome. The turnover tax struggle surrounding the Court's 1966 *Lüttike* ruling illustrates this point. This decision created hundreds of thousands of refund claims for 'illegally' collected German turnover equalization taxes, leading the German Finance Ministry to issue a statement confirming that the CJEU's judgement was to be considered invalid. This course of action triggered an outcry from the lower German courts which refused to not apply a legally valid decision of the European Court. Lawyers from the Ministry of Economy constructed a test case strategy, arguing that the wrong question was asked in 1966, referring to article 95 TEC instead of article 97 TEC. The Court accepted this argument and the plaintiffs lost their legal standing. However, the *Lüttike* ruling remained valid; article 95 TEC is still directly effective and obliges member states to remove national laws that create tariff and non-tariff barriers to trade, even though no new European law has been adopted to replace national policies (Alter, 2009, p. 123).

Lawyers' associations and CJEU judges

Some put the common acceptance of Court rulings by the lower courts and higher courts down to institutional cooperation. Others see this explanation as limited. Contrary to large-scale studies, critical sociologists argue that common acceptance is not merely a consequence of the lower courts' search for more influence at the domestic level. On the contrary, based on a historical and Bourdieusian approach (after the French philosopher and sociologist Bourdieu), these scholars argue that the presence of political entrepreneurs structuring a large network of lawyers in fact enabled the Court to influence the European politics of law. Rasmussen (1986) had already pointed to the close relations between the CJEU and domestic legal experts back in the 1980s. Alter went further by arguing that 'ignoring the role of legal associations served a purpose. Especially while (the CJEU) was seeking to establish its authority, revealing the extensive coordination that gave rise to the (CJEU)'s early legal successes could have implied conspiracy potentially undermining the effort to portray support for an active European court as spontaneously spreading' (2009, p. 63).

Michel Gaudet, the French head of the Commission's legal service by the end of the 1950s (see Chapter 2), is considered a central actor in this game. Using the transnational lawyers association *Fédération internationale pour le droit européen* (FIDE), which brings together national Euro-law associations such as the French *Association française des juristes européens* (AJE), the German *Wissenschaftliche Gesellschaft für Europarecht* (WGE) and the Dutch *Nederlandse Vereniging voor Europees Recht* (NVER), Gaudet developed a doctrinal understanding that distinguishes EU law from national and even international law (Vauchez, 2007, 2010, 2013, 2015; Cohen, 2010; Bailleux, 2013). Critical sociologists argue that the strategy was to depoliticize the European project and to perceive the law as a purely technical question whose teleological and constructive interpretation could be the only one applied. Together with members of the national legal associations (composed of both academics and legal practitioners), Gaudet became one of the principal proponents of a political-judicial vision, whose aim was to promote a uniquely European law at any cost – and one that would allow for a specific European interpretation of law across the territory of the European Communities. Gaudet's position in the European Commission was not an entirely comfortable one at the end of the 1950s. 'European

Community law remained an esoteric topic' for much of the 1960s (Alter, 2009, p. 71). Scholars working on the influence of legal associations in establishing the Court's power have shown how through networking, and in particular by the Commission's president Walter Hallstein, the legal service he chaired gained increasing influence among Commission officials.

The FIDE's congresses at the beginning of the 1960s paved the way for the Court to establish its *Van Gend en Loos* and *Costa vs. ENEL* doctrines. Critical sociologists argue that the extensive influence in the European politics of law, and the establishment of the primacy of EU law over national law, cannot be explained by a mere legal and technical decision. Instead, it was the strategic planning of Gaudet and his colleagues in national European law associations that led to the ground-breaking role the Court acquired. In particular, in *Van Gend en Loos*, the 'meta-narrative' as Vauchez (2010, 2015) calls it, was in fact strategically planned and systematically implemented. This research sees FIDE as the incubator of the future doctrine. Vauchez (2010) argues in this respect that 15 out of 18 of the first cases leading to preliminary rulings between 1962 and 1969 were initiated by Dutch advocates, all of them members of the Dutch branch of FIDE. In November 1961, the Dutch NVER had established a working group to identify which provisions of the Treaty of Rome might be considered to be self-executing, and hence under Dutch law directly applicable by domestic courts. It was a Dutch lawyer and member of the NVER, Ter Keile, who prepared the test case that later became the *Van Gend en Loos* ruling. The referral to the European Court by Dutch judges was based on the question of whether European law could create direct effect (Alter, 2009, p. 74). At the annual congress of 1963, the FIDE adopted a resolution defending the revolutionary character of the *Van Gend en Loos* decision. A similar example can be found in *Cassis de Dijon*, where a meeting of the German European law association constructed the argument for the test case. It was an associative member, Gert Meier, a German lawyer, who brought the case before the German court, which subsequently referred it to the European Court (Alter, 2009, p. 75).

However, the *Cassis de Dijon* ruling on mutual recognition met with important criticism at the domestic level, and the FIDE's role in legitimizing the ruling is harder to prove (Alter & Meunier-Aitsahalia, 1994). Equally, in *Costa vs. ENEL*, both domestic and European associations seemed to play a minor role. It is difficult to ascertain whether all rulings have benefited from associational interest, or if these cases are anecdotal.

More generally, this understanding of legal history cannot solely explain why member states have not reacted with more scepticism, as Bailleux underlines (2013, p. 112). One might argue that the member states' legal apparatuses (courts) were occupied by Europeanist legal actors with a high level of social capital, given their connections with political and economic elites. We know, however, that the interpretation of the primacy of EU law was not agreed upon initially by a majority of national legal scholars in all member states (Alter, 2009). European law and the CJEU doctrine tended to be frequently ignored in the 1960s and 1970s. Those national judges unaffiliated to Euro-law associations were reluctant to refer cases to the CJEU. Moreover, national high court rulings often contradicted the CJEU doctrine, as mentioned earlier in the chapter.

Exchange programmes between the CJEU and national judges

Another explanation for the acceptance of CJEU's rulings, in particular among higher courts, can be found in network approaches. Aware of potential conflicts, constitutional courts and the CJEU have established a series of exchanges or dialogue of judges (Mattli & Burley, 1993; Dehousse, 1998; Alter, 2009; Stirn, 2009). While visiting programmes for national judges have existed at the European Court since it was set up, the beginning of the 2000s saw an increasing number of formal meetings as well as a new practice of informal meetings and workshops (Leron, 2014).

The main function of these meetings is to anticipate and prevent potential conflicts. By this informal judicial dialogue, the CJEU can influence the articulation of EU and national legal orders. If there is a conflict, it must be kept in this extra-legal sphere.

National judges have underlined the usefulness of this cooperation and even asked for it. One of the French members of the *Conseil d'État*, Jean-Marc Sauvé (2008), argues that besides institutional or vertical judicial cooperation between supreme jurisdictions (through preliminary questions before the CJEU for instance), legal professionals should also put in place an informal, horizontal cooperation between administrative supreme judges of the EU.

In 2000, a pan-European *Association of State Councils and Supreme Administrative Jurisdictions of the European Union* was established by a group of judges, with the aim of fostering exchange programmes, to consider different public law approaches and see if they could be reconciled, to allow a convergence towards common practices. It has since fostered bilateral working meetings. New member state judges have visited older member states' jurisdictions. Since 2008, this judge exchange programme has become more systematic. The association participates in the European Judicial Training Network (EJTN), created in 2000 with financial support from the Justice Programme of the EU and conceived to be 'the principal platform and promoter for the training and exchange of knowledge of the European judiciary' (http://www.refj.eu/en/About/About-EJTN/).

Private law supreme courts of the EU have acted in a similar way and gathered in the *Network of the Presidents of the Supreme Judicial Courts of the European Union*. In April 2007 the network launched a mega search engine on national case law (http://www.reseau-presidents.eu/rpcsjue/) that allows for national case law search engines to be cross-searched. It is a powerful tool for applied comparative law, and part of the new trend of judicial collaboration in the EU (Leron, 2014; Hübner, 2015).

Conclusion

How and why the CJEU has managed to influence the member state level to such an extent requires a complex and nuanced analysis. Normative, institutional and sociological factors have influenced the CJEU's success as an international and constitutional Court. It is the interplay of these factors that has allowed the Court to become an influential player in the EU's political system. The CJEU partially empowered domestic lower courts and legal actors, created salience for specific issues through heated debate on rulings in the national realm (such as *Laval* (C–341/05)) and influenced EU public policies through its rulings and/or the threat of a possible ruling.

One of the most important factors over time has been the capacity of the Court to avoid widespread non-compliance with EU law. Once domestic courts had accepted its jurisprudence and engaged with the preliminary rulings procedure, the Court began to broaden its scope. Had member states simply continued to stick to national law, in contradiction with EU law, the CJEU would have had no enforcement instrument – apart from the infringement procedure, which would also have been weaker. However, with domestic courts enforcing CJEU actions, governmental non-action had high political and financial costs.

The resistance of constitutional courts, particularly strong in the early days of Court activism in the 1960s and 1970s, has also slowly decreased, despite considerable enlargement of the EU in the 2000s bringing in 13 new central and eastern member states. As the chapter has shown, for constitutional judges, a strategy of 'dialogue and persuasion' has been more effective than actions risking 'open conflict' over where ultimate authority lies (Bobek, 2008a; Stone Sweet, 2013, p. 495). Exceptions remain, of course, as seen with the German FCC and the Czech Constitutional Court.

This chapter has discussed the paradox of CJEU influence at the domestic level. The next chapter analyses how private actors have, individually and collectively, contributed to the Court's capacity to influence EU policies.

Chapter 6

The Court and Interest Groups

As we have seen in the preceding chapters, the Court's power is dependent on actors appealing to the Court. Among those bringing cases before the Court are the member states and the EU institutions. However, another category of actors – interest groups – has consistently brought cases, either directly or indirectly, through the preliminary procedure. The aim of this chapter is to analyse why and how interest groups have used the legal opportunity structure provided by the CJEU, and in turn, to what extent interest groups have themselves been influenced by the Court's rulings.

Any discussion of the politics of law in the EU that didn't consider the relationship between interest groups and the Court would paint an incomplete picture of the Court's role in the EU's political system. The CJEU has had a great impact thanks to the role of private and public interest groups, who have used the Court as a means to advance their own position. These groups have heavily influenced the CJEU's case law and considerably helped carve out specific areas of legislation, ranging from intellectual property rights to gender equality. Clearly, European integration has benefited from the relationship between interest groups and the Court.

Interest groups have been active since the beginning of the European integration process. During the 1970s they adopted litigation strategies to plead their cause (Harlow, 1992, 1997; Dehousse, 1998; Cichowski, 1998, 2007; Mazey, 2001; Wernicke, 2009), such as in the field of equal treatment (for example, the *Defrenne* cases; see Chapter 2). After firms and trade unions came environmental, consumer and other interest groups (Alter & Meunier-Aitsahalia, 1994; Alter & Vargas, 2000; Hilson, 2002; Vanhala, 2009; Jacquot & Vitale, 2014). The extensive interpretation of *direct effect* promoted by the Court has allowed a number of groups to defend their individual rights. The Court fostered integration by deciding that specific national regulations contradicted European law, and therefore needed amending or repealing. However, the Court's decisions have not always been in favour of the plaintiff. Therefore, going to Court is, for many interest groups, just one strategy among many (Hilson, 2002; McCown, 2009).

This chapter takes an overview of existing interest group studies linked to the role and rulings of the CJEU. This is necessary in order to understand, on the one hand, the impact that European law has on the domestic level through interest group activity, and on the other hand, the degree to which the EU has become a 'normalized' political system where non-state actors play a crucial role in all aspects of political life, beyond the lobbying strategies with which they are usually related.

Interest groups are understood in this chapter as 'organised private actors seeking to influence political decision-making' (Beyers, Eising & Maloney, 2008; Grossman & Saurugger, 2012). According to Beyers, Eising and Maloney (2008), they are characterized by three features: organization, political interests and informality. *Organization* relates to the nature of the group and excludes unorganized broad movements and public opinion. *Political interest* refers to the attempts by these organizations to influence policy outcomes. Finally, *informality* relates to the fact that interest groups do not normally seek public office or compete in elections, but pursue their goals through frequent informal interactions with politicians and bureaucrats.

Interest groups can be economic in nature, such as firms and industrial federations, or be public interest groups such as NGOs and associations, universities or foundations. Hence, one of the defining factors of 'interest groups' is their collective nature (Beyers, Eising & Maloney, 2008). However, judicial systems are 'inherently individualistic, and collective bodies interested in using the courts as a vehicle to pursue goals must conform to this' (Vanhala, 2010, p. 12). It is precisely here that interest group litigation strategies become very specific compared to those usually used in decision-making processes. In order to refer a case to the Court, the group must represent an individual actor or have legal personality and be directly concerned by the issue.

This chapter is divided into four sections. The first presents the various legal and political incentives, in order to explain why groups use the Court. The second section analyses the resources groups have at their disposal. The third section looks in-depth into specific cases and explores the different litigation strategies groups used at EU level: test cases, sequential litigation strategies, and simultaneous litigation strategies. The last section puts the relationship between the Court and interest groups into the wider perspective of the politics of law in the EU.

Incentives to litigate

Interest groups have different ways and means to represent their interests in the European system. Litigation strategies are one of several so-called 'action repertoires'. First, groups may follow a 'national route', lobbying individual member governments for national regulations, and pressing their governments to champion EU-level policies in the Council of Ministers, whereas, second, interest groups may simultaneously pursue a 'Brussels route' by lobbying the European Commission, which in most policy areas possesses the sole right of initiative in EU policy-making and has been the subject of increased lobbying activity in the past two decades. Third, interest groups may appeal to the European Parliament, which emerged as the object of increased lobbying at the end of the 1990s and has since demonstrated considerable sympathy for the demands of diffuse interests, especially within the relevant parliamentary committees. Fourth, and finally, interests can and do appeal to national courts as well as to the CJEU, which in the EU legal system has the power to both enforce and interpret the treaties and EU secondary law (Pollack, 1998; Greenwood, 2011; Grossman & Saurugger, 2012).

In this sense, in public policy terminology litigation strategies are clearly part of the implementation phase of policy. They come into play when public policy has already been defined. But litigation strategies can, as we will see, also be considered as an agenda-setting process, when interest groups act proactively and, by resisting the implementation of a law, end up being taken to Court. The remaining part of this section examines four, direct or indirect, litigation routes at the disposal of interest groups.

Judicial review of EU legal acts

When the Court was established in 1952, some member states, in particular France, were sceptical about the idea that private parties could take cases directly to the CJEU. Since then, and as we have shown in Chapter 2, things have changed. Today, interest groups can bring claims before the CJEU against those legal acts adopted by EU institutions. Studies show that while public interest groups increasingly rely on litigation (Jupille & Caporaso, 1998), a large majority of EU interest groups remain reluctant to use litigation strategies to defend their interests at the EU level (Kelemen, 2002).

Article 263 TFEU, which is concerned with the CJEU's judicial review of EU legal acts, divides potential direct applicants into three groups (Eliantonio & Kas, 2010, p. 121; see also Chapter 3). The member states, the Council, Commission and European Parliament are regarded as 'privileged applicants', meaning that they are entitled to bring actions under article 263 TFEU without any restrictions. The European Court of Auditors and the European Central Bank are regarded as 'semi-privileged applicants'; they are entitled to bring actions only if they do so for the purpose of protecting their prerogatives. Natural and legal persons, and among them interest groups, are considered to be 'non-privileged applicants'.

The rules governing the legal standing of non-privileged applicants can be found in article 263 (4) TFEU. Natural and legal persons can seek judicial review in only three types of cases. First, if a decision is directly addressed to the applicant, he/she can challenge the decision, without any restrictions. Second, if a decision is addressed to third parties or a decision was in the form of a regulation, private parties can challenge it only if they have successfully shown that the measure is of 'direct and individual concern' to them (Chalmers, Davies & Monti, 2010, pp. 416–20; Fairhurst, 2007, pp. 225–54; Craig & de Búrca, 2008, pp. 507–17). Hence, organized interest groups cannot, as such, be considered as private parties, as we have stated above. They can, however, support an individual or a case. The situation is different with regard to companies 'directly concerned' by a decision. Third, although direct complaints may not be possible, article 37 of the Statute of the CJEU grants private parties intervention rights, provided they establish 'an interest in the result in any case submitted to the Court, save in cases between Member States, between institutions of the Union or between Member States and the institutions of the Union'.

The possibility for 'non-privileged' applicants (including individuals supported by interest groups, such as consumer, environmental and industrial groups and trade unions, as well as companies) to go directly to the CJEU concerning decisions of the EU institutions is limited by article 263 TFEU; either the decision is directly addressed to the applicant or the decision is of direct and individual concern to the applicant. This possibility is also subject to the restrictive interpretation given to it by the CJEU. In the leading case *Plaumann & Co. vs. Commission* (25/62), the CJEU asserted that individuals could challenge EU decisions directly before the CJEU 'only if that decision affects them by reason of certain attributes which are peculiar to them or by reason of circumstances in which they are differentiated from all other persons and by virtue of these factors distinguishes them individually just as in the case of the person addressed'.

Specifically, the CJEU has refused to accept collective organizations representing their members as qualifying as 'individually' and 'directly' concerned. For example, the CJEU rejected two cases where French works councils – organizations representing workers, which function as a local/firm-level complement to national labour negotiations – challenged a Commission decision allowing mergers between French companies to proceed (*Comité Central d'Entreprise de la Société Générale des Grandes Sources vs. Commission* C–96/92; *Vittel vs. Commission* C–12/93). It also refused a case where a works council challenged a Commission decision condemning state aid to a particular industry (*Comité d'entreprise de la Société Française de Production vs. Commission* C–189/97).

Preliminary rulings procedure

Preliminary ruling procedures are a central judicial tool for legal action by interest groups in the EU. Groups can use one or several individuals as legal plaintiffs to represent the interest of the organization in the context of this procedure. As in most cases, interest groups are not given direct access to the CJEU but use arguments pertaining to EU law before a national court. For the latter to decide on the case, it may be necessary to first acquire an interpretation of a specific EU rule, which only the CJEU can provide. The interest group – or the interest group supporting an individual – may or may not have the right to directly ask for a CJEU preliminary ruling. The fact that the national court may be obliged to do so, on the basis of article 234 TFEU, is a factor that will be taken into account by interest groups when developing their litigation strategies. As we have seen in previous chapters, the Court's preliminary reference case is considered to be the major source of pro-integrative rulings in the EU (Slaughter, Tulumello & Wood, 1998). The Court has played a central role in the development of EU policy by legitimating, enforcing and broadly interpreting the EU's primary and secondary legislation. Interest groups have played, and continue to play, an indirect, but nevertheless crucial role in this regard.

Preliminary rulings offer the highest number of cases involving public interest groups. The *Defrenne* cases (80/70; 43/75; 149/77) on equal pay between female and male workers are among the most prominent preliminary rulings. It is interesting to note that while women's movements did not introduce or support the case, Belgian trade unions were active supporters of Eliane Vogel-Polsky in her pledge. One of the most important lobbies defending women's rights – the European Women's Lobby – had never used litigation strategies in order to advance their cause at the EU level. The organization at that time combined different classic lobbying strategies such as participation in groups and committees, informal contacts and the production of expertise and counter-expertise, but did not file legal complaints (Jacquot & Vitale, 2014).

Another illustration of how interest groups use the preliminary rulings procedure can be found in the environmental sector. The '*Lappel Bank*' ruling, (*Regina vs. Secretary of State for the Environment* C–44/95) is based on a complaint introduced by the Royal Society for the Protection of Birds (RSPB). The RSPB appealed to the House of Lords to overthrow the decision by the Secretary of State to exclude a portion of the Medway Estuary and Marshes – the Lappel Bank area – from the Special Protection Areas (SPA) designation. The House of Lords asked the CJEU for a correct interpretation of article 4 of the Wild Birds Directive (79/409/EEC), in particular whether economic reasons could be taken into account in the designation of SPAs. The Court stated in its answer that economic interests could not override ecological objectives when constructing SPAs (Cichowski, 2007, p. 151).

While CJEU preliminary rulings can empower actors and push their governments into compliance, they don't always favour the plaintiff (Conant, 2002; Anagnostou, 2014). Yet a comparison of a series of cases – *Commission vs. Germany* (C–112/05), *Laval un Parteneri Ltd* (C–341/05), *Commission vs. Belgium* (C–503/99), *Commission vs. Germany* ('*Volkswagen*') (C–95/12), *Rüffert* (C–346/06), *Commission vs. Luxembourg* (C–319/06) – has shown that, while the Court's decisions went against public interest groups, the mitigated reception they received at the domestic level reinforced the domestic coalition in favour of the public interest group under scrutiny (Blauberger, 2014).

Opposition to the Court's jurisprudence stretched across all major parties in *Laval* and '*golden shares*' cases (*Commission vs. Germany* C–112/05 and C–95/12). The *Laval* case refers to a preliminary reference from the Swedish Labour Court to the CJEU. At its origin was a conflict between the Swedish building workers' union and a Latvian construction company over the building of a school in Sweden. Instead of reaching an agreement with the Swedish unionists, the company signed an agreement with the Latvian trade union. The Swedish trade unionists blocked the construction site and denied the validity of the agreement. The CJEU's decision, while acknowledging the fundamental right of trade unions to take collective action, found the blockade of the construction site 'disproportionate'. Furthermore, it criticized the lack of precise provisions on the definition of 'minimum pay' in Sweden, given that no such minimum wage exists, as well as the existence of the so-called 'Lex Britannia', which permits collective action irrespective of existing collective agreements under foreign law (Blauberger, 2014, p. 476). In reaction to the *Laval* ruling, even the conservative Swedish prime minister sided with the Swedish trade unions.

The 'golden shares' cases concerned shares that give government organizations, or other shareholders, the right of decisive vote in a shareholder meeting. In a case brought against Germany (C–112/05), the Court ruled in 2007 on a state measure (the VW-law) designed to give public authorities special rights in the Volkswagen AG, which they would not normally have under German company law. Following this judgement, Germany repealed the provisions of the VW-law that granted German authorities the special right to appoint representatives to the supervisory board and limited shareholders voting rights at the level of 20 per cent. In 2013, the Court found these amendments sufficient to comply with the previous judgement (C–95/12). Only the German liberal party (FDP) welcomed the Court's rulings. Everyone, even those social democrat *Länder* governments not directly affected by the ruling, went ahead with their own legal reforms to counter the Court's rulings, and thus empowered the German trade unions that opposed the idea of golden shares.

Non-compliance: indirect access to the infringement procedure

Interest groups can forward a case of member state non-compliance to the Commission. They can file complaints with the Commission, leading to infringement proceedings (pursuant to article 258 TFEU) that may ultimately result in new CJEU case law. Article 258 TFEU states: 'If the Commission considers that a member state has failed to fulfil an obligation under the Treaties, it shall deliver a reasoned opinion on the matter after giving the State concerned the opportunity to submit its observations. If the State concerned does not comply with the opinion within the period laid down by the Commission, the latter may bring the matter before the Court of Justice of the European Union.' Hence, in cases of member state non-compliance, the Commission can initiate an infringement procedure with a letter of formal notice, which can then be followed up by a reasoned opinion, a seizure of the CJEU and, finally, a ruling. If the member state does not react to the ruling, a second infringement procedure may be initiated and financial sanctions imposed (art. 260 TFEU). This can all be done on the incentive of the interest groups, be they public interest groups (Cichowski, 2007) or companies (see Genschel, Kemmerling & Seils, 2011, in the field of tax regulation). This incentive can only be indirect, however; interest groups can only file complaints with the Commission. Contrary to the annulment procedure, they cannot act as litigants in infringement cases.

Class action

The fourth possibility refers to a more complex procedure. Interest groups may lobby for the legal system to 'accommodate' group demands, such as through the possibility of initiating class action (Kelemen, 2011). Class actions allow government-authorized public interest groups (for example, a consumer group) to bring a legal action on behalf of the collective interest they represent (collective redress). For the time being, this last option is only possible at the domestic level, where relevant legal changes have been in recent years. Expanding mass consumer markets with consumers shopping cross-border and on the Internet created a potential for large groups of consumers to be harmed by the same or a similar illegal practice of a trader. At the European level, the Commission has been exploring the idea of introducing collective action mechanisms in consumer and competition policy since 2008. It has launched consultations with stakeholders, leading to comparative studies on consumer redress or competition policy. In a 2008 white paper addressing the issue of class action in the field of competition policy, the Commission attempted to distance itself from the US approach, based on the strong role of lawyers actively convincing consumers to search for class action, by emphasizing the central role of public authorities in the overall enforcement of European competition rules. In keeping with this theme, its white paper made clear that its aim was not to substitute public enforcement, noting repeatedly that EU and US systems had fundamentally different objectives (Commission, 2008). The 2014 *Damages Directive* (Directive 2014/104/EU) is the result of this process. Without opening the possibility for class action at the CJEU level, it aims at harmonizing class action practices at the member state level. It allows citizens and companies to claim damages if they are victims of infringements of EU antitrust rules, such as cartels and abuses of dominant market positions.

TABLE 6.1 *Legal routes for interest groups*

Judicial review of the legal acts adopted by EU institutions Art. 263 TFEU	Non-privileged applicants: – the decision must be addressed to the applicant – the decision must be of direct and individual concern for the applicant
Preliminary rulings procedure Art. 234 TFEU	Article 234 allows the CJEU to rule on points of EU law referred to it by national courts. Interest groups file a complaint with the relevant national court, which may decide to transfer the question to the CJEU
Non-compliance: Indirect access to the infringement procedure Art. 258 TFEU	Interest groups can file a complaint with the EU Commission. In cases of member state non-compliance, the Commission can initiate an infringement procedure (Letter of formal notice, followed up by a reasoned opinion, a transferral to the European Court of Justice and a ruling by the CJEU)
Class action	Only possible at the domestic level

We can see from the study of the different incentives to litigate that four conditions have to be met in order to be able to use international legal mechanisms to influence domestic policy (Alter, 2000, p. 489): (1) there must be a basis in European law that creates legal status and promotes the litigant's objectives; (2) litigants must use this law as the legal basis and adopt a litigation strategy; (3) if the case is brought before a national court, the latter must refer the case to the CJEU or else apply its jurisprudence; and (4) domestic actors must follow through on the legal victory to place the necessary pressure on national governments so that they actually take their position into consideration. Various factors influence each of these steps, creating cross-national and cross-issue variation in the influence of EU law on national policy.

Interest groups and their resources in litigation cases

Legal incentives are the key variable when seeking to explain the judicial activism of interest groups. However, non-state actors must also have access to resources to be able to fight a case before the Court or a national jurisdiction. Not all interest groups have the same resources at their disposal; a distinction between the different types of resources is important in order to understand the context in which interest groups gain access to the Court (providing that access is legally possible).

Resources favouring access to the Court

We can distinguish four types of resource: financial, organizational, social and societal. Financial resources are the money needed to bring a case before a jurisdiction and develop 'sustainable' litigation strategies. It refers to the costs of paying for legal counsel or in-house lawyers and necessary expertise. Organizational resources refer to the organizational strength of interest groups and their longevity. Hence, in the field of social policy, scholars have found that well-established groups, such as trade unions, have greater success with litigation strategies (Alter & Vargas, 2000). Furthermore, well-organized, financed and structured groups generally have legal services at their disposal, which makes long-lasting legal procedures easier to follow. At the same time, however, groups with significant influence over the policy-making process are also said to be less likely to turn to litigation strategies. As Alter and Vargas (2000,

p. 472) point out: 'The greater the political strengths of a group, and the more access the group has to the policy making process, the less likely a group is to mount a litigation campaign.'

A recent series of studies question this hypothesis, however. Scholars suggest that the best explanation for legal mobilization activity may lie in the dynamic interaction between the structural features that shape access to the legal system on the one hand, and an organization's structure and internal position towards the law on the other. Vanhala's study on two resourceful French environmental associations, both enjoying strong relations with the ministry of environment and a strong record of referring cases to the courts (Vanhala, 2016), illustrates this particularly well. She builds on work that argues that paying due attention to the influence of agent-level characteristics within a particular legal and political setting can offer better explanations for when and why groups turn to courts rather than focusing on external, structural factors alone (Epstein, Kobylka & Stewart, 1995; Edelman, Leachman & McAdam, 2010; Doherty & Hayes, 2014).

Social resources are those that allow interest groups to access and potentially influence the decision-making process through their extensive social network. This comprises former colleagues, training partners or any other individuals connected through a contact or professional cooperation. Finally, societal resources allow interest groups to play an active role in society; this role allows them to weigh more heavily during electoral campaigns and, hence, to exert a greater influence on public policy-making. This can be exemplified by the impact of anti-nuclear groups in Germany, as opposed to France. Environmental groups fighting nuclear energy have far more societal resources in Germany than in France, and therefore, can have much more impact (Grossman & Saurugger, 2012).

With regard to litigation strategies, these different types of resources have received different levels of attention. Until the beginning of the twenty-first century, financial resources were considered to be the most crucial of all, offering interest groups access to litigation strategies (Harlow & Rawlings, 1992; Conant, 2002; Bouwen & McCown, 2007). For a long time, social and societal resources were not studied, with the notable exception of the famous *Defrenne* case on gender equality rights (Mazey, 1998). They have only received increasing attention (Hilson, 2002; Cichowski, 2007; Vanhala, 2012; Jacquot & Vitale, 2014) in the last ten years. Financial resources remain a crucial factor in long and complex litigation procedures, where advocates have to be paid and hearings prepared. These resources might not be as easily available to some public interest groups or small businesses. On the interest group 'elite level', however, the differences between public interest groups such as Greenpeace and private interests such as Business Europe, the European-level confederation of businesses, and the European Federation of Pharmaceutical Industries Associations (EFPIA) are limited. These groups possess the financial resources necessary to hire specialized lawyers from law firms in Brussels to defend their case in Court. Small groups, whether they represent public or private interests, can't generally afford these law firms. At the same time, however, financial resources alone do not explain the differences in access completely (and even less the outcomes of these litigation cases). Support from agencies and large-scale bureaucracies can be equally important, as shown in studies linked to equality policies (equal pay, equal treatment) by Cichowski (2007), Hilson (2002) and Vanhala (2010).

Access to the Court strengthening interest groups' resources

Although resources are an important explanatory variable when seeking to analyse how and why non-state actors use the CJEU, the road to the Court – through preliminary ruling procedures or Commission-induced non-compliance procedures – can also shift the domestic balance of power in favour of non-state actors, and in

TABLE 6.2 *Resources*

Organizational	Organizational strength and longevity
Financial	Level of funds available in support of lobbying actions
Social	Allow interest groups to access and potentially influence the decision-making process through their extensive social network
Societal	Allow interest groups to make demands and exert influence in society

so doing modify the resources of groups. In this case, resources are not a factor influencing litigation strategies but are actually influenced by judicial politics, and need to be understood in order to explain the politics of law in the EU.

A number of examples illustrate interest group empowerment through the Court. They concern environmental issues, women's rights protection, animal welfare and lesbian and gay movements. The main argument found in these cases is that litigation strategies are used by domestic groups to circumvent national governments and to influence national policies (Börzel, 2006; Vanhala, 2009).

For example, the British Gender Equality Movement used the EU legal system in the 1980s to circumvent opposition to UK gender equality policies within the national judicial hierarchy, by linking their demands to those of the UK Equal Opportunities Commission (EOC). Throughout the 1980s, the EOC adopted a litigation strategy that targeted British policies contributing to gender discrimination in the workplace. It enjoyed considerable success in challenging the Conservative government's social policy, and allowed British trade unions to gain some of the powers that Margaret Thatcher's government had cut back, in some cases quite severely (Harlow & Rawlings, 1992, pp. 283–4; Kilpatrick, 1998; Mazey, 1998; Alter & Vargas, 2000, pp. 457–9). The EOC-funded test cases were referred to the Court through the preliminary ruling procedure by British industrial tribunals seeking a broader interpretation of equality rights. These cases would later become crucial CJEU rulings, such as *Drake vs. Chief Adjudication Officer* (180/85), as well as *Marshall vs. Southampton and South-West Hampshire Area Health Authority* (152/84) (where the EOC was actually a latecomer, the first two rounds of litigation having been funded by Marshall himself).

In the *Drake* case, the EOC supported Mrs Drake, a married and part-time-employed woman whose invalid mother came to live with her and her husband. When Mrs Drake applied for an invalid care allowance under the UK Social Security Act, she was told that married women who lived with their husbands were not entitled to such an allowance, contrary to their husbands in the same situation. The question brought before the Court was whether the risk of invalidity in the person of Mrs Drake's mother was covered by Directive 79/7/EEC, and whether Mrs Drake, who had given up her employment to support her invalid mother, could receive an invalid care allowance. The Court defined working population broadly and argued that although Mrs Drake and her mother were not the same person,

Mrs Drake's situation (giving up employment to care for her invalid mother) fell under the social security scheme. Discrimination on the grounds of sex was contrary to the directive. Alter and Vargas stress several factors which contributed to the impressive influence of the EOC in the British legal system (2000, p. 464). First, the EOC employed a strategy of forum shopping, targeting tribunals that were considered sympathetic to the EOC's policy objectives and that would therefore be receptive to EU law arguments. Second, a growing number of legal scholars supported the notion that British equality laws should be interpreted in accordance with European principles (Gormley, 1986; McCrudden, 1987). Alter and Vargas quote the Law Society's president, Martin Mears, declaring in this regard that tribunals had been 'hijacked by the discrimination industry' (Dyer, 1995, p. 8, in Alter & Vargas, 2000, p. 464).

As a weapon of the weak, however, the law is not systematically successful, as Jacquot and Vitale have shown in their study of Roma and women's groups at the European level (Jacquot & Vitale, 2014). It is particularly the groups' contrasting relationships to the law, based on organizational characteristics and group identity, that explain why umbrella organizations – the European Women's Lobby (EWL) and the European Roma and Traveller Forum (ERTF) – use litigation strategies to varying extents. Groups adapt their strategies to the changing institutional context in a highly reflexive manner. A clear-cut differentiation between domestic groups using litigation strategies and European groups using lobbying strategies is thus exaggerated. The EWL has never used legal activism, whereas the ERTF considers law and litigation as a resource and uses it extensively. Litigation can be seen as a 'means of differentiating and positioning the group within a competitive interest groups environment' (Jacquot & Vitale, 2014, p. 600).

In general, resources can be understood as tools for non-state actors to change European law through litigation, but these resources must be used strategically. Alone, they are not sufficient explanatory factors for change. How then, more precisely, do interest groups select and determine their litigation strategies?

Litigation strategies

In the literature we can identify two litigation strategies: proactive litigation strategies and reactive litigation strategies (Vanhala, 2011, p. 7). Proactive litigation strategies describe those situations in which groups act as the litigant, seeking to take their cause to the courts. Reactive litigation strategies are a response by groups that choose to engage in civil disobedience. In these situations, groups purposefully flout laws they consider to be unjust or immoral, with the aim of being brought before a judge. Although both strategies co-exist with regard to EU law, proactive litigation strategies seem the prominent strategy pursued, and very few systematic studies exist that analyse reactive litigation strategies. Bouwen and McCown (2007) and McCown (2009) distinguish three types of proactive litigation strategies: test cases, sequential litigation strategies and simultaneous litigation strategies.

Test cases

In case law systems, that is, in systems such as in the United States or the EU where judges use precedent-based reasoning to decide cases, a test case can be defined as a legal action whose purpose is to set a precedent. It has significance not only for the person bringing it but for others too. An actor files a lawsuit in order to see if the court considers a certain law or a certain legal precedent applicable in specific circumstances. A test case strategy seeks rulings which establish untested points of law; confirm or challenge an existing interpretation of the law; challenge an existing practice; and/or force or incite policy-makers to act.

Test cases in the EU can be found in a large number of policy fields. In areas such as social and environmental policies or the free movement of goods, interest groups have taken part in test cases.

In social policy cases, labour unions, minority groups and women's rights movements have actively supported the plaintiff when filing the case with the national-level court responsible. One of the most well-known test cases is in the field of gender equality rights (see also Chapters 7 and 8). The first landmark ruling in this area was the abovementioned *Defrenne* case of 1971 (80/70), where a Belgian flight attendant, Mrs Defrenne, had been required by her employer, Sabena Belgian Airways, to accept early retirement (at the age of 40) or else change jobs within the company with a loss in pay. The reason for this proposition was that, contrary to male flight attendants, women over the age of 40 were not considered attractive enough for the job. In 1966, Belgium had not yet adopted a single measure included in article 119 TEC. A Belgian feminist lawyer, Eliane Vogel-Polsky, chose a litigation strategy and recruited Gabrielle Defrenne as a test case. She sued, pointing out that Sabena imposed no such rule on male stewards, and calling for Sabena's policy to be outlawed on the basis of article 157 TFEU (then art. 141 TEC). The Belgian court referred the case to the CJEU, which ruled that Sabena's policy was indeed discriminatory, and required the company to compensate Mrs Defrenne for loss of income (in fact there were three CJEU judgements, in 1971, 1976 and 1978). More importantly, however, the Court also held that article 141 TEC had *direct effect* within the member states, conferring rights on individuals despite the lack of transposition of article 141 TEC into Belgian national law (Hoskyns, 1996; Cichowski, 2007). The second CJEU *Defrenne* ruling established the direct effect of article 119 TEC while the third ruling asserted that equal treatment is a fundamental EU principle – both provided the legal basis for the development of EU secondary legislation on gender equality during the 1970s and 1980s (Hoskyns, 1996).

Cichowski has pertinently underlined that 'the transformation of article 141 (now art. 157 TFEU) had consequences not only for secondary legislation in the 1970s and 1980s, but also for the litigating environment' (2007, p. 98; Vanhala, 2012, 2016). The Equal Treatment Directive, which followed the *Defrenne* rulings, is today 'included' in the TFEU as an equal rights principle and allows litigants and their lawyers to act strategically by invoking this right. In this sense, it provides the Court with a powerful tool to decide on the case.

In the field of pregnancy rights, another field of social policy, trade unionists and individual activists have also used available legal resources and EU rules to bring legal claims before their national courts. The CJEU's rulings have expanded the meaning and scope of EU social provisions, starting with the *Dekker* case (C– 177/88 Dekker) (see also, McCown, 2009), the first such case on this issue. A Dutch court brought the case before the CJEU in 1988. Mrs Dekker had applied for a job with a Dutch company, VJV. The recruitment board found her to be the most qualified of all applicants, but the management board rejected her on the grounds that she was three months pregnant. The case was referred to the CJEU under article 141 TEC (now art. 157 TFEU) and the Equal Treatment Directive. In its ruling, the Court found that discrimination in employment and recruitment on the grounds of pregnancy constituted direct sex discrimination, contrary to the Equal Treatment Directive. Similar rulings were issued in the *Herz* case (C–179/88), *Habermann-Belterman vs. Arbeiterwohlfahrt* (C–421/92) and the British *Webb* case (C–32/93), to quote but a few. In all cases, the litigants were supported by well-organized trade unions that had the necessary financial and social resources to see the cases through to the end (see also Vanhala, 2010).

In the field of environmental rights, Cichowski (2007, p. 122) has shown that the situation differs with regard to the national origin of environmental groups. Hence in Spain, while NGOs have actively filed lawsuits with regard to the implementation of the EU Access to Environmental Information Directive (Council Directive 90/313/EEC), national courts have not sent the cases to the CJEU, reflecting the general trend of national judges not to make preliminary references. However, this led to increased activism and transnational cooperation, with the Spanish NGO Asociación Ecologista de Defensa de la Naturaleza (AEDENAT), together with the Dutch NGO Stichting Natuur en Milieu, producing a user's guide to filing complaints and appeals against the improper implementation of the EU directive on Access to Environmental Information (Cichowski, 2007, p. 125).

In countries where environmental interest groups are well organized and preliminary references widespread, non-state actors have had more success in getting their cases referred to the Court. An example here is the *Danish Bottles* decision of 1988 (302/86), which upheld a Danish recycling programme deemed in conflict with free trade law. The Court argued, in its judgement, that national environmental protection measures could in certain instances remain in place despite obstructing free trade.

How do individuals use secondary legislation that has not granted individual rights to bring legal actions against their own national governments? Often interest groups file complaints with the Commission leading to infringement procedures that ultimately result in CJEU case law (Cichowski, 1998, 2007, p. 142). European federations, companies and national and transnational NGOs use the Commission's complaints procedure to provide detailed compliance information that is otherwise difficult to collect for the Commission. There are plenty of examples involving environmental NGOs and European federations – such as pharmaceutical industries, banks and shipbuilders – unhappy about national fiscal systems that distort competition (Cichowski, 2007; Genschel, Kemmerling & Seils, 2011). However, filing a complaint is just one step in the lobbying process. During the trial, if the Court decides that the case can be heard, the European policy process might already lead to a revision of the directive or a new decision. Thus, interest groups must be very attentive in following these processes correctly. This is an illustration of the range of action strategies that interest groups have at their disposal – filing a complaint is just one of several lobbying mechanisms often used at the same time. It is clear that only resourceful groups – those with substantial assets, with financial support from other sources (charities, foundations and so on), or with close links to the administration in charge – have a chance of their test case strategies being successful.

Case studies provide very interesting insight into how interest groups use non-compliance as a legal strategy to influence decision-making procedures at the EU level. However, we might take this qualitative analysis further and complement it with quantitative data that establishes correlation between yearly infringement procedures and the number of complaints filed by interest groups with the Commission.

Sequential litigation strategies

Sequential litigation strategies are chosen to lock in decisions. Financial resources and a powerful legal service are usually required. Rulings favourable to litigants are followed up by other rulings, which, if favourable to the litigant, make legislative over-ruling more complicated and therefore less likely (McCown, 2009). This strategy is particularly successful if resourceful interest groups are able to bring several cases swiftly before national courts, which are then referred to the CJEU. Non-state actors may be successful before the courts but also at policy-making level, when either the national or EU legislator chooses to amend the law in accordance with their positions. This strategy is used by so-called 'repeat players' (as opposed to 'one-time shooters') and refers to both large corporate actors and public interest groups. Corporate actors have been instrumental in pushing the French administrative Court (*Conseil d'État*) to comply with European law since the late 1980s (see Chapters 2 and 5). Corporate interests, in France, found themselves in a legal context whereby they had a competitive disadvantage compared to corporate interests operating in member states where direct effect and supremacy doctrines were fully respected (Mattli & Slaughter, 1998, p. 188). To remedy this situation, the tobacco producers Philip Morris and Rothmans – classical repeat players – launched systematic attacks on government decisions that they felt were contrary to European law. Their aim was to trigger a domino effect of CJEU verdicts condemning France for the breach of European law. This strategy finally led to the decision by the *Conseil d'État* confirming the primacy of the EU directive over national law, even if the national law came after the EU directive (*SA Rothmans International France et SA Philip Morris*, 1992).

Simultaneous litigation strategies

Simultaneous litigation strategies or 'joining cases' increase the consistency, coherence and salience of legal interpretations. According to McCown (2009), they also maximize the immediate applicability of any legal change. However, simultaneous litigation strategies demand an immense coordination effort, and so are generally nested in a wide range of lobbying activities. The case of taxation is an example illustrating this specific point. While the Commission has been very slow in attempting to create a common taxation policy (because of political resistance), simultaneous litigation strategies have led to CJEU rulings initiated by banks and auditing firms, such as PriceWaterhouse Coopers. A key ruling stated that while direct taxation falls under member state competences, member states must avoid any discrimination on grounds of nationality (Genschel, 2007; McCown, 2009; Genschel & Jachtenfuchs, 2011). From 1958 to 2007, the corporate tax jurisprudence of the CJEU increased constantly, with a particularly high number of cases from 1998 onwards (from 1958 to 1997 the Court dealt with 6 cases on corporate tax issues, while from 1998 to 2007 it handled 37 cases). Of the 43 cases between 1958 and 2007, some 31 were 'lost' by the member states (Genschel, Kemmerling & Seils, 2011), which defended their right to make their own taxation laws in complete freedom. Through rulings such as *Wielockx* (C–80/94), *Asscher* (C–107/94) and *Royal Bank of Scotland* (C–311/97), the CJEU made tax law, in place of the Commission and member states, and did so thanks to interest group activism through the preliminary ruling procedure. This has led scholars to argue that 'tax jurisdiction shopping has been elevated to the status of constitutional right' (Genschel, Kemmerling & Seils, 2011, p. 16). While in some cases it allowed restrictions to the four freedoms because they served public interest requirements (Nicolaïdis & Schmidt, 2007), the Court nevertheless seems to have accorded a higher priority to

TABLE 6.3 *Litigation strategies*

	Definition	Examples
Test cases	A legal action whose purpose it is to set a precedent.	*Defrenne vs. Sabena* 80/70; 43/75; 149/77 *Dekker* C–177/88 *Herz* C–179/88 *Webb* C–32/93
Sequential litigation strategies	To lock in a decision: a series of cases is introduced one after another. A strategy that seeks to reinforce the impact of the ruling by enlarging its scope.	
Simultaneous litigation strategies	'Joining cases' aims to increase the consistency, coherence and salience of legal interpretations.	C–80/94 *Wielockx*, C–107/94 *Asscher*, C–311/97 *Royal Bank of Scotland*

the protection of taxpayers' (individual but particularly collective) treaty-based rights of mobility than to member states' public policy requirements.

The Court, interest groups and the politics of law in the European Union

Given the incentives for interest groups to litigate, their access strategies and resources and litigation strategies, to what extent do these factors influence the politics of law in the EU?

According to Lisa Conant (2002), it is the action of interest groups, more than any other factor, that explains why national governments go along with CJEU judgements. While national judicial enforcement and institutional barriers to overturning judgements (see Chapter 2) provide the most consensual arguments to explain member state behaviour, Conant claims that CJEU rulings have to be mediated at the national level by interest groups in order for judgements to be 'efficient'. Hence 'variation in the ability and interest of societal actors to coordinate their demands will influence how much pressure governments face in the wake of innovative legal interpretation' (Conant, 2002, p. 17). In others words, 'the utility of the CJEU interpretation as a source of political leverage depends on the characteristics of the actors who engage law' (ibid.).

In her study, Conant concentrates on CJEU rulings on trade liberalization in the fields of telecommunications and electricity, and on access to public sector employment and social benefits. She argues that how these two areas of CJEU rulings were received (following the limited implementation of EU law) can be explained in two ways: on the one hand, by the important institutional commitment provided by relevant interest groups in telecommunications and electricity policies; and on the other, by the lack of institutional commitment on account of weakly organized and poorly mobilized interest groups and social movements (social and employment policies). Likewise, Conant argues that two factors explain interest group success, or as she calls them, 'potential beneficiaries and losers' (Conant, 2002, p. 23) when it comes to litigation strategies: public opportunity structures and the organizational capacity of those groups. Hence, instead of being the domain of the politically disadvantaged, the law is at the service of the privileged: 'Litigation is most likely to create political pressure that promotes broader reforms when deployed by actors with substantial material and organizational resources' (ibid.).

Cichowski (2007) and Vanhala (2010) both agree with Conant's argument, according to which relations between interest groups and the CJEU are the key factor for explaining the development of supranational governance in the EU, and the politics of law in the EU more generally. Like Conant, Cichowski asserts that two factors – organizational capacities of interest groups and institutional support – are the two most relevant variables that account for variation in the use of preliminary rulings by non-state actors. However, she argues, contrary to Conant, that it is not the interests of the most powerful actors that influence the Court's ruling, but whether or not the interest groups have access to EU law in the first place. In analysing the preliminary ruling procedures on social provisions from 1970 and environmental protection from 1976 (both until 2003), Cichowski shows that NGOs and trade unions helped the Court develop its case law, which in turn triggered a steady rise in the amount of preliminary references sent from national courts to Luxembourg. The better organized the mobilized interests, and the higher the legal resources by way of government agency legal support, the higher the number of preliminary references. Hence, those trade unions and social NGOs that benefited from significant government agency legal support were better able to indirectly access the CJEU through the preliminary ruling procedure. On the contrary, environmental NGOs suffered from the absence of well-structured legal expertise. Furthermore, contrary to the many options available within the equal rights legislation within EU social policy, there were difficulties bringing claims before national courts under EU environmental law. This also explains why there were twice as many references in the field of social provisions (307) as in environment (148) (Cichowski, 2007, p. 246).

Thus, organizational and institutional opportunity structures seem to be the main factors explaining interest group access to the Court. Cichowski's data also suggest that, in particular, vague EU laws have given the CJEU the opportunity to make expansive rulings (rather than constrain the Court), regardless of member state opposition or of national laws that currently govern these practices (Cichowski, 2007, p. 246). Her study convincingly countered the argument that the policy positions of member states, and particularly the most powerful ones, determine the Court's rulings. In analysing the 'amicus briefs' sent to the Court on issues concerning preliminary references in the field of environmental and social cases brought before the national courts by NGOs and trade unions, Cichowski found that although the Court was informed about the preferences of the most powerful member states, it did not hesitate to act in opposition to those interests. Where member states overruled the Court's decision, the Court continued to make rulings that were expansive with regard to the precision, scope and enforceability of EU law. Furthermore, rulings invoking treaty-based principles and areas governed by unanimity voting have presented a greater challenge to EU policy-makers seeking to reverse adverse judicial decisions through corrective legislation or treaty amendments (see also Chapters 4 and 5).

This perspective is arguably very insightful when we seek to understand the relationship between the Court and interest groups, and how over time it has enabled CJEU rulings to have an impact (without the constraining force of the police or military, which might otherwise coerce member states to comply). This is similar to Stone Sweet and Brunell's (1998) argument whereby the transnational activity of EU actors, based on interest group action, is crucial for explaining the success of CJEU rulings. In this sense, the EU is not distinct from other liberal democratic systems, since overt coercion rarely plays a significant role in fostering obedience. Courts rely predominantly on consent, but it is this consent that needs to be explained.

Conclusion

We have seen that public and private interest groups, NGOs and economic interests use the CJEU to expand EU law and the Court's power. These actors use the relationship between the Court and European law for their own benefit, and through their actions enlarge EU law and the Court's power. An approach that recognizes political and institutional opportunity structures helps us to understand how resources and access points enable interest groups to gain access. However, it is difficult to say whether public or private interest groups are the most influential in their litigation strategies, and whether one policy field is more open to interest group litigation than another. It is equally difficult to say how precisely the Court's rulings have changed the overall balance of power between public and private interest groups in the EU.

Analysing the relationship between the CJEU and interest groups also leads us to the question of whether such interaction fosters the democratic character of the EU, or, on the contrary, constitutes a threat. Alternatively, we might see this relationship as a development that we observe in all liberal democracies, that is, a process concerned with the mainstream transformation of democracy rather than one that seeks to undermine it. The judicial policy-making of the Court might be considered as a way of promoting democracy, insofar as the interaction between the Court and civil society shows how courts can provide participatory opportunities for citizens and groups 'by engaging them in the development, monitoring and enforcement of law' (Cichowski, 2007, p. 260). At the same time, European law provides opportunities for citizens and public groups to 'seize' or make effective use of the Court, just as it does for companies, banks and industrial federations. The Court enables both public and private interests to develop European law. The fact that non-state actors are able to trigger referrals to the Court and mount legal challenges makes them crucial actors in the politics of law of the EU.

Chapter 7

The Constitutional Role of the Court

The CJEU has often been depicted as being 'activist' (Chapter 2), insofar as it not only 'speaks' but 'makes' the law. At first sight, activism runs counter to the legal tradition in civil law countries, where core principles are codified into a system of written rules, which serve as the primary source of law. This contrasts with common law systems based on judge-made decisional law and the doctrine of judicial precedent. The legal system within which the CJEU operates is therefore at odds with the legal traditions in EU member states, with the exception of Ireland and the United Kingdom. In civil law countries, the courts are meant to be the 'mouth' of the law or the Constitution, and 'legal interpretation is supposed to distil an objective deductive operation' (Rosenfeld, 2006, p. 640). In common law countries, judges 'make or infer or construct the law [...] by a process of interpretation, accretion, experimentation, argumentation, and trial and error' (Rosenfeld, 2006, p. 635).

However, this distinction is misleading and does not correctly characterize the role of judges in contemporary legal systems. To consider courts as no more than the mouthpiece of the law is naïve. Courts do more than simply 'speak' the existing law (Shapiro, 1981). Even the French Constitutional Court has clearly 'made' law, such as in its landmark 1971 *Liberté d'association* decision, transforming its role from mere guardian of the boundary between executive and legislative power to a guarantor of individual rights against legislative infringement. The idea that international tribunals are more inclined to law-making than domestic ones must therefore be seriously questioned (Alter & Helfer, 2010, p. 563). Activism is not connected with the international or domestic character of the court, but rather, with factors such as the compulsory jurisdiction of the courts (Posner & Yoo, 2005); the possibility for private litigants to access the courts (Helfer & Slaughter, 1997;

Keohane, Moravcsik & Slaughter, 2000); the difficulty for political authorities to overrule the courts (Stephan, 2002; Steinberg, 2004; Ginsburg, 2005); and, finally, the blocking of decisions at the political level, which provides room for the courts to play a compensating role and 'make' law where political institutions failed to do so (Weiler, 1981, 1991).

As long as the law is not written in a perfectly clear and precise manner, judges cannot prevent themselves from 'making' law, that is, from explaining how law should be understood and implemented. As far as the CJEU is concerned, this function is displayed at both the constitutional and legislative level. Through its legal doctrines, the CJEU has helped to transform the EU into a polity – or an organized and sophisticated system of governance – and in so doing, played a role close to that of constituent power, as we argue in this chapter. Yet the CJEU has also contributed to the development of several EU public policies, acting as a policy-maker at the legislative level, which we discuss in Chapter 8.

Though the CJEU was not established as a constitutional court, it has developed into a powerful and bold adjudicator, which is not surprising given that tribunals devoted to constitutional review, such as the German Constitutional Court, have achieved enormous influence since the Second World War. The constitutional role of the CJEU is based on the assumption that EU treaties are constitutional by nature, even if they are not strictly called a 'constitution' (Stein, 1981; Weiler, 1991; Hartley, 1996; Terpan, 2015b). Other scholars have criticized this argument on the grounds that the EU is not a state and therefore should not be analysed through the lens of constitutional law (Everson, 1998, p. 108, quoted in Shaw, 1999; D'Onorio, 2005). For the purpose of this book, we consider that constitutionalism *is* possible within the context of international organizations generally (Fassbender, 1998; Cass, 2005; Trachtman, 2006; Fassbender, 2007; Terpan, 2015a), and more particularly, in a post-national organization such as the EU (Constantinesco, 1995; Gerkrath, 1997; Shaw, 1999; Arnold, 2011). The Court itself sees its role as partly constitutional.

The treaties provide the various functions of a constitution (Sunstein, 2001): organizing the hierarchy of legal norms; defining the conditions of exercise of political power; distributing competences among different levels of governance and administration; and protecting the rights and freedoms of individuals. Acting as a constitutional adjudicator, the European Court has interpreted treaty provisions over time, often departing from the text and taking into account the objectives and the system of the treaties. This bold case law has resulted in the establishment of two major constitutional principles (*direct effect* and *primacy*), the organization of horizontal and vertical powers, and the progressive inclusion of fundamental rights in EU law.

Legal methods of the Court: treaties as a constitutional integrative system

Since the origins of European integration, the Court has worked to develop the treaties into a sort of de facto European constitution (Stein, 1981). Since the mid-1980s, it has referred to the treaties as 'the Constitutional Charter of the European Communities' ('*Les Verts*' 294/83; Opinion 1/91), making it clear that a European constitution could exist even if a document formalized as such has not been adopted (Terpan, 2015a). Not only has the Court used the concept of 'constitution' to describe the European treaties, but it has developed a series of other 'constitutional' concepts such as 'primacy', 'direct effect', 'implied powers', 'effectiveness' and 'useful effect' ('*effet utile*') in order to build a European legal order, as we have shown in previous chapters. The use of legal concepts is not specific to the European Court, of course, but it is of particular relevance in this case because the Court has had to build this new legal order by starting from scratch. The CJEU judges 'have not inherited a legal system in which they had predetermined roles and which was composed of well-developed concepts grounded in the system's tradition and backed up by homogeneous linguistic practices. The legal system was to be created and endowed with authority conventionally ascribed only to state laws' (Leczykiewicz, 2008, p. 786).

Moreover, the European Court has chosen to interpret the treaties in a rather bold manner. Legal reasoning is made up of six different possible interpretation criteria (Bengoetxea, 1993; Bengoetxea, McCormick & Moral Soriano, 2001; Itzcovitch, 2009). Four of them give rise to activism (functional, teleological, consequentialist and systemic criteria), while the remaining two are a sign of self-restraint (literal and historical criteria).

First, a functional interpretation (Bengoetxea, 1993) assumes that, in case of doubt, a legal provision must be interpreted in such a way as to ensure its 'effectiveness' or 'useful effect' ('*effet utile*').

Second, a teleological (or purposive) interpretation (Pollicino, 2004) implies that interpretation is consistent with the goals and purposes explicitly or implicitly established by the treaties. Third, a consequentialist interpretation (McCormick, 1994, 2005; Conway 2014) takes into consideration the foreseeable consequences of the interpretive decision. The CJEU has widely used the three methods. For example, 'useful effect' was invoked in the jurisprudence dealing with the direct effect of directives (*Van Duyn* 41/74). And, in *Van Gend en Loos* (26/62), the Court used both the teleological criterion (in using sentences such as 'The objective of the EEC Treaty ...' and 'according to the spirit, the goals and purposes of the Treaty ...', making a reference to the preamble of the treaty: 'an ever closer union') and the consequentialist one (the frequent use of the modal verbs 'could' or 'would' shows that the Court anticipates the consequences of its decisions). Finally, the systemic (or contextual) interpretation takes into consideration the normative context in which the legal provision is placed and makes interpretive links between different provisions belonging to the same legal order. Systemic interpretation has been widely used by the European Court in a very broad manner, including most of the interpretative techniques familiar to national legal cultures (*a contrario* interpretation, recourse to analogy, *a fortiori* reasoning and *ad absurdum* argument). In *Van Gend en Loos*, for instance, the Court mentioned the 'general scheme' of the treaties, invoking quite clearly the systemic criterion.

The last two methods cannot be considered as judicial activism. The literal (or textual) criterion must stick to the text and should not allow for any 'external' criteria to interfere. The historical argument, typical of the French exegetic school and the tradition of the so-called legislative legal positivism, prescribes that legal provisions be interpreted in a way that corresponds to the will of the legislator.

The CJEU has refused to limit its legal reasoning to literal and historical arguments, choosing instead to use the systemic criterion in combination with the three – or some of the three – most audacious criteria (teleological, consequentialist and functional). For instance, the teleological interpretation can easily be combined with the systemic one, given that treaty objectives are part of a system constructed by legal doctrine. Similarly, the consequentialist interpretation can overlap with the systemic interpretation when the consequences taken into consideration are not the practical effects 'out there' in the world, but the internal legal effects within

TABLE 7.1 *Types of interpretation*

Interpretation Criteria	Activism / Self-Restraint	
teleological	++	Activism
functional	++	
consequentialist	++	
systemic	+	
historical	- -	Self-Restraint
literal	- -	

the European legal system (Itzcovitch, 2009). This use of audacious criteria is consistent with the idea of the court being an activist, as it offers significant room for manoeuvre to the judges, contrary to textual and historical arguments.

The use of legal concepts and interpretive methods supports the idea of a European Court being an 'activist'. A way of measuring the possible activism of a tribunal is to look at the distance between *interpretation* on the one hand, and the textual basis and *original intentions* of the drafters of the treaties on the other – hence the greater the distance between interpretation and original intention(s), the greater the activism. As for the CJEU, this distance is assumed to be high because of the extensive/dynamic interpretation of the Court (Bengoetxea, 1993), complemented by its large use of systemic reasoning. This conclusion is drawn from the analysis of landmark rulings. A more systematic and longitudinal study of the Court's case law is needed, however, in order to demonstrate whether the Court has been – and still is – an activist (Saurugger & Terpan, 2015). Understanding the Court's legal reasoning – that is, the collective reasoning of the Court's judges and law practitioners – is necessary when seeking to measure Court activism, beyond its degree of opposition to the largest member state positions (Carrubba Gabel & Hankla, 2012). The Court's cognitive frame can therefore be understood as the doctrine constructed by the European judges through legal interpretations, and constraining the judges' ability to act. Of course, the judges, while deciding on a case, also make strategic decisions with regard to the Court's external political, social and economic environment. Only by linking both aspects – the legal cognitive frame and the strategic position with regard to other actors – can we understand the Court's place in the constitutionalization of the European political system.

Describing the CJEU as activist often elicits criticism of the Court's legal reasoning, both from a political and a legal perspective. From a political standpoint, the Court is sometimes viewed as undermining the democratic foundations of the political system. This was the point that Lüder Gerken (Director of the Centre for European Policy) and Roman Herzog (former German president and former judge at the German Constitutional Court) made in the campaign 'Stop the ECJ', which they launched in September 2008 in the newspaper *Frankfurter Allgemeine Zeitung*. From a 'legal positivist' standpoint, the CJEU is seen as straying from what a court is strictly supposed to do in a system based on the rule of law (Conway, 2012).

Both arguments are built on fragile assumptions. By pointing at activism, they suggest that the Court goes beyond its 'proper' judicial function. What is the 'proper' function of a Court, however? Judicial interpretation stems from dialogue with EU institutions and national legislatures, the implementation of a 'normatively open' and often contradictory set of documents (the EU treaties), and interaction with other legal orders. Given all the factors at play, a consensus on the Court's 'proper' function is, not surprisingly, difficult to achieve (Dawson, 2014). For the purpose of this book, we do not explore activism as a means to criticize the Court for going beyond its proper function, but rather, as a way to point to its propensity to widely interpret EU norms and 'make' law, something that implies neither a negative nor positive judgement on the Court's behaviour.

The doctrines of direct effect and primacy

In its landmark rulings of the early 1960s (*Van Gend en Loos* 26/62 and *Costa vs. Enel* 6/64) (Chapter 2), the Court stated that EU law, by imposing obligations and rights on both individuals and member states, and limiting the sovereignty of member states, constituted an autonomous body of law, distinct from international law. In the same cases, it 'gave birth to' the doctrines of *direct effect* and *primacy*, making a key contribution to the integration process.

Direct effect

In international law, the assumption is that treaties do not have direct effect; treaties with direct effect are the exception. In the absence of direct effect, treaty provisions and other international rules cannot be directly invoked before a national court. Direct effect depends on direct applicability, which means that international rules can be applied at national level even if they have not been transposed or incorporated into domestic law. In monist states, where international law is part of the domestic law, direct applicability is inherent to the legal system, and direct effect is possible, although not automatic. In dualist states, which consider international law separate from domestic law, direct applicability, and thus direct effect, are impossible (Chapter 5).

European treaties, since they were established, have not made a clear choice between the two approaches. On the one hand, a dualist country such as the United Kingdom adopted a specific legal act (European Communities Act 1972) in order to make European law applicable at the domestic level. On the other hand, EU treaties contain two provisions that lean towards monism: the direct applicability of EU regulations (art. 288 TFEU); and a mechanism that envisages the direct application of European rules by national courts (art. 267 TFEU). However, the European Court considerably reinforced direct effect in the EU with the monistic reading of European law in its landmark ruling *Van Gend en Loos* (26/62), and thereafter with its case law.

The *Van Gend en Loos* ruling (Tizzano, Kokott & Prechal, 2013) is based on the assumption that provisions of European law have direct effect unless the European Court says otherwise. The case concerned a decision by Dutch customs to increase custom duty to goods imported in the Netherlands, despite article 12 EC (art.12 of the EEC Treaty, now art. 28 TFEU) having forbidden the raising of duties (for more details on the case see Chapter 2). The Court of Justice had to issue a preliminary ruling on the question of whether article 12 had direct effect. There were two possible interpretations. The first, supported by the advocate-general and three member states, was that article 12 did not create a legal norm of a general nature, but rather, placed an obligation on the member states. In the Treaty of Rome, only regulations were – and still are – explicitly granted 'direct effect'. Nothing was said about treaty provisions and directives.

The Court of Justice, going beyond literal interpretation, chose a second option, based on the 'spirit, the general scheme and the wording' of the treaties. Instead of concentrating purely on specific treaty provisions, it contextualized its arguments with regard to the treaties in general. Several arguments were put forward to demonstrate that the Treaty of Rome is 'more than an agreement which merely creates mutual obligations between the contracting states'. As such, it constitutes 'a new legal order of international law for the benefit of which the states have limited their sovereign right, albeit within limited fields, and the subject of which comprises not only member states but also their nationals'. The Court based its decision on the general aims of the EEC Treaty, referring to its preamble and to article 177 (now art. 267 TFEU), which was taken as an indication that the member states had acknowledged the fact that citizens could invoke Community law (Burley & Mattli, 1993).

The preamble of the Treaty of Rome refers not only to governments but also to peoples. The sovereign rights transferred to the Community were those of the nationals, not those of the governments. The nations are called upon to cooperate through the intermediary of the European Parliament and the (European) Economic and Social Committee. The procedure of preliminary ruling links the national courts to the application of European law. It confirms that the member states have acknowledged that European law possesses an authority that can be invoked by private litigants before national courts (Claes, 2006). From these arguments the Court deduced that, although it is the member states that are the subject of the negative obligation included in article 12 EC (prohibition to raise custom duties), this does not imply that their nationals cannot benefit from the obligation. Crucially, article 12 TEC contains an obligation requiring no further intervention on the part of the states and institutions for it to be effective and used by applicants before national courts.

The major novelty of the doctrine was not the 'discovery' that EU law could have direct effect (self-executing provisions were not an unknown phenomenon prior to 1963), but the confirmation that it is up to the European Court to decide whether specific provisions of the Treaty of Rome have direct effect (De Witte, 2010, p. 10); it cannot be left to national courts because they would not give a unified interpretation of EU law. The member states that communicated their observations to the Court during the *Van Gend en Loos* proceedings had a different view. According to them, possible violations of the treaty at the national level could only be ascertained by the European Court in the context of infringement procedures, and not through preliminary references. On the contrary, the Court found the two different channels not to be mutually exclusive: 'the vigilance of individuals concerned to protect their rights amounts to an effective supervision in addition to that entrusted by articles 169 and 170 EC (now art. 258 and 259 TFEU) to the diligence of the Commission and the member states' (*Costa vs. Enel* 26/62). Through this channel, those individuals deprived of a role within the framework of the infringement procedure were able to compensate for the Commission's weakness; indeed, it is difficult for the Commission to monitor and pursue all violations of European law.

Although Belgium, the Netherlands and Germany originally opposed the direct effect of article 12 TEC (now art. 28 TFEU), they have never tried to overrule the Court on this point (Chapter 5). The national courts have also readily accepted the Court's reasoning. Thus, the Court's jurisprudence has fostered the considerable expansion of European rules having direct effect.

In *Van Gend en Loos*, the European Court had set out three criteria to be tested in order to determine whether or not an EU rule had direct effect: the relevant provision had to be clear, unconditional and absolute. This test became somewhat more lenient in subsequent jurisprudence with direct effect being granted, in some cases, to European rules where there was a certain lack of clarity (*Ianelli & Volpi SpA vs. Ditta Paolo Meroni* 75/76; *Defrenne vs. Sabena* 43/75), where the rules were not unconditional (*Reyners* 2/74), or where they were relative rather than absolute (*Salgoil vs. Italian Ministry of Foreign Trade* 13/68). These case rulings in the 1960s and 1970s significantly enlarged the volume of European rules that private parties could invoke before national courts.

Moreover, in the aftermath of *Van Gend en Loos*, the European Court extended the application of direct effect to a wide range of treaty articles, and to other sources of EU law such as directives and international agreements (that is, binding sources of EU law that were not explicitly granted direct effect by the treaties). A directive is the second type of secondary legislation adopted by EU institutions on the basis of the treaties. Contrary to regulations, a directive only includes objectives or general rules, and leaves it to national authorities to define the way these objectives will be achieved. As the treaty specified that directives needed to be transposed by national parliaments into national law before they could be considered to have an effect at the domestic level, the Court's decision to grant direct effect to EU directives in the case of *Van Duyn* (41/74) was arguably quite audacious.

Indeed, the *Van Duyn* jurisprudence was particularly controversial because, apparently, the very nature of directives – the possibility for the member states to choose the forms and methods of transposition – seemed to exclude the possibility of direct effect. The Court's central argument was that for a directive to be effective there needs to be the possibility for individuals to claim rights before a national court after the deadline for transposing the directive has expired. The only limit of this jurisprudence was linked to the horizontal effect of EU law (the possibility for a private party to invoke an EU rule against another private party), which, in the case of a directive, was not acknowledged by the Court, contrary to vertical direct effect (the possibility for a private party to invoke an EU rule against a state). In few cases has the Commission actually found a directive to have directly affected the relations between private parties, but such 'incidental' horizontal effect (Craig & de Búrca, 2011, p. 207) has been the exception rather than the rule.

The direct effect doctrine has had tremendous consequences. It has encouraged the uniform interpretation of EU law at the domestic level, coupled with the principle of consistent interpretation, whereby EU and national law must be interpreted consistently (*von Colson*, 14/83). Furthermore, it has transformed basic principles guiding the action of member states and European institutions into a freedom or right that private parties can invoke before national courts. In so doing, it has 'fostered a kind of indirect alliance between the private litigants and pro-integration forces' (Dehousse, 1998, p. 47). Many individuals have used it to attack national rules, especially protectionist trading rules, and have thus become the agents of the decentralized implementation of European law. Owing to direct effect, a wide range of European norms can be effectively used as a 'shield' or 'sword' before a national court, or else employed in a non-judicial context (as a tool supporting a lobbying strategy for instance). These European norms can either be applied instead of the inadequate national norm, or merely be used to help sideline a national norm without replacing it. Thanks to direct effect, a Belgian air hostess obtained recognition of the right to equal treatment with her male colleagues (*Defrenne* 43/75); an importer of French spirits gained access to the German market for his products ('*Cassis de Dijon*' 10/78); and football players in the EU obtained the right to move from one club to another at the end of a contract without a transfer fee (*Bosman vs. Royal Club Liégeois* C–415/93).

Primacy

In 1957, the Treaty of Rome did not foresee possible conflicts between EU law and national legislation. Almost 50 years later, the treaty establishing a Constitution for Europe made clear that EU law had primacy over national law, though the treaty was ultimately rejected by French and Dutch voters in national referenda. Instead of acknowledging primacy in the provisions of the EU Treaty, the follow-up Lisbon Treaty (2009) merely added a declaration (no. 17) to the treaties stating that, 'in accordance with well-settled case law of the Court of Justice of the European Union, the treaties and the law adopted by the Union on the basis of the treaties have primacy over the law of member states, under the conditions laid down by the said case law'. The declaration makes a point similar to the Opinion of the Council Legal Service on the primacy of European law (Opinion of the Council Legal Service 2007), which asserts that

> it results from the case-law of the Court of Justice that primacy of EC law is a cornerstone principle of Community law. According to the Court, this principle is inherent to the specific nature of the European Community. At the time of the first judgment of this established case law [...] there was no mention of primacy in the treaty. It is still the case today. The fact that the principle of primacy will not be included in the future treaty shall not in any way change the existence of the principle and the existing case-law of the Court of Justice (declaration no. 17 annexed to the TEU and TFEU).

Although not explicitly stated in a treaty provision, it is clear that the member states and the Council have aligned themselves with the Court, acknowledging the constitutional role the Court has played in formulating the principle since the early 1960s.

Under article 4 of the Treaty on European Union, the member states 'shall take any appropriate measure, general or particular, to ensure fulfilment of the obligations arising out of the treaties or resulting from the acts of the institutions of the Union'.

This obligation has existed since the original Treaty of Rome in 1957. It was clear early on that national law would have to be put aside where incompatible with European law. It was not clear, however, whether national courts would play a crucial role in honouring and ensuring the effectiveness of European law; this obligation to 'take any appropriate measure...' seemed to be aimed at national governments only. Faced with the ambiguity of the Treaty of Rome, the Court, in the *Costa vs. Enel* case (6/64), turned to the 'spirit' of the treaty and held that the treaty had created its own legal order; the member states had accepted a permanent limit to their sovereignty rights; and if European law were to be effective, then national courts had to apply it in the face of incompatible national law. According to the Court, direct effect implied primacy. Though primacy was not explicitly stated in the treaties, it would develop into a general principle of European law (see Chapter 2). Later, in the rulings on *Internationale Handelsgesellschaft* (11/70) and *Simmenthal* (106/77), the Court was very explicit in explaining that the whole of European law had precedence over the whole of national law, including constitutional provisions. This was reiterated in a recent ruling on the compatibility of the French 'priority question of constitutionality' with the principle of primacy (*Melki and Aldeli* C–188 and C–189/10).

Hence, the Court has opted for a primacy principle with absolute scope, instead of allowing areas where national law could prevail over conflicting European law. The only limit that has been accepted by the CJEU over time is when primacy clashes with other principles of EU legal order. In *Kühne and Heitz* (C–453/00), the Court tolerated a breach of Union law because the principle of legal certainty, which is a general principle of EU law, would otherwise have been violated. However, here it is the CJEU itself that defines the scope and limits of the principle of primacy, and determines whether the EU's interest in securing the effective and uniform interpretation of its legal order is outweighed by the need to respect competing EU norms, such as legal certainty. It remains with the Court to decide upon this limit and ensure consistency in respect of other EU norms.

Other limits may arise from the relationship between the EU law and national courts. National courts did not easily accept the audacious reasoning of the CJEU in *Costa vs. Enel*, or in subsequent rulings (see Chapter 5). For example, it took time for the French

Conseil d'État (highest administrative court) to admit that European law had primacy over subsequent national law. It was only with the *Nicolo* case (20 October 1989) that it stopped limiting primacy to conflicts between European law and prior national rules. In the United Kingdom, primacy was accepted but on the grounds that national courts had to abide by the European Communities Act of 1972, adopted to give effect to European law.

Most national constitutional courts continue to limit the effect of the primacy principle when it comes to possible conflicts with national constitutions. They oppose the idea that primacy has a relative rather than an absolute scope. Two main limits are placed on the primacy principle. The first concerns fundamental rights and has been expressed by the German Constitutional Court in particular, in the so-called *Solange* jurisprudence. The second limit brought by national constitutional courts was about the sharing of competences between the EU and the member states. As exemplified by the German Constitutional Court's decisions on *Maastricht* and *Honeywell*, the primacy of European law and case law could not be accepted in cases where EU institutions went beyond the competences conferred by the treaties. Thus, a clear signal was sent to the European Court and the Commission that there would now be a strict control of the dynamic extension of existing treaties, that is, the open-handed treatment of article 352 TFEU; the doctrine of implied powers; and treaty interpretation allowing the maximum exploitation of Union powers ('*effet utile*') (see 'Horizontal and vertical separation of powers' below).

In a nutshell, there is still a difference between the absolute primacy doctrine advocated by the Court, and the relative primacy defended by national constitutional courts. The latter, however, have moved progressively closer to the Court. The primacy principle is now accepted on principle by national courts. It is only in very specific cases – when there is an important risk of contradiction with national constitutions – that it is hotly debated and sometimes ultimately discarded.

Horizontal and vertical separation of powers

The CJEU has helped to clarify the distribution of power and competences in the EU, both horizontally (between EU institutions) and vertically (between EU institutions and the member states). This is a classic function for any court dealing with constitutional issues.

Horizontal separation of powers: the balance between the Commission, the Parliament and the Council

The CJEU has regulated the working relationship between the three main institutions (Commission, Parliament and Council) through the application of the principle of inter-institutional balance, now enshrined in article 13-2 TEU. This provision reads: 'Each institution shall act within the limits of the powers conferred on it in the Treaties, and in conformity with the procedures, conditions and objectives set out in them. The institutions shall practice mutual sincere cooperation.'

Three constitutional obligations follow from this provision (Schütze, 2012, p. 85), each applied and specified by the Court. First, it is not possible for an institution to extend its powers through constitutional practice (*Wybot vs. Faure* 149/85). Second, each institution 'must exercise its powers with due regard for the powers of the other institutions' (*Parliament vs. Council 'Chernobyl'* C–70/88). And third, each institution is embedded in the normative procedures of the EU. Even when a procedure gives weak powers to an institution, these powers must be observed.

The principle of inter-institutional balance has been at the heart of a number of legal disputes brought by the Commission, Parliament and Council, as well as the member states. Many of these highly politicized cases (Cullen & Charlesworth, 1999; McCown, 2003, p. 977) have protected the Parliament's right to take part in the decision-making process (Lenaerts, 1991; McCown, 2001). Even the right to be consulted 'represents an essential factor in the institutional balance intended by the treat(ies)' (*Roquette Frères vs. Council, 'Isoglucose'*, 138/79). Moreover, the right to be re-consulted whenever the final version of the legal text departs substantially from the text on which the Parliament has already been consulted, has also been recognized, except in cases where the amendments correspond essentially to the wishes expressed by Parliament itself (C–65/90, C–388/92, C–417/93, C–21/94, C–392/95). In order to help the Parliament protect its own powers, the Court has given further standing to the Parliament, rewriting the constitutional provisions of the treaties (*'Titanium Dioxide'* C–300/89; McCown, 2003, p. 977). The Parliament has used this power extensively, attempting to change the legal basis of a piece of legislation from one requiring consultation to one allowing for co-decision or co-operation (*'Titanium Dioxide'* C–300/89; *'Waste*

Directive' C–155/91, *Parliament vs. Council* C–187/93). The principle of inter-institutional balance, as applied by the Court, has been instrumental in helping the Parliament (originally the weakest institution) to make its voice heard, especially in the period when it had little capacity to exert legislative powers.

The Parliament is not the only institution that has benefited from the Court's case law. The Court has chosen to interpret the Commission's powers in relation to competition policy rather widely (C–271, 281 and 289/90). In addition, the Court has put limits on the Parliament's power with regard to budgetary procedures (C–34/86), as well as legislative procedures (the formal obligation to consult the Parliament does not mean that the Council must take into account the views expressed by the Parliament (*Parliament vs. Council* C–417/93). The Council and the member states benefited from the Koester ruling (25/70) where the Court ruled against the argument that comitology procedures failed to respect the Commission's powers; it found comitology rules to be in respect of the executive's role and status.

Vertical separation of powers: competence sharing between the EU and the member states

Like any international organization, legally speaking the EU only exerts the competences that have been conferred upon it by its constitutive charter (Treaty). However, the limits between EU and national competences are not easy to establish, and the Court's interpretations are necessary to be able to draw the line between them. The European Court has been active in defending an extensive interpretation of EU competences and subjecting national prerogatives to strict scrutiny (Dehousse, 1998, p. 56).

EU policy competences have been extended through the Court's judgements, which have recognized the principle of *implied powers*, and *parallelism* between internal and external powers. In the *ERTA* case (22/70), the Court had to rule in a dispute between the Commission and the Council about an international agreement on road transport. The Commission claimed that the matter fell under Community competence on transport policy. The Council argued that there was no explicit provision in the treaty granting the Community the right to conclude international agreements in this field. The Court decided in favour of the Commission, arguing that 'the authority to enter into international agreements [...] arises not only from an express conferment by the Treaty [...] but may equally flow from other provisions of the Treaty and from other measures adopted, within the framework of these provisions, by the Community institutions'. The Court continued by saying that 'with regard to the implementation of the provisions of the Treaty the system of internal Community measures may not therefore be separated from that of external relations'. According to the implicit powers theory – another cognitive and legal frame that constrains the judges' rulings – competence in external matters now derives, be it implicitly, from explicit internal competence. This principle has been completed and refined in subsequent decisions (Opinion 1/76; *Kramer* 3, 4 and 6/76). Yet the Court has not always ruled in favour of an extensive interpretation of EU competences. Indeed, in the '*Open Skies*' cases (C–466, 467, 468, 469, 471, 472, 475 and 476/98), it made clear that EU external competence cannot be established in a field where no secondary law has been adopted. In so doing, it established limits to the extent to which the principle of *competence parallelism* can be applied.

Other than the principle of 'parallelism', the Court has allowed the Commission to make proposals based on an extensive interpretation of existing competences. This was the case in a series of rulings dealing with education matters. Here the Court accepted initiatives based on a broad interpretation of the treaty provision on vocational training (*Gravier* 293/83). For instance, the Erasmus programme, aimed at enhancing the mobility of students, was launched on the basis of the treaty provision dealing with vocational training. In so doing, the Court opened the door to an EU education policy, which was finally given a clear legal basis in primary law following the entry into force of the Maastricht Treaty.

Elsewhere, the Court has not been particularly strict when reviewing article 352 TFEU, which contains a flexibility clause allowing the Council to legislate outside the list of competences conferred upon the EU by the treaties. According to this provision, the Council can adopt 'appropriate measures' if action by the Union proves necessary. It can do so within the framework of policies mentioned in the treaties in order to attain one of the objectives set out in the treaties, and where the treaties themselves have not provided the necessary powers. The Court could have controlled EU institutions more closely so as to prevent them from using article 352 TFEU. Instead it has largely allowed for the extension of EU competences based on this provision.

Similarly, the CJEU has not exercised a strong control over the way EU institutions apply the principle of subsidiarity. This principle, introduced by the Maastricht Treaty (1992), defines the circumstances in which it is preferable for action to be taken by the Union, rather than the member states. For several years the Court has not looked deeply into the way EU institutions justified legislative action; the mere existence of a justification was enough for the Court to make a legislative proposal consistent with the subsidiarity principle. In the case of *Vodafone* (C–58/08), however, the CJEU's control has been tighter, signalling a new period of greater judicial scrutiny. Since then, the Court has controlled not only the existence of a justification but also its content. Potentially, such a control could significantly increase the number of applicants, block the whole judiciary system of the EU (Lenaerts & Corthaut, 2004) and limit legislative action at EU level while protecting national competences. In fact, the *Vodafone* ruling has not entailed stronger restrictions on EU institutions, as the Court can always decide in favour of EU competence stretching.

Undoubtedly, the fact that the bold jurisprudence of the Court has favoured an expansion of EU competences corroborates the idea of judicial activism. However, the European Court has not been the only one to use the doctrine of implied powers; both the US Supreme Court and the International Court of Justice have used it with regard to the US constitution and the United Nations (UN) Charter respectively.

Furthermore, the European Court seems to have been less able and willing to extend EU competences since the 1990s. The Court is less able to do so because the EU already enjoys a great deal of legal competences, and as such the Court has few remaining opportunities to offer bold and wide interpretations of the treaties with regard to competence extension. It might also be less willing to extend competences because, as often said, the Court has become more cautious and exercised self-restraint, accepting that the climate of European integration has changed and is generally far more Eurosceptic than it used to be (Chapter 2). This assumption may be wrong in other policy areas, where the Court is still 'activist', as we will see in the final sections of this chapter; it seems to be true regarding the extension of competences.

The Court and the protection of human rights

Finally, the European Court has contributed to the constitutionalization of the European integration process by strengthening the protection of human rights. Originally, the treaties did not include a catalogue of rights and freedoms. The Court has compensated for this absence through the application of general principles of European law. In a way, an 'unwritten bill of rights' (Schütze, 2012, p. 411) has emerged thanks to the Court's jurisprudence. What triggered such an attitude remains unclear. A first thesis stresses that the Court has been 'on the offensive' when it comes to human rights, spreading legal norms at national level. Those who argue that the Court has developed the protection of human rights while seeking to achieve the economic goals of the treaties (Coppel & O'Neill, 1992) oppose those who refute this 'instrumentalization' (Weiler & Lockhart, 1995). A second thesis posits that the Court has developed its human rights jurisprudence 'defensively', that is, to cope with the risk that national courts might refuse to apply European law for reasons linked to the protection of human rights – in particular in Italy and Germany, where human rights are sensitive for historical reasons. These two explanations are not incompatible. The Court's activism has always been linked to the opportunities that the social and political environment provides over time.

As we have seen in Chapters 2 and 5, the interaction between the European Court and national courts increased in the 1960s and early 1970s. In particular the relationship between the Court of Justice and the German Constitutional Court (FCC) contributed widely to the development of fundamental rights within the EU.

The case of *Internationale Handelsgesellschaft* (11/70) was the first step in a process through which the European Court ensured the effective application of human rights in the EU using so-called general principles of European law. Later, the Court specified the sources where fundamental rights principles were to be found. In the *Nold* ruling (4/73), it stated that it was 'bound to draw inspiration from constitutional traditions common to the member states' and mentioned for the first time 'international treaties for the protection of human rights on which the member states have collaborated or of which they are signatories'. In *Rutili* (36/75) and *Hauer* (44/79), it clarified that, of all international treaties, the European Convention on Human Rights (ECHR) is fundamental, and can be invoked to support the existence of general principles of European law.

With the entry into force of the Lisbon Treaty, the EU was endowed with a whole catalogue of fundamental rights. The Charter of Fundamental Rights of 7 December 2000, as adapted at Strasbourg on 12 December 2007, has the same legal value as the treaties.

A declaration annexed to the final act of the intergovernmental conference that adopted the Lisbon Treaty makes clear that the Charter (while remaining a separate document) is legally binding. Thus, the European Court has become the guardian of the Charter, or at least the guardian of some of the Charter's provisions. There are limitations to the legal effect of the Charter. Articles 6, 52–2 and 53 of the Charter make a distinction between two kinds of provisions: rights and principles. Rights have direct effect and can be invoked before a court, while principles resort to soft law and cannot be brought before a court. Notwithstanding this limitation, now that the Charter has been given legal force, the European Court is unlikely to resort to general principles of EU law as much as it used to do, though this is still possible. Article 6 TFEU dealing with European human rights refers to the European Charter as well as to general principles stemming from the ECHR, which result from constitutional traditions common to the member states.

The autonomy of the European legal order

In *Van Gend en Loos*, the European Court made it clear that EU law had to be accepted as a new legal order, quite separate from international law. More than ever, this notion is central to the CJEU's case law, as seen in the *Kadi* ruling of 3 September 2008 (C–402/05 P & C–415/02 P). In this case, the CJEU held that the EU regulation allowing listing and asset freezes against Mr Kadi and other persons suspected of terrorist activities breached fundamental rights under EU law, although this regulation implemented UN agreements. EU 'constitutional' law (treaty provisions and principles of EU law) was considered superior to international rules adopted in the UN framework.

The protection of the EU's legal autonomy seems to be an area where the Court remains wholly active and where it does not hesitate to attract criticism, as Opinion 2/13 on the accession of the EU to the European Convention on Human Rights recently reminded us.

The idea of the EU acceding to the EcHR dates back to the late 1970s and was first pushed by the Commission. In the early 1990s, the Council asked the CJEU for a legal opinion on the issue. In Opinion 2/94, the main argument developed by the Court, which opposed such accession, was the lack of a proper legal basis to be found in the treaties. The Treaty of Lisbon, however, provided for such a legal act through article 6(2) TEU, which explicitly foresees the possible accession of the EU to the ECHR. As a consequence, negotiations with the Council of Europe started in 2010 and came to an end with the signing of a draft agreement (April 2013). The Commission asked the CJEU for an Opinion on the Draft Agreement, which was released in December 2014 (Opinion 2/13).

Contrary to advocate-general Kokott, the Court held that the draft agreement was not compatible with the EU treaties for a series of reasons. The central argument put forward by the Court was that the EU's accession to the ECHR could endanger the autonomy of EU law. Protocol 16 to the ECHR was of particular concern because it entitled the highest courts of member states to ask questions on the interpretation or application of fundamental rights to the European Court of Human Rights (ECtHR). According to the judges in Luxembourg, the EU's monopoly on dispute settlement was threatened. The member states were obliged to settle disputes concerning the interpretation or application of the treaties using article 344 TFEU. However, according to article 33 ECHR, it was possible for one member state to start proceedings against another, or even the EU itself, before the ECtHR. Hence, the CJEU argued in favour of excluding the ECtHR's legal competence under article 33 ECHR for disputes between EU member states or between the latter and EU institutions in areas covered by EU law.

Scholars and experts composing the legal doctrine have been very critical with regard to Opinion 2/13. The Opinion seemed to give utmost priority to the autonomy of the EU legal system, regardless of the objective of EU accession to the ECHR, which is, yet, grounded in the Treaty. In order to avoid pronouncing the draft agreement incompatible with the treaties, another option for the Court, as suggested by advocate-general Kokott, would have been to propose reasonable amendments that would render it compatible. The CJEU's opinion illustrates how it continues to take an active position on issues central to the European integration process and to defend its position in the integration process. The autonomy of the legal order and the monopoly of the CJEU in interpreting EU law enable it to adopt such a position. We can therefore understand why the Court, although a consistent defender of fundamental rights since the 1970s, has acted to prevent EU accession to the ECHR, regardless of the added value it might bring to the protection of human rights.

Conclusion

Through its 'constitutional' rulings, the CJEU has contributed enormously to the transformation of the EU into a polity, and in so doing, to its distancing from classic international organizations. The principles of *direct effect* and *primacy* have ensured a high level of member state compliance with EU law, something that would have been much more difficult had the EU relied solely on the infringement procedure. The Court's case law, and its rulings pertaining to the distribution of powers, has also had pro-integration effects, although not systematically. The Court has expanded the European Parliament's power and the EU's competences more generally.

The protection of human rights by the Court has been linked to the integration process. When the Court wanted national courts, and the German FCC in particular, to abide by the principle of *primacy*, it had to demonstrate its own ability to protect fundamental rights to the same extent that national constitutional courts could. Extensive jurisprudence transforming rights and freedoms into general principles of European law has had another consequence when we consider the EU as a polity: the EU is now governed by the *rule of law*, itself a central feature of democracy in post-Second World War regimes.

The constitutional case law of the Court has led to two rather contradictory kinds of comments regarding its impact on the integration process. First, the Court has been presented as an 'activist' given its audacious jurisprudence and capacity to distance itself from the explicit content of treaty provisions. Activism may have decreased since the early 1990s but it has not disappeared. This is a problem for some scholars whose main criticism has been that the judges are neither representing the European peoples nor taking into account the political will of the peoples' representatives (Rasmussen, 1988; Vauchez, 2014); they tend to forget, however, that constitutions are not actually complete at the moment of their enactment, but rather, are open texts that need to be adapted and interpreted over time (Beck, 2012). Besides, as the legal scholar Jo Shaw put it, 'the Court does not consistently track either an integrationist or a disintegrationist *telos*, but is subject to a number of varying political influences from within and without the Union' (Shaw, 1999, p. 584; see also de Búrca, 1998, p. 232). Most of all, the use of interpretive techniques that depart from the literal wording of the law is a factor that brings together, rather than separates, the European Court from its national constitutional interlocutors (Dawson, 2014). All highest courts have to grapple with the indeterminacy of legal rules and make interpretations; and the act of making these interpretations closely resembles law-making.

Second, the Court is also viewed as making an important contribution to European democracy through the judicial enhancement of EU rules (Mancini & Keeling, 1994). This line of argument is based on the assumption that a central feature of democracy is an independent judiciary capable of ensuring that law is applied consistently and fairly within that court's jurisdiction. The problem here is not the CJEU's so-called activism, but its ability to be 'obeyed' by the member states in the absence of public awareness around what exactly it is ruling on – the possibility of public sanctions is the main incentive for national governments to accept the Court's decisions (Carrubba, 2003, pp. 96–7).

The Court's competence to review and invalidate legislation does not necessarily signal a 'democratic deficit', but is in fact 'indispensable for the democratic legitimacy of the EU's legal system as a whole' (Hong, 2010, p. 695). Even though democracy may be defined as 'government by majority', it also requires the guarantee of minority rights by a counter-majoritarian force. Thus, the role of the CJEU can be seen as an integral part of the very checks and balances mechanisms that give the EU its legitimacy (Moravcsik, 2002, p. 614). From this standpoint, the Court must assert its political independence vis-à-vis the member states, especially the larger ones (see Chapter 5), and effectively play a political role: 'Given the urgent need for checks and balances in a mega-leviathan like the EU', as Hong puts it, 'the [CJEU] has to play a political role, lest it lose its entire raison d'être' (Hong, 2012, p. 716). The (pro-integration) motivations of activist judges cannot be ignored, nor can the Court's contributions to the development of democracy and law in the EU. Its constitutional role remains significant, but nonetheless often gets overlooked by scholars working on judicial politics.

Chapter 8

The Court in Policy-Making

While many scholars acknowledge the contribution the Court has made to the 'constitutionalization' of the European Union (see Chapter 7), the extent to which it takes part in the policy process remains uncertain. In the treaties we see instances of 'negative integration' (Scharpf, 1999) where member states have been prevented from adopting discriminatory behaviour with a view to establishing the internal market. Such prohibitions have been made more effective as a consequence of judicial interpretations of the treaty provisions. The *Cassis de Dijon* ruling (120/78) concerning the free circulation of French blackcurrant liqueur is one of several cases that has illustrated the readiness of the Court to make sure that the objectives set out in the treaties are achieved. In this case, the Court established the principle of *mutual recognition*, which reduced the need to harmonize trade standards (see also Chapter 2). At the same time, when it comes to 'positive integration' – where new rules are created to influence member state behaviour – the Court has also played a crucial role in a number of policy areas where it has interpreted existing rules and triggered new legislation.

This chapter analyses the Court's influence on the legislative process. It asks two key questions. First, has the European Court's impact been achieved through law-making (Alter & Helfer, 2010)? More generally speaking, has CJEU case law been the means by which the Court's judges have successfully instilled legal federalism in the functioning of the EU? Second, has the CJEU gone beyond its delegated function of adjudication, to transform itself into a policy-maker, thus competing with other EU political institutions? By extension, does it challenge (or complement) the role of the Commission as policy initiator, and the Council and Parliament as co-legislators?

Adopting an area-specific approach, in this chapter we argue that the European Court's rulings have had a tremendous impact in several policy areas such as internal market, equality law, and social and health policy. Thereafter, we examine the functions that the

Court exerts in European policy-making, from setting the agenda to forcing the legislator to act.

Areas of policy-making

In this section we focus on several policy areas where the Court has widely ruled and exerted a very significant policy-making function: free movement of goods, competition, free movement of persons and services, EU equality law, social and health policy (Garrett, 1992; Dehousse, 1998; Tallberg, 1999; Wollenschläger, 2011; Martinsen, 2015b; Dougan, 2009, 2013; Hartlapp, 2014; Shuibhne, 2015; Thym, 2015; Verschueren, 2015), environmental policy (Kramer, 2012), home affairs (Peers, 2011) and economic and monetary union. These are not the only fields where the CJEU has had an impact, but these policies illustrate crucial aspects of the process. We choose to focus on the internal market (free movement of goods, competition, persons and services) because of the central role this policy area has played since the early years of European integration. EU equality law, as well as social and health policies, are good examples of the way the CJEU has managed to use internal market rules in order to develop its case law in related fields. Environmental law is the area where the largest number of CJEU rulings is issued every year. Home affairs and economic governance are new areas of competence for the Court, showing that, even when member states refuse judicial control in the first place for sovereignty reasons, progressive judicialization may occur.

Free movement of goods

According to the Treaty on the Functioning of the European Union (TFEU), the internal market is 'an area without internal frontiers in which the free movement of goods, persons, services and capital is ensured in accordance with the provisions of the Treaties' (art. 26). Since the beginning of the European communities, the Court has seen in the four freedoms (of goods, persons, services and capital) both negative obligations resting upon national governments and the possibility for individuals to enforce their rights before a tribunal (*Van Gend en Loos* 26/62). The internal market has also been used as a means to enlarge the integration process to other areas; there are hardly any fields of competence where it is not possible to make some kind of connection to these essential four freedoms.

With the free movement of goods, the TFEU prohibits quantitative restrictions and customs duties on imports and exports, as well as charges and measures having an equivalent effect. A *charge* with equivalent effect to custom duties is a levy imposed by a member state on goods when they cross a border. The specificity is that this levy is not formally presented as a custom duty, but has the same blocking effect on the free movement of goods. A *measure* with equivalent effect to quantitative restrictions can take very different forms such as import inspections and controls, language requirements, requirements as to the labelling of products, and so on. The measure has the effect of hindering the free movement of goods. The Court, together with the Commission, has provided extensive interpretations of these charges and measures of equivalent effect in order to achieve the goals set out in the treaties. These interpretations have been aimed at fighting protectionism 'in disguise' (Davies, 2003; Syrpis, 2012).

Non-tariff barriers have proven more difficult to eradicate than tariff barriers, due to the high number of national rules applying in this field. The Court has interpreted the above-mentioned notion of measures as having the equivalent effect to quantitative restrictions. It has ruled that it is applicable both to national measures discriminating against imported products and to national measures capable of hindering (directly or indirectly, actually or potentially) intra-European trade (*Dassonville* 8/74). From this rationale, proving that the measure is an actual hindrance is not necessary, as long as it is potentially capable of having such effects. The *Dassonville* case concerned the trade of Scotch whisky. To sell whisky in Belgium, a certificate of authenticity was required by the Belgium authorities, while in France a trader could sell the same whisky freely. The case was referred to the Court of Justice, which found that the Belgian legislation represented a measure having equivalent effect to a quantitative restriction on trade.

Later, in the case of *Cassis de Dijon* (120/78) (see Chapter 2 for more details on the case), the Court stated that obstacles resulting from disparities between national laws relating to the marketing of products must be accepted in so far as they are recognized as necessary in order to satisfy mandatory requirements. These mandatory requirements are the effectiveness of fiscal supervision, protection of public health, fairness of commercial transactions and protection of consumers. In so doing, the Court added a new series of derogations – the so-called 'rule of reason' – to the free movement of goods, complementing those already under article 36 TFEU (public morality, public policy and public security; the protection of health and life of humans, animals and plants; the protection of national treasures possessing artistic, historic or archaeological value; and the protection of industrial and commercial property). Aside from these derogations, for the Court there is no valid reason why 'provided that goods have been lawfully produced and marketed in one of the member states, they should not be introduced into any other member state' (principle of mutual recognition, *Cassis de Dijon* 120/78). Goods that have been lawfully marketed in one member state benefit from a presumption of compliance with mandatory requirements, unless this is rebutted by evidence. However, the burden of proving that a national measure limiting access to a specific good is necessarily is a heavy one.

There are limits to the idea that the Court has constantly ruled in favour of removing barriers to intra-European trade. The principle of mutual recognition has had to be balanced with the need to respect both the mandatory requirements ('rule of reason') and exceptions provided by article 36 TFEU. Moreover, the Court has put limits on its own interpretation since the early 1990s and the *Keck and Mithouard* rulings (C–267 and 268/91). Mr Keck and Mr Mithouard had broken French law by reselling products in an unaltered state at prices lower than their actual purchase price. When prosecuted before the *Tribunal de Grande Instance* of Strasbourg, they argued that the French prohibition on resale at a loss was contrary to the provisions of the Treaty of Rome establishing the free movement of goods. The French Court referred the argument to the CJEU in the form of a preliminary question. The CJEU held that,

> a national provision restricting or prohibiting certain selling arrangements is not such as to hinder directly or indirectly, actually or potentially, trade between Member States within the meaning of the *Dassonville* judgment, so long as those provisions apply to all relevant traders operating within the national territory and so long as they affect in the same manner, in law and in fact, the marketing of domestic products and of those from other Member States.

Hence, the French prohibition on resale at a loss was not considered a measure that had equivalent effect to quantitative restrictions. More generally, in later jurisprudence, the Court found that arrangements for sale (dealing with the where, when, how and by whom of selling goods) fell outside the scope of article 34 TFEU prohibiting quantitative restrictions and measures having similar effect.

Yet, before and even after *Keck*, it remained a hard task to define the scope of prohibition (Weatherhill, 1996). This difficulty is exemplified by the Sunday trading cases (Arnull, 1991). In *Torfaen Borough Council vs. B&Q plc* (C–145/88), the CJEU held that British rules prohibiting large multiple shops from opening on Sunday might be justified with regard to 'national or regional socio-cultural characteristics', and left the referring British court to examine the rules in light of their proportionality. This led to a situation where different British courts came to different conclusions in different cases (Steiner & Woods, 2009). The CJEU later clarified the situation and found that, like similar rules in other countries (*Conforama* C–312/89, *Marchandise* C–332/89), the British prohibition was justified and proportionate (*Stoke-on-Trent City Council vs. B&Q plc* C–169/91).

In spite of the cautiousness we mentioned with regard to 'rule of reason' (*Cassis*) and the scope of the prohibition of quantitative restrictions (*Keck*), the free movement of goods is clearly an area where the Court has acted as a policy-maker. This is confirmed by the fact that little secondary legislation of direct importance has been adopted in this area of EU law, with the exception of Directive 70/50, Regulation 764/2008 and Directive 98/34 (Foster, 2014, p. 305). Secondary law has not been as necessary since the jurisprudence of the Court has been sufficient to eliminate the main barriers to trade.

Market-oriented rulings and competition law

More generally, the Court has ruled on the conditions for the establishment and functioning of a competitive internal market, such as in the *Vodafone* 'roaming' case (C–58/08). In 2002, the EU adopted a regulatory framework for electronic communications, networks and services which laid down maximum charges that mobile phone operators could charge for calls made and received by users outside their own network. The regulation also imposed a ceiling for wholesale roaming charges – the price paid by the consumer's network to the foreign network that the consumer is using. The leading European mobile telephone operators challenged the validity of the regulation before the High Court in the United Kingdom. The High Court referred a question on the validity of the regulation to the CJEU. The Court replied that the European legislature had not infringed the principles of subsidiarity and proportionality. This case provides a good example of how the CJEU sets the limits of what is – or is not – justified on the grounds of treaty provisions, in order to help establish the internal market.

Similarly, the Court has ruled on competition policy, an area where the Commission enjoys very important powers (Faull & Nikpay, 2014). The TFEU prohibits anti-competitive agreements, decisions and concerted practices, as well as abuses of a dominant position, mergers and acquisitions. In the original Treaty of Rome, there was no explicit mention of mergers and acquisitions. However, in *Continental Can* (6/72), the European Court held that 'one cannot assume that the Treaty, which prohibits [...] certain decisions of ordinary associations of undertakings restricting competition without eliminating it, permits [...] that undertakings, after merging into an organic unity, should reach such a dominant position that any serious chance of competition is practically rendered impossible'. This ruling set the basis for the EU's mergers and acquisitions policy, which was further developed through secondary law (Regulation 4064/89, replaced by Regulation 139/2004).

The Judges in Luxembourg exert an advanced control over the decisions taken by the Commission in competition law. For example, in 2002 the General Court (at the time called the Court of First Instance) decided to overturn the Commission's veto of a 5.7 billion euro deal between the French electrical groups Schneider Electric and Legrand (*Schneider Legrand,* T–351/53). Similar annulments of restrictive decisions by the Commission were decided in *Airtours* (T–342/99), *Tetra Laval Sidel* (T–5/02) and a series of other cases. Generally speaking, the CJEU – and more precisely the General Court acting as a court of first instance in competition cases – is far less restrictive than the Commission with regard to competition policy.

The CJEU also controls the policy of the Commission on state aid and its compatibility with EU competition policy. In the case of *Altmark* (C–280/00), the Court of Justice held that public service compensation does not constitute state aid when four cumulative conditions are met. First, the recipient undertaking must have public service obligations, and the obligations must be clearly defined. Second, the parameters for calculating the compensation must be objective, transparent and established in advance. Third, the compensation cannot exceed what is necessary to cover all or part of the costs incurred in the discharge of the public service obligations, taking into account the relevant receipts and a reasonable profit. Finally, where the undertaking which discharges public service obligations is not chosen pursuant to a public procurement procedure, the level of compensation needed must be determined on the basis of an analysis of the costs of a typical well-run company. In addition to this case law aimed at bringing legal certainty into the way state aid is provided, the Court has contributed to the emergence of the notion of services of economic general interest, alongside the Commission. In *Corbeau* (320/91) and *Almelo* (393/92), it allowed for exceptions to competition rules only in so far as the restriction on competition was necessary to ensure the performance of a task in the general economic interest that had been entrusted to the undertaking by the state.

Free movement of persons and services

Similarly, the CJEU has ruled in favour of the free movement of persons, using the principle of non-discrimination on the grounds of nationality (art. 18 TFEU) in the case of workers (*Netherlands vs. Reed* 59/85), services (*Reyners* 2/74) and right of establishment (*Commission vs. UK – Nationality of fishermen* C–246/89). The Court has narrowly interpreted those situations where a member state can benefit from derogation to the free movement of persons on grounds of public policy, public security and public health. Thus, in *Van Duyn* (41/74), the Court held that being a member of the Church of Scientology could not be considered a genuine and serious threat to public policy. In the same vein, criminal convictions (*R vs. Bouchereau* 30/77) as well as prostitution activities (*Adoui and Cornouaille vs. Belgium* 115 and 116/81) are not examples of personal conduct that justify a restriction of the free movement of persons.

The *Reyners* case was one of the first landmark rulings with regard to the free movement of persons. In *Reyners*, the Court considered that the ban on national discrimination had direct effect and could be invoked by individuals before national jurisdictions, instead of having a legal effect on national governments alone. This implied that nationality was not a barrier for an appropriately qualified Dutch lawyer to access the Belgian Bar.

A few Commission proposals aimed at giving effect to the treaty provision prohibiting national discrimination in this field were actually pending at the time the Court gave its decision in *Reyners*. The Court's decision has meant less need, or at least less urgency, for further European legislation. Most of all, the Commission had realized in the late 1970s that the harmonization approach used in the 1960s and early 1970s, which examined one profession at a time on a case-by-case basis, was far too slow. The new approach following *Reyners* involved the enactment of mutual recognition directives and their application to many professions.

A similar parallel between the Court's rulings, and the proposal and adoption of new directives, can be seen in area of services with the *Viking* and *Laval* cases, ruled in 2005 (*ITWF & FSU vs. Viking* C–438/05; *Laval* C–341/05) (Reich, 2008; Davies, 2008; Joerges & Rödl, 2009) a few months before the Directive 2006/123 on services, otherwise known as the Bolkestein Directive after the Dutch Commissioner who first sponsored it. The negotiations over this directive opened up a wider European debate on social dumping, ultimately leading to the rejection of the Constitutional Treaty by French and Dutch voters in 2005. Originally, the proposal for the directive was based on a principle stipulating that service providers should apply social rules of their country of origin. Fearing a race to the bottom (the directive would benefit those countries with a low level of social protection), in the final version of the directive the Council together with the Parliament finally decided to apply the rules of the host country.

A few months before the adoption of the Services Directive, in *Viking* and *Laval* the CJEU was asked to clarify the extent to which collective action may be used to resist social dumping within the EU (see Chapter 5). Trade unions and workers in old member states felt that firms and workers from the new member states threatened their economic and social position, owing to the increasing practice of social dumping. In its decisions, the CJEU tried to strike a balance between the competing positions of old and new member states, by essentially leaving decisions as to the justifiability of collective action to the national courts, when they potentially conflicted with the free movement provisions (Zahn, 2008). These decisions have been considered problematic because they do not ensure legal certainty with regard to the right to strike (Zahn, 2008; Seikel, 2015). Having failed to set up clear criteria, the European Court has given considerable leeway to the national courts, which may lead to different outcomes in the member states, in favour either of trade unions or of business. This situation triggered the adoption of the Services Directive, which finally took into account, and attempted to solve, the problem of social dumping (Crespy, 2012). This example illustrates once more the importance of linking the legal framework on which the Court's rulings are based to the external environment in which the Court is embedded. The Court does not rule in a political vacuum, only based on legal doctrine or legal normative frames (see Chapter 1); nor does it rule only based on a strategic positioning vis-à-vis the member states or European institutions. The use of the CJEU's decisions by the European institutions – first and foremost the European Commission, but also increasingly the European Parliament (Martinsen, 2015a, 2015b) – is a central element of the EU's law-making.

Hence, free movement is an area where the CJEU has clearly been very active. For example, the Court has enlarged the free movement of persons to non-EU citizens, when there is legal ground to move in this direction. Wiesbrok (2013) has argued that, in the face of a reluctant legislator, the Court has taken an audacious stance with regard to Turkish migrants. It has interpreted the rights of Turkish migrants extensively, under the EU-Turkish Association Agreement of 1963, the Additional Protocol of 1970, and Decision n°1/80 of 19 September 1980 of the Council of Association, established by the Association Agreement. In so doing, the Court has left it to the discretion of the member states to regulate on the entrance and residence of Turkish nationals in their respective territories (Hillion, 2007). In other cases related to Turkish citizens, it has allowed for the transformation of status from family member/student to worker (*Payir and Others* C–294/06; *Hava Genc* C–14/09) and applied standstill clauses (clauses forbidding the introduction of new restrictions) to conditions of entrance (*Soysal and Savatli* C–228/06, *Sahin* C–242/06, *Commission vs. The Netherlands* C–92/07).

The Court's activism with regard to the free movement of persons and services has nevertheless been balanced with a more lenient approach towards national measures. A number of rulings in this field can be considered as the equivalent to *Keck and Mithouard* in the area of goods. In *Volker Graf vs. Filzmoser Maschinenbau* (C–190/98) and *Dip Spa* (C–140-2/94), for example, the CJEU found that measures with effects that are too uncertain and/or indirect do not qualify as obstacles to the free movement of persons.

In *Sayn-Wittgenstein* (C–208/09), the CJEU took a position on the Austrian legislation on the abolition of the nobility, which has constitutional status according to article 149(1) of the Austrian Constitution. Mrs Sayn-Wittgenstein, an Austrian national residing in Germany, was professionally active in the luxury real estate sector under the name Ilonka Fürstin von Sayn-Wittgenstein. This name could not be used in Austria where citizens are not authorized to bear titles of nobility such as 'von' or 'Fürstin' (duchess) since Austria is no longer an empire but a republic. The CJEU held that the restrictive measure taken by the Austrian government and preventing Mrs Sayn-Wittgenstein from using her full name, although potentially hindering her right to move and reside freely, was 'not out of proportion as regards their objective of protecting the principle of equal treatment'. Moreover, the EU is committed to respecting the national identities of its member states, which includes the status of the State as a republic. This example illustrates that the CJEU's rulings do not systematically diminish national sovereignty.

EU equality law

In the treaties we find several express bans on discrimination, many of them on the grounds of nationality, others on the grounds of sex, age or religion. In particular, article 10 TFEU is a general provision aimed at combatting discrimination across a range of issues. In addition, the Charter on Fundamental Rights provides a section prohibiting discrimination on any grounds. For its part, the CJEU acknowledges the existence of a general principle of equal treatment (*Chazi* C–149/10). This is hardly surprising, given that the Court has widely used treaty provisions on non-discrimination in the area of free movement of persons, as well as other policy domains.

One area of equality law where the Court has been particularly active is sex discrimination, or gender discrimination, as the EU now calls it (see Chapter 6). The reasons for including a provision for equal pay between men and women in the original Treaty of Rome appear to go back to an original request of the French government. As French law provided for equal pay between female and male workers, it was feared that French industry would be at a disadvantage if equal pay was not enforced in the other member states, especially in Germany (Foster, 2014, p. 436). The Court, however, declared in its famous *Defrenne* rulings, that the treaty provision on equal pay formed part of the social objectives of the

Community (43/75) and of fundamental rights within Community law (149/77). The Court ruled that this provision was sufficiently clear and precise to have *direct effect*, and therefore was binding for national governments and could be invoked by individuals before national courts (see Chapter 2 for more details). This paved the way for many more cases on equal pay.

In parallel, a directive on equal pay (75/117/EC) was adopted to specify how the principle should be implemented. A directive on equal treatment (76/207/EC) extended the ban on discrimination on the grounds of gender into many areas of employment: access, appointment, dismissal, retirement, training and working conditions. A social security directive (79/7/EC) applied the principle of equal treatment to the field of social security and other elements of social protection, and another directive (92/85/EC) was adopted a few years later to protect pregnant and breastfeeding workers. The adoption of these directives was prompted either by the case law of the CJEU or out of fear, from the part of the member states, that the Court might soon rule on the subject (Martinsen, 2015). In return, the Court has continuously issued rulings in favour of women's rights, as in *Barber* (262-88, equal pension rights for women and men) and *Kreil* (C–285-98, women's access to work in the German army) (Costello & Davies, 2006). More recently, in *Commission vs. Greece* (C–46/07), the Court held that the provisions of the Greek code on pensions which stipulated that women were entitled to a different retirement pension at a different age and under different conditions from men were a breach of EU law.

Other seminal rulings in this domain, such as *Kalanke* (C–450-93, positive action incompatible with gender equality) and *Rinke* (C25-02, full-time training requirement for part-time workers), would appear less audacious, however, since the Court was more respectful of member states' prerogatives. However, the Court has allowed differences in pay or treatment that discriminate indirectly against women where they have been objectively justified by the employer (*Bilka-Kaufhaus Gmbh vs. Weber von Harz* 170/84) using economic factors and social-policy aims (see also Genschel, 2011; Genschel, Kemmerling & Sils, 2011; Bonjour & Vink, 2013; Hervey & McHale, 2015).

Similarly, in *D. and Sweden vs. Council* (C–122/99 P & C–125/99 P), an EU official of Swedish nationality claimed from his employer, the Council, a household allowance for married EU officials provided for by the staff regulations. The Court of Justice ruled that, although an increasing number of member states had legally recognized various forms of union between same-sex partners, it was impossible to consider them as equal to marriage. As the intention of the EU legislature was that only married couples could claim for household allowances under the staff regulation, only this legislature (Council and Parliament) could adopt measures to change the situation in favour of non-married couples. Most certainly, this ruling can be seen as an example of the self-restraint exerted by the Court in recent years.

In the 1990s, the Court extended the principle of non-discrimination on the grounds of gender to LGBT (Lesbian – Gay – Bisexual – Transgender) rights. In *P v S & Cornwall County Council* (C–13/94), the European judges ruled that discrimination of a person who has undergone a sex change operation equated to discrimination on the grounds of belonging to a particular sex, thus stretching the scope of Directive 76/207 on equal treatment for men and women (Van Der Vleuten, 2010, 2014; de Waele & Van der Vleuten, 2011). The British government's opinion was that the directive did not concern discrimination of transsexuals. According to the Court, on the contrary, it is not only the rights of women that need to be protected but the rights of all citizens suffering from sex discrimination.

In 2000, the EU adopted the Employment Equality Directive covering discrimination on the grounds of religion or belief, disability, age and sexual orientation (2000/78/EC). Arguably, the new legislation mirrored the Court's philosophy found in rulings such as *P v S and Cornwall County Council*. In this directive, as well as in case law, the trend has been to favour the principle of non-discrimination on several grounds, not only nationality and gender. The *Maruko* ruling (C–267/06) provides a good example of discrimination on the grounds of sexual orientation. The claimant had entered into a civil partnership with another man, on the same legal conditions as a marriage between heterosexuals. When his partner died, he applied for a widower's pension. The state pension fund denied the right to benefit from such a pension on the grounds that such an entitlement was possible for surviving spouses but not for surviving civil partners. The CJEU held that it constituted direct discrimination since Germany had chosen to provide the same legal conditions to both married heterosexuals and homosexuals couples in a civil partnership (Steiner & Wood, 2009, p. 653).

Also in 2000, a directive was adopted against discrimination on the grounds of racial or ethnic origin (2000/43/EC), which was not limited to the field of employment. In *Feryn* (C–54/07), the CJEU ruled that a public statement made by the director of a company, where he said he did not wish to employ immigrants, was indeed a form of direct discrimination in accordance with the directive. In most cases, the Court has interpreted the provisions of the 2000 directives in a way that enlarges rather than restricts the protection provided in the fields of race, disability, sexual orientation and age (Howard, 2011).

In *Mangold* (C–144/04), the existence of a general principle prohibiting discrimination on the grounds of age was upheld, independent of the Employment Equality Directive (Schiek, 2006). The European Court considered the principle of non-discrimination on the grounds of age to be a fundamental principle of European law. This law stems from the constitutional traditions of the member states and various international instruments applicable to the EU institutions and member states. The 2000 Employment Equality Directive is an expression of this general principle, though the principle itself does not rely on the directive in order to exist.

The *Mangold* ruling triggered a strong reaction in Germany, with German high-level personalities launching the 'Stop the ECJ' campaign against the judicial activism of the Court (see Chapters 5 and 7). Some of the Court's advocates-general also disagreed with *Mangold* in their conclusions on subsequent cases (*Lindorfer* C–277/04, *Palacios de la Villa* C–411/05). The debate on the legitimacy of the CJEU aside, it is clear that the *Mangold* case opened the door for some sort of new judicial policy-making. Lawyers felt that, were the Court to continue in the direction, it would likely end up generating a whole body of non-discrimination law going beyond existing secondary legislation through the direct application of the general principle of non-discrimination (European Network of Legal Experts in the Non-discrimination Field, 2006).

In the *Mangold* case, the Court was far from oblivious of the respective positions of other actors. The Commission and the member states (or at least some of them) had defended an extended version of the equal treatment principle. In 2008 the Commission proposed to implement the principle of equal treatment between persons irrespective of religion, belief, disability, age or sexual orientation outside the labour market (Commission, 2008, p. 426). This proposal supplemented the existing European legal framework that only covered such discriminations (on the grounds of religion, belief, disability, age or sexual orientation) in areas of employment, occupation and vocational training. The grounds of the 2008 proposal were similar to those of the Employment Directive, while its scope of application was as large as that of the Race Directive. With unanimity required, so far the directive has not been adopted, due to the opposition of Germany and other member states.

With the adoption of the Lisbon Treaty, national governments have improved on the anti-discrimination rules. In a way, one might argue that the Court's ruling in *Mangold* was made in anticipation of the Lisbon Treaty. Indeed, article 10 TFEU, a new provision introduced into the TEU by the Lisbon Treaty, states that 'in defining and implementing its policies and activities, the Union shall aim to combat discrimination based on sex, racial or ethnic origin, religion or belief, disability, age or sexual orientation'. Furthermore, article 21 of the Charter of Fundamental Rights, transformed into a binding commitment by the Lisbon Treaty, prohibits 'any discrimination based on any ground such as sex, race, colour, ethnic or social origin, genetic features, language, religion or belief, political or any other opinion, membership of a national minority, property, birth, disability, age or sexual orientation'. Thanks to the Lisbon Treaty, the approach towards non-discrimination moved from one limited to nationality and sex in the context of employment, towards a broader concept of equal treatment encompassing very different grounds and applying to different domains. In so doing, the signatories of the new treaty were very much on the same line as the *Mangold* ruling.

Social and health policy

The CJEU has been instrumental in extending the scope of the four fundamental freedoms to politically and economically highly sensitive areas of social policy such as the right to strike and the regulation of working conditions for posted workers (workers posted abroad by their employers) (*Laval* C–341/05, *Rüffert* C–346/06). The *Kohll/Decker* jurisprudence probably offers the best example of judicial activism in the field of social and health policy (Obermaier, 2008b). In *Kohll* (C–158/96), a Luxembourg citizen saw his national health insurance provider refuse to authorize and reimburse his dental treatment after seeing an orthodontist in Germany. In *Decker* (C–120/95), Nicolas Decker was refused reimbursement by his Luxembourg health insurance for a pair of glasses he had bought in Belgium using a prescription from a Luxembourg ophthalmologist. The reasons for restricting a patient's mobility, as stated by several member states during the proceedings, was either that the freedom to provide services did not apply to national social protection systems or that, if it did apply, then prior authorization procedures for healthcare expenditure abroad was needed, that is, Mr Decker should have asked his health insurance provider if he could look for glasses outside Luxembourg, and if the cost of purchase would be reimbursed.

The CJEU, with the support of the Commission, applied the principles of free movement of services and goods to the Luxembourg healthcare system. France, Germany, the United Kingdom and other member states that had commented on these cases in written and oral proceedings, argued that the Court had quite unjustifiably interfered in the organization of domestic social protection systems, and that its ruling imposed on Luxembourg could not be applied to their own social protection systems. Yet the Court gradually extended the legal principles to other member states and to similar cases. In its subsequent jurisprudence until *Stalemaki* in the first decade of the twenty-first century (*Aikaterini Stalemaki vs. NPDD Organismos Asfaliseos Eleftheron Epangelmation*, C–444/05), it 'came to include all healthcare systems, public and private provision, and gradually limited the justified scope of national conditions' (Martinsen, 2015a, p. 145).

This evolution can be seen as a 'de-territorialization of welfare' (Martinsen, 2005a; Vollaard, Van de Bovenkamp & Martinsen, 2015), and as a process through which the Court has had tremendous influence (Martinsen, 2005b; Martinsen, 2015b). Here we can arguably see the Court as a real 'activist' court in its successive rulings.

On the other hand, the *Kohll* and *Decker* cases did not come as a surprise, considering the long-standing jurisprudence on the free movement of persons and services (Schmidt, 2009). What is curious, in reality, is that questions around the compatibility of prior authorization rules were not submitted to the Court earlier (Greer & Jarman, 2012; Greer & Almagro Iniesta, 2014).

Furthermore, the Court in *Kohll and Decker*, and the later case law on healthcare systems and the free movement of persons, has exercised self-restraint by accepting, contrary to other policy areas, that restrictions on free movement can be justified on economic grounds where there is the risk of seriously undermining the financial balance of the social security system; the need to maintain a balanced medical and hospital service open to all; and the need for capacity planning within the healthcare sector. As Martinsen put it, the Court has 'entered a conflict-ridden terrain between the market freedoms of the European Union and the redistributive competences of the member states' (Martinsen, 2015a, p. 142). When adopting its first rulings in the 1990s, the Court did not envisage the difficulties they would create (Greer & Jarman, 2012, p. 267). As the member states reacted, sometimes strongly against it, the Court added clarifications to existing rules in further rulings. Deviations from internal market principles were allowed and specified. Obermaier explains the 'fine-tuning' of the Court's case law as a result of some very negative reactions by the member states towards the *Kohll/ Decker* jurisprudence, and of the need to be pragmatic in order to ensure compliance from recalcitrant member states (Obermaier, 2009). Eventually, the Court's case law triggered a legislative procedure, which led to the adoption of the Patients' Rights Directive in Cross-border Healthcare (2011/24/EU). This directive has not aligned with the Court's case law as the Commission proposed, but rather, has responded to the case law by allowing more national control of cross-border care (Martinsen, 2015a, p. 181).

Environmental policy

The number of CJEU cases concerning environmental issues is vast, both quantitatively and qualitatively. In 2006, more than 700 judgements related to over 50 different EU legislative acts (Jacobs, 2006). Hence, environmental law has become one of the main sources of judicial review in the EU.

The Court's jurisprudence has helped in finding a balance between the protection of the environment on the one hand, and the requirements of the internal market and freedom of trade, on the other (Kelemen, 2001). In the *ADBHU* case (240/83), the CJEU held that the free movement of goods, together with the freedoms of competition and trade, are not 'to be viewed in absolute terms but are subject to certain limits justified by the objectives of general interest pursued by the Community'. It also asserted that the protection of the environment was 'one of the Community's essential objectives'. In *Commission vs. Denmark* (302/86), also known as the *Danish Bottles* case, the Court added environmental protection to the list of mandatory requirements derived from *Cassis de Dijon* (see above, free movement of goods) that justify derogating to the free movement of goods.

Apart from balancing environmental protection with the internal market, the CJEU has also influenced the enforcement of environmental law. In fact, the first ruling where the Court imposed a fine on a member state for non-compliance with one of its judgements was actually decided in an environmental case. It concerned Greece and the dumping of waste in Crete (*Commission vs. Greece*, C–45/91). The reasons for the large number of environmental cases at EU level are diverse. Environmental case law has increased in parallel with the development of secondary legislation in this field. Since the Council and the Parliament have widely legislated in areas dealing with waste disposal as well as the protection of air, water and birds, the CJEU has the task of ensuring compliance with a large number of environmental directives. Although there is wide variation across countries (Vanhala, 2012), NGOs have widely used litigation strategies at national level, leading national courts to make preliminary references before the CJEU. The enforcement of the Wild Birds Directive provides a good example, among others, of the way in which interest groups use legal means to defend their cause (see Chapter 6).

Enlarging the Court's jurisdiction to new areas: home affairs and economic governance

In the 1990s, the scope of EU competences was enlarged to new policy areas. Until fairly recently, the CJEU had no jurisdiction over these fields. Justice and home affairs, as well as economic governance, were kept away from the Court. The member states carefully avoided any judicial control in order to preserve their sovereignty. This has changed over time with these areas being incorporated into the mainstream of Community decision-making (the so-called 'Community method'). This evolution shows how difficult it is to insulate policy areas from supranational influence in the longer term.

Justice and Home Affairs (JHA) was developed as the third pillar of the EU in the aftermath of the Maastricht Treaty (adopted in 1992, ratified in 1993). The Community method was not used in these fields until the Amsterdam Treaty (adopted in 1997, ratified in 1999) for immigration and asylum policies, and the

Lisbon Treaty (adopted in 2007, ratified in 2009) for EU criminal justice policy. The Treaties of Amsterdam and Lisbon have – cautiously – opened up JHA to judicial review.

Regarding immigration measures, the grand chamber of the Court of Justice ruled on the Family Reunification Directive in *Parliament vs. Council of the European Union* (C–540/03). The European Parliament challenged the provisions of the directive insofar as they did not sufficiently protect the family life of the migrants. Indeed, the Council had made concessions to the member states and allowed children above the age of 15 to remain separated from their migrant parents. The CJEU held that the directive had not breached article 8 of the ECHR on the right to respect for family life. This shows us that the Court does not systematically rule in favour of the supranational institutions (Commission and Parliament) when they oppose the Council (and indirectly the member states).

In a more recent judgement (*Elgafaji vs. Staatssecretaris of justice*, C–465/07), this time in the field of asylum, the grand chamber gave an interpretation that respected high levels of human rights. It confirmed that the Refugee Definition Directive 2004/83/EC provides for humanitarian protection to any person fleeing the dangers of civil war. Contrary to the member states, which argued that the obligation only concerned those who could show they were being, or had been, individually targeted, the judges confirmed that EU law on this issue went beyond existing refugee law (and article 3 of the ECHR in particular), in so doing, affording sufficient protection to those fleeing civil wars and domestic armed conflict.

Contrary to asylum law, criminal justice is an area that has been relatively protected from the Court's activism, at least since the Lisbon Treaty. Yet, even before the treaty entered into force, the CJEU had managed to get a firm grip on criminal justice policy, with a view to protecting fundamental rights and/or developing first EU initiatives in this field.

In the controversial *Criminal Proceedings against Maria Pupino* (C–105/03), a schoolteacher was sued in Italy for having assaulted a child. The prosecution wanted the child to give evidence outside the trial hearing, which appeared to be a much more sensitive treatment of a witness (as testifying in a trial can be a traumatic experience, for a child in particular). Normally, under Italian law, this was only allowed in cases of sexual assault. Yet an EU framework directive provided for a higher level of protection of witnesses than

Italian law. This text had been passed within the third pillar of the EU (police and criminal justice) and as such was not given direct legal effect. The CJEU established a preliminary ruling asserting that a framework decision, for which the TEU prohibited direct effect, could nevertheless have indirect effect. The duty of sincere cooperation required the framework decision to be followed as far as possible. Hence national courts had to take it into account when applying and interpreting national law. This 'radical' case (Steiner & Woods, 2009, p. 601) transformed soft law measures (the framework decision) into harder ones, and decreased the distinction between 'third pillar' law (much more intergovernmental and out of judicial control) and 'Community' law (fully controlled by the CJEU and national courts).

Another ruling, *Advocaten voor de Wereld VZW vs. Leden van de Ministerrad* (C–303/05), concerned the legality of the framework decision on the European arrest-warrant (EAW) with regard to EU primary law. For a wide range of categories of crimes, the framework decision removed the double criminality rule. According to the rule, a state could normally refuse to extradite suspects if the conduct recognized as a criminal offence in the state requesting extradition (requesting state), is not recognized as a criminal offence in the state being asked to effect the extradition (sending state). Under the EAW, the sending national court has no obligation to assess the crime with which the suspects are charged. A Belgian lawyers' association argued that the framework decision had been passed in breach of the general principles of European law. In other words, the fact that suspects could be sent back so easily to the requesting state was in breach of the ECHR, national constitutions and general principles of EU law. The CJEU, on the contrary, held that the requesting member state, when receiving the suspect, must always abide by these principles. This implies that national courts must trust each other to uphold key principles of fundamental rights. The German Constitutional Court, however, annulled the implementation of the EAW system, on the grounds that fundamental rights were not sufficiently ensured (BVerfG 2735/14 of 15 December 2015, 'Solange III'). This is a clear indication of how fragile the primacy principle is in the area of criminal justice.

Economic governance is another field where the competence of the CJEU has been enlarged. When the signatories of the Maastricht Treaty introduced economic and monetary union (EMU) into primary law, they decided that economic coordination should function under the so-called 'new modes of governance' and therefore not be controlled by the European Court. However, economic governance has been transformed in the wake of the economic and financial crisis, and once again legal integration has been used to foster integration (Saurugger & Terpan, 2016b; Saurugger, 2016). The revision of the Stability and Growth Pact, the main legal basis for economic coordination across the member states, started with the adoption of the European Semester in October 2010, was followed in 2011 by the 'Six-Pack', composed of five regulations and one directive, and thereafter in 2013 by two regulations known as the 'Two-Pack'. At treaty level, the member states, with the exception of the United Kingdom and the Czech Republic, signed the Treaty on Stability, Coordination and Governance (TSCG), also known as the 'Fiscal Compact', in March 2013. In addition, a European Financial Stability Facility (EFSF) was established by the member states in 2010, and then transformed into a European Stability Mechanism (ESM), to help the member states deal with the sovereign debt crisis.

These new economic governance rules have strengthened the CJEU's influence. According to the 'Fiscal Compact' (TSCG), national budgets should be 'balanced' or in surplus – the so-called 'golden rule' – and provide for an automatic correction mechanism. Both provisions had to be embedded in national law during a period of one year after the entry into force of the treaty. Compliance with budgetary rules is controlled at the national level by independent institutions, and at EU level by the Commission. Furthermore, the CJEU may control the inclusion of the 'golden rule' in national law and submit an enforcement ruling that sets a deadline for compliance. If non-compliance continues after the expiration of the deadline, a penalty of up to 0.1 per cent of GDP can be applied to the state concerned.

The CJEU has never ruled on the application of the Fiscal Compact, but has been asked to control the financial mechanisms set out by EU institutions to solve the debt and deficit problems. There have been two rulings as a result: *Pringle* (C–370/12) and *Gauweiler et al. vs. Deutscher Bundestag* (C–62/15).

The *Pringle* ruling provided an answer to the question referred to it by the Irish Supreme Court, as to whether the setting up of a permanent international body competent to grant financial assistance to Eurozone members in financial difficulties went against the very foundations of EMU, which aimed at ensuring price stability through sound government budgets. In its ruling, the CJEU confirmed the competence of the EU member states to conclude the ESM Treaty and its compatibility with the TFEU. A first group of scholars praised the efforts of the CJEU to save the Euro, even if the legal reasoning used in *Pringle* might be criticized (Craig, 2013; Fahey and Bardutzky, 2013). A second group of scholars was much more critical, considering that the ruling undermined the constitutional commitment of the EU to monetary stability (Beck, 2014; Everson, 2015). Welcomed or criticized, the *Pringle* ruling was considered by a large majority of experts as a bold interpretation of EU law.

The CJEU's second ruling with regard to the new economic governance mechanisms, *Gauweiler et al. vs. Deutscher Bundestag*, dealt with the Outright Monetary Transactions (OMT), which are indirect bond-buying performed by the European Central Bank (ECB). This case was of crucial importance because, for the first time in the history of European integration, the German Federal Constitutional Court (FCC) had made a request to the CJEU for a preliminary ruling. The FCC asked whether the ECB had transgressed the limits of its powers derived from the treaties. The OMT Programme launched in September 2012 was part of a series of measures taken by the ECB in response to the euro crisis to accompany the loan facilities (European Financial Stability Facility and European Stability Mechanism). The Court delivered its final decision on 16 June 2015, finding the programme to be compatible with EU law. Indirect bond-buying through the OMT programme would indeed have an effect on member states' access to credit, but that effect was not deemed to be the same as if buying bonds directly from member states (monetary financing). The TFEU has forbidden monetary financing, in order to encourage the member states to pursue a prudent budgetary policy; it has not forbidden indirect monetary, says the Court, and therefore the OMT programme was considered legal.

Both the *Gauweiler* and *Pringle* decisions, in a context of crisis, have contributed to move the EMU towards more integration and more coercive forms of regulation (Saurugger & Terpan, 2016b).

Functions of policy-making

Apart from case studies dealing with the contribution of the CJEU in different policy areas, another way to analyse the CJEU as a policy-maker is to look at the functions carried out with regard to

EU legislative activities. Four main functions can be distinguished. First, the Court finds new areas of policy-making; second, it compensates for the lack of EU legislation in specific fields; third, it shapes EU legislation by interpreting imprecise rules and principles; and, finally it incites the legislator to adopt or revise EU secondary law.

Finding new areas of policy-making

One of the Court's main functions is agenda setting. The Court has helped launch policy actions in areas where the treaties have been 'silent' or ambiguous. This is the case with the *Mangold* ruling (C–144/04) where the Court enlarged the scope of EU gender equality law to non-discrimination on the grounds of age.

Another example is in the field of competition law and, in particular, merger control. The original Treaty of Rome had given the Commission several powers in the field of competition policy, but it said nothing about controlling the mergers and acquisitions of companies. In *Continental Can* (6/72), as in *Van Gend en Loos*, the Court argued that 'it had to go back to spirit, general scheme and wording of article 86 EEC [now art. 102 TFEU], as well as to the system and the objectives of the Treaty'. Using a teleological and systemic interpretation (see Chapter 7), and against a literal reading of the treaties, it ruled that the Commission should be given the power to control the mergers and acquisitions of companies (Monti, 2007; Jones & Davies, 2014). Following the Court's decision in *Continental Can*, as well as another important ruling on the same matter, *British American Tobacco* (142 and 156/84), the Commission pushed forward its proposal for a regulation on merger control, finally adopted by the Council in 1989. Hence, the CJEU has been instrumental in empowering the Commission with important control powers in this field.

Compensating for the lack of EU legislation in specific fields

When the treaties provide the competence and legal basis for policy actions but the EU legislator does not make use of it, it sometimes happens that the Court fills the gap and compensates for the lack of legislation through innovative rulings. This was the case with the free movement of goods and the principle of *mutual recognition*, in particular. Considerable disparities used to hinder the completion of the internal market in the 1960s and 1970s. The only instrument that the treaties provided for the removal of obstacles to the free movement of goods, was the approximation of national legislation. However, reaching agreement on harmonization was very difficult, and when it was, it often ended up being outdated because of more recent technological advances. In the *Cassis de Dijon* case (120/78), the Court circumvented the problem by establishing the principle of *mutual recognition*. As such, if a product has been lawfully produced and marketed in one member state, there is no valid reason why it should not be introduced into the market of another member state. Later, the Commission decided to endorse the position of the Court in *Cassis de Dijon* and further developed the principle of *mutual recognition* through secondary legislation. There was certain resistance in the Council of Ministers, however, with the member states reproaching the Commission for having gone beyond the Court's position. In the mid-1980s, the Commission succeeded in convincing the Council to launch an ambitious programme aimed at completing the internal market by 31 December 1992 (Dehousse, 1998, p. 87). Not only had the *Cassis de Dijon* ruling established an important legal principle, but it also triggered a 're-launch' of the European integration process and gave credit to the idea of 'integration through law' (Cappelletti, Seccombe & Weiler, 1986, 1987).

The compensatory function of the Court should thus be seen in conjunction with the troubles affecting the Council of Ministers since the 1965 'Empty Chair' crisis. The Luxembourg Compromise, reached in January 1966 between the six member states to end the crisis, complicated the decision-making process. While the treaties allowed for decisions to be taken by qualified majority voting (QMV), the Compromise favoured the practice of unanimity. Subsequently, the role of the Court as a policy-maker arguably compensated for the inertia of the European political institutions between 1966 and 1986 in terms of sustaining the momentum for integration.

The Court has continued playing this compensatory role since the mid-1980s and the generalization of qualified majority voting in the EU, which has been applied to many more areas in recent years. For example, and as seen before, the Court's interpretation that dismissing transsexuals, for the very reason that they are transsexuals, was a case of sex discrimination covered by secondary law prompted the EU to develop legislation regarding lesbians, gays, bisexuals and transgender (LGBT) people in the 1990s (Holzhacker, 2012).

Shaping legislation by interpreting imprecise rules and principles

Through the interpretation of both the treaties and EU secondary law, the Court can shape the content of EU policies, and such activity is often seen as a form of activism (Rasmussen, 1986, p. 29). The Court's interpretations, and the alliance between the Court and the individual, have had the effect of partially disempowering the legislator of its law-making function. For example, as seen above, the Court has interpreted EU law in a way that is favourable to Turkish migrants, contrary to the positions defended by the member states in the Council. More generally, some authors have argued that the single market had more to do with the case law of the Court than with secondary law adopted by 'political' institutions (Gormley, 1985, p. 249; Grimmel, 2012).

The Court's shaping of legislation takes place at both the European and the national level. At the European level, it is often said that the European Court adopts a more precise and trenchant position than the EU legislator, which is not surprising since the latter continually risks a veto from the member states, while the Court can rule more autonomously (Dehousse, 1998, p. 79; see also Chapter 5). Another reason why the Court's interpretations are difficult to override is that many are anchored in the EU treaties. The Court often shapes legislation, based on rules derived from this primary law. Therefore, simply adopting new legislative rules may not be enough to override an earlier decision by the Court.

At the domestic level, as we have argued in Chapter 5, compliance with CJEU's rulings is widespread, although not automatic. The effect that these rulings have on national laws and practices is not necessarily always the same. Interest groups active at the domestic level can experience power shifts in both directions as we have seen in Chapter 6. Studying the impact of the *Laval* (C–341/05) and *Rüffert* (C–346/06) cases (rights to strike and free movement of workers) in Denmark, Sweden and Germany, Seikel (2015) argues that the domestic effects of supranational case law were determined by the way labour and capital pursued their interests. The Court rulings affected labour and capital asymmetrically. They shifted the veto positions in the domestic arena, changing the balance of power in favour of business. This created disparities among the member states depending on the way business/labour relationships were structured in each country.

The Court's activist function of shaping legislation can be explained by the very nature of European law. Indeed, the treaties make frequent recourse to legal concepts such as 'measures of equivalent effect to custom duties' and 'measures of equivalent effect to quantitative restrictions' in the area of the free movement of goods, as well as 'dominant position' in the field of competition. As Dehousse (1998, p. 73) has argued, 'the programmatic nature of the treaty, combined with the relative imprecision of its clauses, leaves considerable discretion to the interpreter'. Moreover, 'the open-textured character together with the purpose-oriented nature of the treaty, has lent itself quite well to the kind of teleological interpretation proposed by the (CJEU)' (Dehousse, 1998, p. 76). In the same vein, Stone Sweet (2004, p. 24) has described the treaties as an 'incomplete contract' that must be further clarified by both legislative and judicial means. The specificity of preliminary rulings (Chapter 4) further explains the propensity of the Court to make 'abstract' rulings: when answering questions submitted by national courts, the CJEU does not necessarily decide upon the case, but rather, provides interpretations in general terms so that national courts can use them when applying EU law to specific cases.

Forcing or inciting the legislator to act

The CJEU may trigger the legislative process in two different ways. First, the Court can be used by the Commission to back up and legitimate its legislative proposals. Dehousse (1998, p. 89) takes the example of insurance law. The Treaty of Rome envisaged the progressive abolition of restrictions on the freedom to provide services within the Community. However, in the early 1980s the problem of insurance regulation had not been solved. The member states continued to make conditions on the freedom of establishment meaning it remained subject to prior authorizations by national bodies. The adoption of a co-insurance directive did not manage to prevent the member states from using these authorizations as protectionist measures. The Commission began a series of infringement proceedings against the member states for having failed to fulfil the obligations incumbent upon them by virtue of the co-insurance directive. Although careful not to act as the Commission mouthpiece, the

Court advocated an alternative approach and opened the door to the use of the *mutual recognition* principle (*Commission vs. Germany* 205/84). In the years following the Court's judgement, the Council adopted a series of directives on the subject, which came about partly because the Commission had managed to use the Court as a means to back up and legitimate its proposals.

Second, the Court may be used by the Commission to force the legislator to act. As we have seen, directives such as those dealing with gender equality tend to have been prompted by concerns that the Court may one day end up ruling on the subject. Blauberger and Weiss (2013; also Weiss and Blauberger, 2016), in an article on defence procurement, explain how the Commission made strategic use of judicial politics to change the opportunity structure of member states, and force the adoption of the 2009 directive on defence and security. The Commission threatened to leave the regulation of defence procurement to the European Court, while at the same time offering the member states the chance to restore legal certainty and political control by setting rules for defence procurement themselves. Convinced that the Court's jurisprudence could potentially harm national security interests, the member states finally agreed on the Commission's proposal to legislate after many years of refusal.

Whether it is by backing policy initiatives or threatening member states with the prospect of new secondary law at the EU level, the Court is usually able to influence the adoption of secondary law. Furthermore, when the CJEU's interpretations and doctrines are incorporated in the policy-making process, then it has far more influence on integration (Blauberger, 2009, 2012; Wasserfallen, 2010; Martinsen, 2015a, 2015b). Indeed, when faced with the Court's decisions, governments have different options, which range from the most resistant to the least resistant. First they can simply ignore them. Second, they can choose to apply the Court's decisions only to those parties involved in a specific case. Third, they might restrict the application of judgements by limiting the range of legal principles in national legislation. Fourth they could pre-empt future interventions by adjusting national regulations in an 'EU-friendly' way, and adopt new principles as broader policy guidelines. In other words, as Seikel (2015, p. 3) has argued, outcomes can vary between non-compliance, EU-compatible re-regulation, and regulatory surrender. National governments are more likely to fully comply with EU rules when they derive from both the Court's jurisprudence *and* the secondary legislation.

Using the case study of social policy – where the Court has traditionally advocated far-reaching European coordination rules, while member states have defended national prerogatives – Wasserfallen (2010) shows that rulings can provide important early guidance and direction when EU legislation is missing. They can also pave the way for the eventual adoption of secondary legislation. However, the adoption of directives or regulations may not be necessary for jurisprudence to have an impact. The application of case law at national level is uncertain in the absence of secondary law. Confronted with 'undesirable' jurisprudence, national governments usually respect the individual decisions of the CJEU, but don't necessarily adapt national legislation to make it fit with the Court rulings. Conant (2002) describes this phenomenon as 'contained compliance'. In short, Court decisions have a greater and more effective impact on EU legal integration when the Council and the Parliament take on board lower-level judicial and political issues, and the sensitivities of the national policy-making context (Wasserfallen, 2010, p. 1129).

Conclusion

Judicial activism is not easy to measure. Lawyers do it by analysing and criticizing the legal reasoning of the CJEU. They usually draw general conclusions from the study of specific rulings, which is arguably not wholly convincing as an analytical approach. Political scientists usually see Court activism in terms of how it opposes the position of the member states, but this perspective is not entirely satisfying either. Indeed, national governments may defend legal arguments that correspond with their short-term interests though they contradict the treaties, if interpreted literally (Grimmel, 2012).

The already difficult task of properly analysing judicial activism is complicated further by the fact that authors often see activism in normative terms, either positively (Weiler, 1991) or negatively (Rasmussen, 1989). As such, the Court might be criticized because its (democratic) activism does not tally with the definition of 'democracy' commonly understood as being about giving power to the people (participatory democracy). Others argue, on the contrary, that judicial control is an important component of democracy, as defined by checks and balances and the rule of law. Apart from the legitimacy debate, the Court has also been criticized for the content of its rulings, which do not necessarily fit with those ideals defended by 'normative-driven' scholars. 'What is deplored is not so much the fact that judges arrogate excessive powers but rather that they put these powers in the service of a bad cause' (Dehousse, 1998, p. 121). This stance may not be surprising given that the literature on judicial activism in the EU developed in the early 1990s, at a time of decreasing consensus (that is, increasing scepticism) over the European integration process.

The emergence of non-binding new governance methods in the 1990s and 2000s challenged the traditional ideals of EU law by suggesting that soft norms could provide a viable alternative. Indeed, soft law in the form of non-binding norms exclude traditional institutions such as courts. New modes of governance (including OMC) in different fields such as social and economic policies, as well as 'high politics' areas such as common foreign and security policy, might therefore be seen as an alternative to hard law and the community method (Hillion and Wessel, 2009; Wessel, 2015). One might consider that the member states, which have been pushing them, have done so in an attempt to oppose possible activism by the CJEU. However, the Community method and hard law have been extended in recent years to areas such as justice and home affairs, fiscal governance and fundamental rights (the Charter on Fundamental Rights becoming a binding commitment) (Kelemen, 2011). This suggests that the member states are still willing to grant the CJEU new and important areas of jurisdiction, albeit carefully and somewhat grudgingly. While opposing judicial activism in certain policy areas, the member states continue to accept it in others, where soft law can be progressively transformed into hard law (Terpan, 2015) and/or where EU competences have been extended through successive treaty revisions.

Chapter 9

Conclusion

Is judicial integration still the basis of European integration?

Is European integration still based on 'integration through law' or has law become less central to European integration since the early 1990s, given the growing political resistance to the EU? As we have seen throughout the book, as far as judicial powers are concerned, the EU can be considered as one of the most highly institutionalized supranational political systems in the world (Stone Sweet & Caporaso, 1998; Alter, 2001, 2009; Kelemen, 2011). The CJEU started out as an international court but today it is both the constitutional and the administrative court of the EU. It seeks to find a legal balance between European integration, member state sovereignty and citizens' rights. However, judicial integration has been increasingly challenged since the early 1990s on various grounds. A number of new European public policies have developed outside the realm of hard law, through the use of soft law and non-legislative instruments of 'new public governance'. All these instruments, contrary to hard law, are beyond the Court's control. In the meantime, the end of permissive consensus – the rather loose but passive support of European citizens for the continual widening and deepening of the European integration process – has put pressure on the supranational institutions, and in particular, the CJEU. A higher degree of public scrutiny in recent years appears to have led the Court to exert self-restraint rather than activism. The chapters have shown that, while this can be observed in several cases, the CJEU remains instrumental in deepening European integration, and is still a core institution of the EU system. This last chapter argues in favour of a continued judicialization of the EU and explains the approach we used to come to this conclusion.

Combining law and politics to better understand the CJEU

We have argued that in order to understand the Court's power and influence, it must be placed in both the legal and the socio-political context within which its acts. Its initiatives, and the repercussions of its actions, are embedded in a wider political system, bringing together EU member state governments, national lower-level courts and constitutional courts, citizens, interest groups and companies.

The book has aimed to show that only through a combination of law and politics, or in other words, by way of legal and political studies, can the Court's activism and its limits be properly understood and explained. The delegation of judicial powers to the Court in the Treaty of Rome created a dynamic through which the Court, with the support of other European institutions and domestic courts, was able to extend its influence through a series of landmark rulings in the 1960s and 1970s. Integration through law became a specific part of the identity of European integration, which was very different from integration processes in Latin America or South-East Asia.

In order to conceptualize the interaction between law and politics, we have argued for an understanding of the CJEU that combines consideration of its normative and legal bases with a systemic approach looking at interactions between the Court and other actors. The Court applies the law as it appears in both the treaties and secondary legislation. It also develops its own legal doctrines, especially through general principles of European law, in order to interpret EU law. These doctrines can be used strategically by the Court to achieve its goals. From this perspective, legal norms enshrined in the treaties and secondary legislation, as well as legal doctrines developed by the CJEU, do not solely constitute the *environment* in which the Court is embedded, but are also *tools*, for they can be consciously used by the Court to attain its goals.

What do we understand by 'integration through law'?

Nobody could deny the European Court's high degree of influence from the 1950s until the 1980s. This influence came largely unexpectedly. This has certainly been one of the most fascinating puzzles in European studies, but also in the politics of law more generally. As we have underlined, law does not become a constraining force merely because it is the law; judicial organs have to be creative and credible actors, and other actors situated in their environment need to accept the rulings. This is even more so when those actors have to apply a text of a general nature, such as a constitution or treaty.

From this perspective, the integration of European states into the EU constitutes one of the central post-war ideas in Western Europe. Supported by the major parties in European member states, and without outward contestation from the populations of the member states, the Treaty of Rome conceived of the Court's role as one of *interpreting* and *assessing the validity* of European law. The Court later overstepped these legal bases, but was, despite resistance from a small number of constitutional courts and member state governments, considered legitimate to fill the political and legal void in this new supranational order. When confronted with decision-making blockades at the Council, in the aftermath of the Empty Chair crisis (1965–66), the Court compensated for the lack of EU legislation through judicial policy-making. This understanding of the Court, which was first based on analyses by Stein (1981), Weiler (1981) and Cappelletti, Secombe and Weiler (1986), has been widely shared and further built upon by a number of scholars who share a common perception of the Court as a political power.

From this perspective, the perceived and perhaps automatically assumed 'neutrality' of the judiciary was the cornerstone of the CJEU's claim to be the sole interpreter of the rule of law. Its inherent legitimacy was difficult to contest politically and not contested by most scholars working on 'integration through law', who generally accepted and sometimes welcomed the audacious jurisprudence of the Court. This understanding of the Court was, however, questioned in Rasmussen's study of the Court in the mid-1980s (Rasmussen, 1986), where it was argued that the Court's authority and legitimacy were in fact undermined by excessive activism, a perception that was later taken up by a series of legal scholars (Arnull, 2013).

Integration through law, while based on the Court's actions, is nevertheless dependent upon the use that is made of these rulings at the domestic level. Governments and domestic courts need to accept the Court's rulings, and, as Chapters 5 and 7 have shown, they do accept the Court's decisions with few exceptions. Interest groups, companies and NGOs have been crucial actors in the ways in which they have used the Court for their own purposes (Chapter 6). Studying their activities helps to explain why CJEU rulings have been largely complied with – notwithstanding the lack of coercive means at EU level (Conant, 2002; Cichowski, 2007; Vanhala, 2010). Hence, the transnational activity of multiple EU actors, based on interest group action, is crucial when explaining the success of CJEU rulings. In this sense, the EU is similar to other liberal democratic systems since overt coercion rarely plays a significant role in fostering obedience. Understanding the systemic interaction between the Court and both private and public actors as 'integration through law' leads us to the question of whether the EU has become more state-like?

The EU and its Court: establishing stateness?

Scholars have attempted to think in more general terms about European integration in a small number of academic research projects since the mid-2000s (Bartolini, 2005; Fligstein, 2008; Leuffen, Rittberger & Schimmelfennig, 2012; Bickerton, Hodson & Puetter, 2015). These studies share a number of characteristics; they ask very broad questions that go beyond the specific nature of a policy sector or a particular group of actors, such as: why heterogeneity matters; under which conditions the demand for differentiation (defined as a claim for the acceptance of national diversity) is translated into actual differentiated integration (mechanisms allowing a flexible participation of the member states in European policies) (Leuffen Rittberger & Schimmelfennig, 2012); and whether the EU is in fact a new state form (Bartolini, 2005).

More particularly, Genschel and Jachtenfuchs (2013) argue that the EU is much more deeply involved in the exercise of core state powers than the 'standard view' in political science would suggest. Their argument is a rationalist one; the demand for integration grows largely from the desire of member states to limit policy externalities and to achieve economies of scale. The demand enables the CJEU to be conferred with powers that go beyond those attributed to any international court (Alter, 2014). Moreover, the process of judicialization did not stop in the 1990s, when political resistance from domestic constituencies increased – a time when many supposed that permissive consensus had come to an end (Hooghe & Marks, 2009). Even campaigns against CJEU activism ('Stop the ECJ!' in Germany) have not prevented the Court from issuing bold decisions, as we have seen in rulings such as the *Viking* and *Laval* cases, *Kadi*, or *Mangold* where the Court stood against member states with large voting power in the Council, such as Germany (see Chapter 8).

It seems that the Court's rulings have given a strong incentive to political decision-makers to tackle follow-up problems of integration by opting for more integration, even though these problems themselves have led the general public to favour less integration (Saurugger, 2016). Once executive, legislative or judicial powers have been delegated to independent agents – be they governmental agencies or courts – these powers are difficult to rescind.

At the same time, however, we observe a paradox; while national governments have delegated powers to the Court, despite the unknown outcome of the rulings (which might in fact go against the interest of the major parties), they also have introduced policy instruments to circumvent the Court.

Hence the same contestation that led member states to turn to the Court, as described above, encouraged EU policy-makers during the 1990s to introduce mechanisms aimed at making EU governance simpler, more flexible and less formal (for a more general debate, see Abbott & Snidal, 2000; Shaffer & Pollack, 2009; Scott & Sturm, 2006; Pauwelyn, Wessel & Wouters, 2012; Terpan, 2015; Saurugger & Terpan, 2016a). The aim was to reduce opposition to integration through so-called 'new modes of governance' that would use coordination mechanisms and soft law instead of coercive tools and hard law (Chapters 4 and 8). In doing so, EU policy-makers sought to slow down the evolution towards stateness. We find three sets of arguments for this phenomenon.

A first category of authors argue that soft law is introduced because, over time, states know it will lead to hard law. In the EU context, the main argument is that governments as well as European institutions, can produce a 'shadow of hierarchy' by threatening to introduce legally binding regulations if actors do not comply with voluntary or soft instruments (Chapter 5).

A second approach considers that governments support soft law out of a desire to protect sovereignty, and more precisely 'because of its low degree of legalization and limited potential for unintended consequences' (Schäfer, 2004). Soft law agreements are easier to conclude and imply lower bureaucratic transaction costs than hard law. Most of all, soft law is favoured when states have considerable interests that they do not want to put at risk.

A third group of authors argue that soft law allows for the creation of shared norms and a sense of common purpose and identity, without the constraints raised by concerns over political litigation. With regard to the EU in particular, scholars stress that 'new modes of governance' trigger more coherence between EU member states because the main mechanism here is *learning* (Radaelli, 2008). This assumption, shared by a number of official Commission documents and discourses, sees in the different forms of learning – by socialization, monitoring, arguing and persuasion – a way of re-orienting initial policy paradigms and positions.

All these conceptual views share the conviction that the introduction of soft law decreases compliance problems. Soft law allows governments in international arenas to choose their own policy instruments for reaching commonly defined goals, thus making the system more efficient. As seen in Chapters 2 and 8, soft law instruments have been introduced in employment, social, environmental and asylum policies. In these contexts, the European Court, and judicial control more generally, is no longer the cornerstone of compliance. As such, in these specific fields, the Court and the legal system lose their position as the central actors in the process of integration through law.

However, we argue more generally that, even if the Court is challenged by the introduction of soft law and increasing public scrutiny and criticism, judicial politics is still a central feature of European integration.

Continued judicialization

The Court, while exerting self-restraint in some cases such as *Keck and Mithouard* (free movement of goods) and *Sayn-Wittgenstein* (free movement of persons), remains active on other occasions, as we have seen in particular in Chapters 7 and 8. More generally, the idea that the Court is still a central actor of integration, given its bold jurisprudence, is defended from various perspectives. First, one sees the CJEU's reach in its questioning of decisions overwhelmingly endorsed by Europe's democratically elected governments (Smith, 2010a). An example is the concern voiced by scholars and the media alike over the *Kadi* ruling (C–402/05) in 2008 where the Court overruled the judgements of the Court of First Instance (now the General Court) and annulled Council Regulation 881/200, which had imposed restrictive measures against persons and entities associated with Osama bin Laden, the Al-Qaeda network and the Taliban. The CJEU found both the judgement and the Council regulation to be a breach of the fundamental rights of the EU (Van den Herik & Schrijver, 2008; Saltinyte, 2010). Second, one sees the

CJEU, in the same *Kadi* case and other cases linked with fundamental rights, as the guardian of the European polity, ensuring that all European rules respect due processes, the rule of law and the fundamental rights of the citizens (de Búrca, 2010). This can also be seen in its Opinion 2/13 on the EU accession to the European Convention for the Protection of Human Rights and Fundamental Freedoms (ECHR), in which it argued that the EU could not adhere to the ECHR. The main issue is that as a consequence of EU accession, the ECHR, and not the CJEU would – indirectly – interpret EU law when ruling on disputes between EU member states or between them and the EU. This would be incompatible with EU law, since only the CJEU can interpret and rule on matters of EU law. Hence defending its own prerogatives and the autonomy of the European legal order is one of the main issues of this bold ruling. Finally, one sees the Court acting strategically with regard to the German Constitutional Court (FCC) in defending fundamental rights in line with the FCC's *Solange* rulings (Murkens, 2009).

Furthermore, the impact of new modes of governance or 'soft law' cannot be seen as indication that the CJEU has been marginalized, for at least three reasons. First, some authors argue that soft law has some efficiency. They point to the shadow of hierarchy coming from the CJEU. In other words, member states prefer to agree on soft law rules for which the CJEU has no say, precisely because, if they fail to do so, the CJEU could issue an activist ruling, as we have seen in chapter eight with the example of defence procurement. Here the Commission made strategic use of judicial politics (*Commission vs. Italy* C–337/05 and *InsTiimi Oy*, C–615/10) to change the opportunity structure of the member states and force the adoption of the 2009 directive on defence and security. Here we see the member states' adopting soft rules as a way to keep control of a policy area and prevent the Court from adjudicating. Nonetheless, this strategy has not been consistently successful.

Second, some policy domains have already evolved from soft law to hard law and, in so doing, have enlarged the scope of the Court's control. Such is the case with immigration, asylum and other fields related to the area of liberty, security and justice, since the Treaty of Amsterdam. Since the Treaty of Lisbon this has also been the case with the European Charter of Fundamental Rights, which has become a legally binding commitment.

Third, law in the form of directives, regulations and decisions still plays a crucial role. This may be due to the fact that the EU responds to conflict and crisis situations with further regulatory integration. As Genschel and Jachtenfuchs (2013, p. 3) underline, conflict and crisis situations 'in turn increase national differences and thus perpetuates the vicious circle of regulatory integration and increasing salient national identities'. Regulatory authorities have the power to overcome political blockades by way of judicial politics exercised by the CJEU. Corporate taxation illustrates this argument (Genschel, Kemmerling, Seils, 2011, pp. 599–600). For many years, member states were unable to agree on a common system of corporate tax legislation. By offering extensive interpretations of the internal market treaty provisions (something that the member states had never imagined), the Court was able to create a set of rulings that, incrementally, drew corporate taxation under the umbrella of European law. Ironically, the potential for integration through judicial rulings has been particularly high where the likelihood of agreement in the Council has been low (Alter, 2009; Garrett & Tsebelis, 2001; see also Chapter 5).

Hence, soft law has not put an end to 'integration through law'. A number of publications since 2010 even insist on the continued *judicialization* of the EU, in an attempt to explain why this process has not stopped (Maduro & Azoulai, 2010; Schmidt, 2012). Two mechanisms are at play in this context (Kelemen 2011): The first mechanism is the process of deregulation and judicial reregulation, which derives from the creation of the European Single Market. This has led to a situation whereby the arrival of new policy players, such as interest groups, companies, NGOs and newly created regulatory authorities, has upset traditional cooperative and informal arrangements that long characterized the policy-making process. By referring cases to the CJEU, these new players have contributed to the reinforcement of the Court.

The second mechanism is the EU's fragmented institutional structure. A weak administrative apparatus has led to the establishment of a powerful judicial system. The fragmentation between the European and national level, as well as among EU institutions, has generated principal-agent problems encouraging the establishment of strict, judicially enforceable goals, based on transparent and accountable procedures. Hence, the greater the distrust between regulators and regulated actors in liberalized markets, the more formal, transparent and legalistic the laws and regulatory processes become; and thus, the more important the judicial apparatus. In fragmented systems, policy-makers have an increasingly difficult job to build the majorities needed to pass their new legislation (Skowronek, 1982; Garrett, Kelemen & Schulz, 1998; Pollack, 2003; Jones, Kelemen & Meunier, 2016). The fragmentation of power insulates the judiciary against being overruled easily, as well as from other forms of political backlash.

Strategic constructivism, the CJEU and the judicial integration of the EU's political system

The paradox of the Court is that it still manages to continue with its activism and enable 'integration through law', while at the same time showing a greater tendency to self-restraint. Thus, is it an activist, or non-activist? Is it independent of, or dependent on, the member states? Does the Court anticipate the member states' reaction? Are its rulings widely accepted, or are its decisions still questioned by constitutional courts?

The book has proposed to solve this problem by taking both the law and the Court's strategic action seriously. In other words, the Court is 'a strategic actor, whose agenda is influenced by legal values, whether these be enshrined in the Treaty or informed by judges' vision of their own role, but whose rulings are also informed by the knowledge that it must come to terms with reality in order to ensure compliance' (Dehousse, 1998, p. 179; Pollack, 2016).

Throughout the book we have argued in this respect that there was no golden age confined to the 1960s and 1970s where the Court *made* law, compared with a more recent period where the Court only *applies* law. Back in the 1960s the nascent CJEU was not evolving rapidly in the political vacuum. In order to act, the Court had to be called upon by other actors (Commission, member states, private parties). Yet, the development of the EU as a complex and sophisticated system of governance increased the importance of the environment on the Court's behaviour. This means that any attempt to understand the Court is a complex endeavour, even more so since it is a legal institution embedded in a political system; we need both a legal *and* a political science point of view.

We have argued throughout the chapters in favour of combining legal and political science points of view within a strategic – or actor-centred constructivist – framework. Such a combined framework allows us to link the legal interpretation of EU law to the strategic (political) positioning of the Court. Judges are embedded in specific cognitive frames, based on legal doctrines that allow them to interpret law. However, as we have pointed out in Chapter 1, these norms don't solely constitute the *environment* in which actors are embedded (constitutive logic), but can also be seen as *tools*, consciously used by these same actors to attain their goals (causal logic) (Gofas & Hay, 2010).

In other words, while the legal framework in which the Court acts remains a crucial element when seeking to explain the Court's rulings, it is its own embeddedness in this environment and its interaction with other actors – member states, European institutions, interest groups and non-state actors more generally – that we must bear in mind when striving for a holistic understanding of why the Court acts as it does.

With regard to the normative frame, the treaties have endowed the Court with the task of ensuring that, in the interpretation and application of the treaties, the law is properly applied. However, the vagueness of treaty provisions (incomplete contract) and the difficulty of applying very general rules to specific practical situations have increased the need for judicial interpretations. For the sake of the unity of European law, this interpretative task has been delegated to the European Court. Thus, studying how it interprets European law is crucial for any solid understanding of the legal integration of the EU over time.

The Court has widely used 'activist' types of interpretation, instead of limiting itself to a literal interpretation that would mean sticking to the text and not allowing for any 'external' criteria to interfere. As we have shown, functional, teleological, consequentialist and systemic interpretations are widespread. While a functional interpretation assumes that a legal provision must be interpreted in a way that ensures its 'effectiveness' or 'useful effect', a teleological (or purposive) interpretation implies that interpretation is consistent with the goals and purposes explicitly or implicitly established by the treaties. The consequentialist interpretation takes into consideration the foreseeable consequences of the interpretive decision. Finally, the systemic (or contextual) decision takes into account the normative context in which the legal provision is placed. The CJEU has widely used the four methods.

Taking these norms of *legal* interpretation into account is crucial if we are to understand the legal embededdness of the Court's rulings (Bailey & Maltzman, 2008). We might then be able to measure empirically the extent to which the Court has enlarged its interpretation of EU law, from a strict textual and static analysis, to a teleological and systemic interpretation that embraces the objectives and the spirit of the treaties.

But such an understanding must also draw on a strategic analysis that questions the *political* interaction between the Court and the member states (Cichowski, 2007; Carrubba, Gabel & Hankla, 2008). Four rulings illustrate well the legal embeddedness and political positioning of the Court. It developed teleological and systemic interpretations that would indicate an activist stance, while fully aware of the respective positions of other actors: *Mangold* (C–144/04), *Commission vs. Italy* (C–337/05), as well as *Pringle* (C–370/12) and *Gauweiler et al. vs. Deutscher Bundestag* (C–62/15).

As we have shown in Chapter 8, in the *Mangold* case (C–144/04) the Court ruled on a principle of equal treatment at the same time as the Commission and some member states defended an extended version of the equal treatment principle. The Commission had proposed a directive on the principle of equal treatment between persons irrespective of religion or belief, disability, age or sexual orientation outside the labour market. However, under the unanimity principle, the proposal had difficulties being adopted, due to the opposition of Germany, in particular. In the 2007 Lisbon Treaty, this principle was finally enshrined; hence the 2005 *Mangold* ruling can be seen as legal 'preparation' for the Lisbon Treaty's principle of equal treatment.

In the specific area of defence procurement, the Court adopted equally audacious rulings, which limited the use by national governments of article 346 TFEU (allowing member states to avoid the EU's public procurement rules in order to protect essential security interests). For decades, the defence sector was considered as beyond the scope of the application of EU law. This exclusion contributed to market fragmentation, lack of competition and a strong national preference in procurement.

In *Commission vs. Italy* (C-337/05) the Court's legal reasoning was based on a systemic logic, arguably reflecting a rather subdued boldness. However, the Court's position can only be understood in the wider context of the European political system (Saurugger & Terpan, 2016c). *Commission vs. Italy* was decided in 2008, at the same time as the Commission proposed the Defence and Security Directive (Blauberger & Weiss, 2013; Weiss & Blauberger, 2016). This ruling paved the way for the Commission to convince member states to adopt procurement rules in the field of defence. At the same time, the Court's decision can be explained by looking at the position taken by other actors – the Commission, but also the European Defence Agency (EDA) and the member states. The latter, in particular, created the EDA with a view to opening the defence market and helping to establish a European armament industry. The ruling was also embedded in the overall development of a Common Security and Defence Policy (CSDP), and the first European civilian and military operations from 2003 onwards. The member states were, to some extent, schizophrenic actors, invoking essential security interests on the one hand, while arguing in favour of a European defence policy and a European competitive armament industry on the other. This ambiguous positioning of the member states leads to a more nuanced understanding of the Court's behaviour in the abovementioned rulings. The CJEU has most certainly opposed the member states' willingness to protect national sovereignty; yet it has been consistent with the objectives set out by the member states within the CSDP and the EDA.

Finally, new economic governance mechanisms were established by the EU as a response to the financial and economic crisis that started in 2008, in an effort to solve the debt and deficit problems. The CJEU was asked to control the legal framework of the financial mechanisms that were set up. Two cases – the *Pringle* (C–370/12) ruling and the *Gauweiler et al. vs. Deutscher Bundestag* (C–62/15) decision – illustrate the extent to which member states and the Court still refer to law when confronted with a crisis. As shown in Chapter 8, in both rulings the CJEU opted for a bold interpretation of EU law, in line with the position of the member states, who had decided to offer a flexible interpretation of the treaty provisions regarding EMU.

The Court in both cases used a functionalist logic, and both reinforced a rules-based economic and monetary union as well as defending a more political understanding of those rules in the wake of the crisis. Aware of the interests of the member states, the ECB and the Commission, the Court legitimized European policy-making by judicial (activist) interpretations.

The Court of Justice of the European Union is a dynamic actor, whose influence has grown since its establishment in 1952. It has forged a very specific identity that goes beyond the power of an international court and that makes it comparable – if not entirely similar – to a domestic supreme court. As for national courts, or institutions more generally, its role, influence and identity must be considered as characteristics that have changed in response to, and as a result of, external and internal constraints. Understanding the Court's actions is only possible by studying the interaction between them, both inside and out. The analysis of political contexts, legal doctrines and those actors that 'use' the Court is essential in order to understand the Court's rulings, its activism and restraint.

While the Court is considered to have become less active, its rulings in specific areas, such as fundamental rights, have increased. The inclusion of the Charter of Fundamental Rights in primary law since the Lisbon Treaty (2009) has opened up the legal possibility for the Court to refer to the charter as a legally binding rule. As such, the Court has ruled in this area since the 1990s. Whether we still see the Court as the central actor in the process of integration through law, or whether we concede that some of its power has slipped away, we must acknowledge its continued status as a vital and strategic supranational actor embedded in a political as well as legal environment in which it continuously strives to interpret the law.

Bibliography

255 Panel (2014). *Third Activity Report of the Panel provided for by Article 255 TFEU*, report published 13 December 2013, SN 1118/2014, 8–9.

Abbott, K. W. & Snidal, D. (2000). 'Hard and soft law in international governance', *International Organization*, vol. 54, no. 3, 421–56.

Adam, C. (2016). *The politics of judicial review: supranational acts and judicial compliance conflict in the EU*, Basingstoke: Palgrave Macmillan.

Adam, C., Bauer, M. W, Hartlapp, M. (2014). 'It is not always about winning – Domestic politics and legal success in EU annulment litigation beyond judicial constraint', *Journal of Common Market Studies*, vol. 53, no. 2, 185–200.

Alter, K. (1996). 'The European Court's political power', *West European Politics*, vol. 19, no. 3, 458–87.

Alter, K. (1998). 'Who are the "Masters of the Treaty"? European governments and the European Court of Justice', *International Organization*, vol. 52, no. 1, 121–47.

Alter, K. (2000). 'The European Union's legal system and domestic policy: spillover or backlash?', *International Organization*, vol. 54, no. 3, 489–518.

Alter, K. (2001). *Establishing the supremacy of European law: the making of an international rule of law in Europe*, Oxford: Oxford University Press.

Alter, K. (2003). 'Do international courts enhance compliance with international law?', *Review of Asian and Pacific Studies*, vol. 25, no. 25, 51–78.

Alter, K. (2006). 'Private litigants and the new international courts', *Comparative Political Studies*, vol. 39, no. 1, 22–49.

Alter, K. (2008). 'Agents or trustees? International courts in their political context', *European Journal of International Relations*, vol. 14, no. 1, 33–63.

Alter, K. (2009). *The European Court's political power*, selected essays: Oxford: Oxford University Press.

Alter, K. J. (2010). 'Tipping the balance: international courts and the construction of international and domestic politics', *Cambridge Yearbook of European Legal Studies*, vol. 13, no. 1, 1–21.

Alter, K. J. (2012). 'The global spread of European style international courts', *West European Politics*, vol. 35, no. 1, 135–54.

Alter, K. (2014). *The new terrain of international law: courts, politics, rights*, Princeton: Princeton University Press.

Alter, K. & Helfer, L. R. (2010). 'Nature or nurture? Judicial lawmaking in the European Court of Justice and the Andean Tribunal of Justice', *International Organization*, vol. 64, no. 4, 563–92.

Alter, K. & Meunier-Aitsahalia, S. (1994). 'Judicial politics in the European Community: European integration and the pathbreaking Cassis de Dijon decision', *Comparative Political Studies*, vol. 26, no. 4, 535–61.

Alter, K. & Vargas, J. (2000). 'Explaining variation in the use of European litigation strategies', *Comparative Political Studies*, vol. 33, no. 4, 452–82.

Anagnostou, D. (ed.). (2014). *Rights and courts in pursuit of social change: legal mobilization in the multi-level European system*, Oxford: Hart Publishing.

Armstrong, K. (1998). 'Legal integration: theorizing the legal dimension of European integration', *Journal of Common Market Studies,* vol. 36, no. 2, 155–74.

Armstrong, K. (2010). *Governing social inclusion: Europeanization through policy coordination*, Oxford: Oxford University Press.

Armstrong, K. (2013). 'The new governance of EU fiscal discipline', *European Law Review*, vol. 38, no. 5, 601–17.

Armstrong, K. A. (2010). *Governing social inclusion: Europeanization through policy coordination*, Oxford: Oxford University Press.

Armstrong, K. & Shaw, J. (1998). 'Integrating law: an introduction', *Journal of Common Market Studies*, vol. 36, no. 2, 147–54.

Arnold, R. (2011). *The Emergence of a European constitutional law*, Brussels: Bruylant.

Arnull, A. (1991). 'What shall we do on Sunday?', *European Law Review*, vol. 16, no. 2, 112–24.

Arnull, A. (1993). 'Owning up to fallibility: precedent and the European Court of Justice', *Common Market Law Review*, vol. 30, no. 2, 247–66.

Arnull, A. (2001). 'Private applicants and the action for annulment since Codorniu', *Common Market Law Review*, vol. 38, no. 1, 7–52.

Arnull, A. (2006). *The European Union and its Court of Justice*, Oxford: Oxford University Press.

Arnull, A. (2013). 'Judicial activism and the European Court of Justice: how should academics respond?', in de Witte, B, Dawson, M. & Muir, E. (eds), *Judicial activism at the European Court of Justice*, Cheltenham: Edward Elgar.

Arnull, A. & Chalmers, D. (eds). (2015). *The Oxford handbook of European Union law*, Oxford: Oxford University Press.

Augenstein, D., (2012). *Integration through law revisited: the making of the European polity*, Farnham: Ashgate. Available at http://cadmus.eui.eu/bitstream/handle/1814/12963/LAW_2009_19.pdf. Date accessed 31 July 2016.

Avbelj, M., & Komárek, J. (eds). (2012). *Constitutional pluralism in the European Union and beyond*, London: Bloomsbury Publishing.

Bailey, M. A., & Maltzman, F. (2008). 'Does legal doctrine matter? Unpacking law and policy preferences on the US Supreme Court', *American Political Science Review*, vol. 102, no. 3, 369–84.

Bailleux, J. (2013). 'L'Europe et ses légistes', *Politique européenne*, vol. 41, no. 3, 88–117.

Bailleux, J. (2014). *Penser l'Europe par le droit. L'intervention du droit communautaire en France*, Paris: Dalloz.

Bartolini, S. (2005). *Restructuring Europe*. Oxford: Oxford University Press.

Bauer M. W. & Hartlapp M. (2010). 'Much ado about money and how to spend it! Analysing 40 years of annulment cases against the European Commission', *European Journal of Political Research*, vol. 49, no. 2, 202–22.

Beach, D. (2001). *Between law and politics: the relationship between the European Court of Justice and EU member states*, Copenhagen: DJOF Publishing.

Beck, G. (2011). 'The Lisbon Judgment of the German Constitutional Court, the primacy of EU law and the problem of Kompetenz-Kompetenz: a conflict between right and right in which there is no Praetor', *European Law Journal*, vol. 17, no. 4, 470–94.

Beck, G., (2012). *Legal Reasoning and the European Court of Justice*, Oxford: Hart Publishing.

Beck, G. (2014). 'The Court of Justice, the Bundesverfassungsgericht and legal reasoning during the euro crisis: the rule of law as a fair-weather phenomenon', *European Public Law*, vol. 20, no. 3, 539–66.

Bell, M. (2008). *Racism and equality in the European Union*, Oxford: Oxford University Press.

Bengoetxea J. (1993). *The legal reasoning of the European Court of Justice: towards a European jurisprudence*, Oxford: Clarendon Press.

Bengoetxea, J., McCormick, N., & Moral Soriano, L. (2001). 'Integration and integrity in the legal reasoning of the European Court of Justice', in G. de Búrca & J. H. H. Weiler (eds), *The European Court of Justice*, Oxford: Oxford University Press, pp. 43–85.

Beyers, J., Eising, R., & Maloney, W. (2008). 'Researching interest group politics in Europe and elsewhere: much we study, little we know?', *West European Politics*, vol. 31, no. 6, 1103–28.

Bickerton, C. J. (2012). *European integration: from nation-states to member states*, Oxford: Oxford University Press.

Bickerton, C. J., Hodson, D., & Puetter, U. (eds). (2015). *The new intergovernmentalism: states and supranational actors in the post-Maastricht era*, Oxford: Oxford University Press.

Black, D. (1976). *The behavior of law,* New York: Academic Press.

Blauberger, M. (2009). 'Compliance with rules of negative integration: European state aid control in the new member states', *Journal of European Public Policy*, vol. 16, no. 7, 1030–46.

Blauberger, M. (2012). 'With Luxembourg in mind ... the remaking of national policies in the face of ECJ jurisprudence', *Journal of European Public Policy*, vol. 19, no. 1, 109–126.

Blauberger, M. (2014). 'National responses to European Court jurisprudence', *West European Politics,* vol. 37, no. 3, 457–74.

Blauberger, M. & Schmidt, S. K. (2014). 'Welfare migration? Free movement of EU citizens and access to social benefits', *Research & Politics*, vol. 1, no. 3.

Blauberger, M. & Weiss, M. (2013). '"If you can't beat, join me!" How the Commission pushed and pulled member states into legislating defence procurement', *Journal of European Public Policy*, vol. 20, no. 8, 1120–38.

Blyth, M. (2002). *Great transformations: economic ideas and institutional change in the twentieth century*, Cambridge: Cambridge University Press.

Bobek, M. (2008a). 'The fortress of judicial independence and the mental transitions of the Central European judiciaries', *European Public Law*, vol. 14, no. 1, 99–123.

Bobek, M. (2008b). 'Learning to talk: preliminary rulings, the courts of the new member states and the Court of Justice', *Common Market Law Review*, vol. 45, no. 6, 1611–43.

Bobek, M. (2008c). 'On the application of European law in (not only) the courts of the new member states: "Don't do as I say"', *Cambridge Yearbook of European Legal Studies*, vol. 10, no.1, 1–34.

Bobek, M. (2013). *Comparative reasoning in European supreme courts*, Oxford: Oxford University Press.

Bobek, M. (2014a). 'Landtová, Holubec, and the problem of an uncooperative Court: implications for the Preliminary Rulings Procedure', *European Constitutional Law Review*, vol. 10, no. 1, 54–89.

Bobek, M. (2014b). 'The Court of Justice of the European Union', Research Paper in Law, 02/2014, Department of European Legal Studies, European University Institute.

Bobek, M. (ed.). (2015). *Selecting Europe's judges. a critical review of the appointment procedures to the European courts*, Oxford: Oxford University Press.

Boerger-De Smedt, A. (2012). 'Negotiating the foundations of European Law, 1950–57: the legal history of the Treaties of Paris and Rome', *Contemporary European History*, vol. 21, no. 3, 339–56.

Bogdanor, V. (2007). *Legitimacy, accountability and democracy in the European Union*, Federal Trust for Education and Research.

Bonjour, S. and Vink, M. (2013). 'When Europeanization backfires: the normalization of European migration politics', *Acta Politica*, vol. 48, no. 4, 389–407.

Börzel, T. A. (2006). 'Participation through law enforcement: the case of the European Union', *Comparative Political Studies*, vol. 39, no. 1, 128–52.

Börzel T. A., Hofmann T. & Panke D., (2012). 'Caving in or sitting it out? Longitudinal patterns of non-compliance in the European Union', *Journal of European Public Policy*, vol. 19, no. 4.

Bouwen, P. & McCown, M. (2007). 'Lobbying versus litigation: political and legal strategies of interest representation in the European Union', *Journal of European Public Policy*, vol. 14, no. 3, 422–43.

Bribosia, H. (1998). 'The Italian Constitutional Court and the relationship between the Italian legal system and the European Union', in A.-M. Slaughter, A. Stone Sweet, & J. H. H. Weiler (eds), *The European courts and national courts*, Oxford: Hart Publishing, pp. 1–39.

Bribosia, E., Scheek, L., & Ubeda De Torres, A. (2010). *L'Europe des cours: Loyautés et résistances*, Brussels: Bruylant.

Broberg, M. & Fenger, N. (2010). *Preliminary references to the European Court of Justice*, Oxford: Oxford University Press.

Brown, L. N. & Kennedy, T. (2000). *Court of Justice of the European Communities*, Hebden Bridge, Sweet & Maxwell.

Bücker, A. (2010). 'The decisions of the European Court of Justice in the Viking, Laval and Rüffert cases from a German legal perspective', in A. Bücker and W. Warneck (eds), *Report 111: Viking – Laval – Rüffert: Consequences and policy perspectives: European Trade Union Institute*, pp. 29–49.

Bulman-Pozen, J., & Gerken, H. K. (2009). 'Uncooperative federalism', *The Yale Law Journal*, vol. 118, no. 7, 1256–1310.

De Búrca, G., De Witte, B., & Ogertschnig, L. (eds)(2005). *Social rights in Europe*, Oxford: Oxford University Press.

Burley, A.-M. & Mattli, W., (1993). 'Europe before the Court: a political theory of legal integration', *International Organization*, vol. 47, no. 1, 41–76.

Caldeira, G. A. (1987). 'Public opinion and the US Supreme Court', *American Political Science Review*, vol. 81, no. 4, 1139–53.

Caldeira, G. A. & Gibson J. L. (1995). The legitimacy of the Court of Justice in the European Union: models of institutional support', *American Political Science Review,* 89, June 1995, pp. 356–76.

Caldeira, G. A. & Gibson, J. L. (1998). 'Changes in the legitimacy of the European Court of Justice', *British Journal of Political Science*, vol. 28, no. 1, 63–91.

Caldeira, G. A. & Gibson, J. L. (1992). 'The etiology of public support for the Supreme Court', *American Journal of Political Science*, vol. 36, no. 3, 635–64.

Caldeira, G. A. & Gibson, J. L. (1997). 'Democracy and legitimacy in the European Union', *International Social Science Journal*, vol. 49, no. 2, 209–24.

Cappelletti, M., Secombe, M. & Weiler J. H. H. (1986). *Integration through law: Europe and the American federal experience: consumer law, common markets and federalism in Europe and the United States*, New York: Walter de Gruyter & Co.

Carrubba, C. J. (2003). 'The European Court of Justice, democracy and enlargement', *European Union Politics*, vol. 4, no. 1, 75–100.

Carrubba, C. J. & Murrah, L. (2005). 'Legal integration and use of the preliminary ruling process in the European Union', *International Organization*, vol. 59, no. 2, 399–418.

Carrubba, C. J., Gabel, M. & Hankla, C. (2008). 'Judicial behavior under political constraints: evidence from the European Court of Justice', *American Political Science Review*, vol. 102, no. 4, pp. 435–52.

Carrubba, C. J., Gabel, M. & Hankla, C. (2012). 'Understanding the role of the European Court of Justice in European integration', *American Political Science Review*, vol. 106, no. 1, pp. 214–24.

Cass, D. (2005). *The constitutionalization of the World Trade Organization*, Oxford: Oxford University Press.

Cattelan V. (ed.) (2012). *Integration through legal education? The role of EU legal studies in shaping the EU*, Bologna: Il Mulino.

Chalmers, D. & Chaves, D. (2012). 'The reference points of EU judicial politics', *Journal of European Public Policy*, vol. 19, no. 1, 25–42.

Chalmers, D., Davies, G., & Monti, G. (2010). *European Union law: cases and materials*, Cambridge: Cambridge University Press.

Chalmers, D., Davies, G., & Monti G. (2014). *European Union law*, Cambridge: Cambridge University Press.

Chalmers, D., Davies, G., & Monti, G. (2010). *European Union law: cases and materials*. Cambridge: Cambridge University Press.

Chalmers, D. (1997). 'Judicial preferences and the Community legal order', *The Modern Law Review*, vol. 60, no. 2, 164–99.

Chalmers, D. (2015). 'Judicial performance, membership, and design at the Court of Justice', in M. Bobek (ed), *Selecting Europe's judges. A critical review of the appointment procedures to the European Courts*, Oxford: Oxford University Press, pp. 51–77.

Christensen, A., & Malmstedt, M. (2000). 'Lex Loci Laboris versus Lex Loci Domicilii: an inquiry into the normative foundations of European social security law', *European Journal of Social Security*, vol. 2, no. 1, 69–111.

Chutkow, D. (2008). 'Jurisdiction stripping', *Journal of Politics*, vol. 70, no. 4, 1053–64.

Cichowski, R. (1998). 'Integrating the environment: the European Court and the construction of supranational policy', *Journal of European Public Policy*, vol. 5, no. 3, 387–405.

Cichowski, R. (2004). 'Women's rights, the European Court and supranational constitutionalism', *Law & Society Review*, vol. 38, no. 3, 489–512.

Cichowski, R. (2006). 'Courts, rights and democratic participation', *Comparative Political Studies*, vol. 39, no. 1, 50–75.

Cichowski, R. (2007). *The European Court and civil society: litigation, mobilization and governance*, Cambridge: Cambridge University Press.

Cichowski, R. & Stone Sweet, A. (2004). 'Sex equality', in A. Stone Sweet (ed.), *The judicial construction of Europe*, Oxford: Oxford University Press, pp. 147–97.

CJEU, (2013). Annual Report 2012, Synopsis of the Work of the Court of Justice, the General Court and the Civil Service Tribunal, Luxembourg.

Claes, M. (2006). *The national courts' mandate in the European Constitution*, Oxford: Hart Publishing.

Clark, T. (2009). 'The separation of powers, court curbing, and judicial legitimacy', *American Journal of Political Science,* vol. 53, no. 4, 971–89.

Clark, T. (2011). *The limits of judicial independence*, New York: Cambridge University Press.

Cohen, A. (2008). 'Scarlet robes, dark suits', EUI Working Papers, RSCAS 2008/35, RSCAS/EUI, Florence. http://cadmus.eui.eu/bitstream/handle/1814/10029/EUI_RSCAS_2008_35.pdf?sequence=1&isAllowed=y. Date accessed 4 April 2016.

Cohen, A. (2010). 'Dix personnages majestueux en longue robe amarante', *Revue française de science politique,* Vol.60, no.2, 227–46.

Cohen, A. (2012). 'The European Court of Justice in the emergent European field of power: transnational judicial institutions and national career paths', in Y. Dezalay & G. Garth Bryant (eds), *Lawyers and the Construction of transnational justice*, London, Routledge, pp. 239–57.

Commission (2008). White Paper on damages actions for breach of the EC antitrust rules COM(2008). 165 final.

Commission (2011). Communication from the Commission – Implementation of Article 260(3). of the Treaty, OJEU C 12 of 15 January 2011.

Commission (2013). 31st Annual Report on the Application of EU Law.

Commission (2014a). Report from the Commission 31st Annual Report on Monitoring the Application of EU Law (2013), COM(2014)12 final.

Commission (2014b). Communication from the Commission, C–6767 final, 17.9.2014.

Conant, L. (2001). 'Europeanization and the courts', in M. Green Cowles, J. Caporaso & T. Risse (eds), *Transforming Europe*, Ithaca, NY: Cornell University Press, pp. 97–115.

Conant, L. (2002). *Justice contained: law and politics in the European Union*, Ithaca, NY: Cornell University Press.

Conant, L. (2006). 'Individuals, courts, and the development of European social rights', *Comparative Political Studies*, vol. 39, no. 1, 76–100.

Conant, L. (2007). 'Review article: The politics of legal integration', *Journal of Common Market Studies*, vol. 45, no. 1, 45–66.

Constantinesco, V. (1995). L'émergence d'un droit constitutionnel européen, RUDH, 445.
Conway, G. (2014). *The limits of legal reasoning and the European Court of Justice*, Cambridge: Cambridge University Press.
Cooter, R. & Ginsburg, T. (1996). 'Comparative judicial discretion: an empirical test of econometric models', *International Review of Law and Economics*, vol. 16, no. 3, 295–314.
Coppel, J. & O'Neill, A. (1992), 'The European Court of Justice: taking rights seriously?', *Legal Studies*, vol. 12, no. 2, 227–39.
Corrias, L. (2011). *The passivity of law: competence and constitution in the European Court of Justice*, Dordrecht: Springer.
Costa, O. (2003). 'The European Court of Justice and democratic control in the European Union', *Journal of European Public Policy*, vol. 10, no. 5, 740–61.
Costello, C. & Davies, G. (2006). 'The case law of the Court of Justice in the field of sex equality since 2000', *Common Market Law Review*, vol. 43, no. 6, 1567–616.
Craig, P. P. (1995). 'The European Court and National Courts, Doctrine and Jurisprudence: Legal Change in its Social Context, Report on the United Kingdom'. *EUI RSC*; 1995/29, http://hdl.handle.net/1814/1404 accessed on 27 July 2016.
Craig, P. (2001). 'The jurisdiction of the community courts reconsidered', in G. de Búrca, & J. H. H. Weiler, *The European Court of Justice*, Oxford: Oxford University Press, pp. 177–214.
Craig, P. (2003). 'Standing, rights, and the structure of legal argument', *European Public Law*, vol. 9, no. 4, 493–508.
Craig, P. (2013). 'Pringle: legal reasoning, text, purpose and teleology', *Maastricht Journal of European and Comparative Law*, vol. 20, no. 1, 9.
Craig, P. & de Búrca, G. (2007). *EU law*, Oxford: Oxford University Press.
Craig, P., & G. de Búrca (2008). *EU law text, cases, and materials*, Oxford: Oxford University Press.
Craig, P. & de Búrca, G. (2011). *EU law*, Oxford: Oxford University Press.
Crespy, A. (2012). *Qui a peur de Bolkestein? Conflit, résistance et démocratie dans l'Union européenne*, Paris: Economica.
Cross, F. & Nelson, B. (2001). 'Strategic institutional effects on Supreme Court decisionmaking', *Northwestern University Law Review*, vol. 95, no. 4, 1437–94.
Cullen, H. & Charlesworth, A. (1999). 'Diplomacy by other means: the use of legal basis litigation as a political strategy by the European Parliament and member states', *Common Market Law Review*, vol. 36, no. 6, 1243–70.
D'Onorio, J.-B. (2005). 'La pseudo-« Constitution européenne » : de l'abus de langage à l'abus de droit', *Recueil Dalloz*, vol. 181, no.20, 1302–07.

Davies, A. C. (2008). 'One step forward, two steps back? The Viking and Laval cases in the ECJ', *Industrial Law Journal*, vol. 37, no. 2, 126–48.

Davies, B. (2012a). *Resisting the European Court of Justice: West Germany's confrontation with European law, 1949–1979*, Cambridge: Cambridge University Press.

Davies, B. (2012b). 'Pushing back: what happens when member states resist the European Court of Justice? A multi-modal approach to the history of European law', *Contemporary European History*, vol. 21, no. 3, 417–35.

Davies, B. (2015). 'Resistance to European law and constitutional identity in Germany: Herbert Kraus and Solange in its intellectual context', *European Law Journal*, vol. 21, no. 4, 434–59.

Davies, G. (2003). *Nationality discrimination in the European internal market*, Amsterdam: Kluwer law international.

Davies, G. (2007). 'The effect of Mrs Watts' trip to France on the National Health Service', *King's Law Journal*, vol. 18, no. 1, 158–67.

Davies, G. (2012). 'Activism relocated. The self-restraint of the European Court of Justice in its national context', *Journal of European Public Policy*, vol. 19, no. 1, 76–91.

Davies, G. (2014). 'Legislative control of the European Court of Justice', *Common Market Law Review*, vol. 51, no. 6, 1579–607.

Dawson, M. (2011). *New governance and the transformation of European law: coordinating EU social law and policy*, Cambridge: Cambridge University Press.

Dawson, M. (2014). 'How does the European Court of Justice reason? A review essay on the legal reasoning of the European Court of Justice', *European Law Journal*, vol. 20, no. 3, 423–35.

De Búrca, G. (1995). 'The language of rights and European integration', in J. Shaw and G. More (eds), *New legal dynamics of European Union*, Oxford: Clarendon Press, pp. 29–54.

De Búrca, G. (1998). 'The principle of subsidiarity and the Court of Justice as an institutional actor', *Journal of Common Market Studies*, vol. 36, no. 2, 217–35.

De Búrca, G. (2005). 'Rethinking law in neofunctionalist theory', *Journal of European Public Policy*, vol. 12, no. 2, 310–26.

De Búrca, G. & Weiler, J. H. H. (eds). (2001). *The European Court of Justice*, Oxford: Oxford University Press.

De Búrca, G. (2010). 'The European Court of Justice and the international legal order After Kadi', 51 *Harvard International Law Journal*, vol. 1, no. 2.

De Waele, H. & van der Vleuten, A. (2011). 'Judicial activism in the European Court of Justice, the case of LGBT rights, Michigan State', *Journal of International Law*, vol. 19, no. 3, 639–66.

De Witte, B. (2010). 'The continuous significance of Van Gend en Loos', in M. Poiares Maduro & L. Azoulai (eds), *The past and future of EU law,*

The classics of EU law revisited on the 50th anniversary of the Rome Treaty, Oxford and Portland: Hart Publishing, pp. 9–15.

De Witte, B., Muir, E., & Dawson, M. (2013). *Judicial activism at the European Court of Justice*, Cheltenham: Edward Elgar Publishing.

De Witte, B. & Vauchez, A. (eds), (2013). *Lawyering Europe: European law as a transnational social field*, Oxford: Hart Publishing.

Dehousse, R. (1998). *The European Court of Justice: the politics of judicial integration*, Basingstoke: Palgrave Macmillan.

Dehousse, R. (2011). *The "community method": obstinate or obsolete?*, Basingstoke: Palgrave Macmillan.

Delmas-Marty, M. (2006). *Le pluralisme ordonné et les interactions entre ensembles juridiques*, Paris: Dalloz.

Delpeuch, T., Dumoulin, L., & De Galembert, C. (2014). *Sociologie du droit et de la justice,* Paris: Armand Colin.

Dinan, D. (2004). *Europe recast: a history of European Union*, Basingstoke: Palgrave Macmillan.

Doherty, B., & Hayes, G. (2014). 'having your day in court: judicial opportunity and tactical choice in anti-GMO campaigns in France and the United Kingdom', *Comparative Political Studies*, vol. 47, no. 1, 3–29.

Dougan, M. (2009). 'Expanding the frontiers of union citizenship by dismantling the boundaries of the national welfare states', in C. Barnard & O. Odudu (eds), *The outer limits of European Union law*. Oxford: Hart Publishing.

Dougan, M. (2013). 'The bubble that burst: exploring the legitimacy of the case law on the free movement of Union citizens', in M. Adams, H. de Waele, J. Meeusen, & G. Straetmans, *Judging Europe's judges. The legitimacy of the case law of the European Court of Justice*, Oxford: Hart Publishing, pp. 127–154.

Dyevre, A. (2011). 'The German Federal Constitutional Court and European judicial politics', *West European Politics*, vol. 34, no. 2, 346–61.

Dyevre, A. (2012). 'Judicial non-compliance in a non-hierarchical legal order: isolated accident or omen of judicial Armageddon?' *Max Planck Institute for International and Comparative Law,* Working paper.

Edelman, L. B., Leachman, G., & McAdam, D. (2010). 'On law, organizations, and social movements', *Annual Review of Law and Social Science*, vol. 6, 653–85.

Eliantonio, M., & Kas, B. (2010). 'Private parties and the annulment procedure: can the gap in the European system of judicial protection be closed?', *Journal of Politics and Law*, vol. 3, no. 2, 121–33.

Ellis E. (2010). 'The impact of the Lisbon Treaty on gender equality', *European Gender Equality Law Review*, vol. 1, 7–13.

Emiliou, N. (1994). 'Opening Pandora's box: the legal basis of Community measures before the Court of Justice', *European Law Review*, vol. 19, 488–507.

Epp, C. R. (1998). *The rights revolution: lawyers, activists, and Supreme Courts in comparative perspective*, Chicago: University of Chicago Press.

Epstein, L., Kobylka, J. F., & Stewart, J. (1995). *A theory of interest groups and litigation,* Greenwich, CT: JAI Press.

Epstein, L. & Knight, J. (1998). *The choices justices make*, Washington, DC: Congressional Quarterly Press.

Eskridge, W. (1991). 'Overriding Supreme Court statutory interpretation decisions', *The Yale Law Journal*, vol. 101, no. 2, 331–455.

Everson, M., & Eisner, J. (2007). *The making of a European constitution: judges and law beyond constitutive power*, London: Routledge.

European Network of Legal Experts in the Non-discrimination Field (2006). European Antidiscrimination Law Review, no.3, available at http://ec.europa.eu/justice/discrimination/files/lawrev3_en.pdf, accessed 31 July 2016.

European Parliament. (2008). Report on the Role of the National Judge in the European Judicial System. A6-0224/2008

Everson, M. (1998). 'Beyond the Bundesverfassungsgericht: on the necessary cunning of constitutional reasoning', *European Law Journal*, vol. 4, no.4, 389–410.

Everson, M. (2015). 'An exercise in legal honesty: rewriting the Court of Justice and the Bundesverfassungsgericht', *European Law Journal*, vol. 21, no. 4, 474–99.

Fahey, E., & Bardutzky, S. (2013). 'Judicial review of Eurozone law: the adjudication of postnational norms in EU courts, Plural-A case study of the European Stability Mechanism', *Michigan Journal of International Law online,* available at http://openaccess.city.ac.uk/6299/, accessed on 31 July 2016.

Fairhurst, J. (2007). *Law of the European Union*, London: Pearson Education.

Falkner, G. (ed) (2011). *The EU's decision traps: comparing policies*, Oxford: Oxford University Press.

Falkner, G. (2015). 'Fines against member states: an effective new tool in EU infringement proceedings?', *Comparative European Politics,* advance online publication 9 March 2015; doi: 10.1057/cep.2015.8

Fassbender, B. (1998). 'The United Nations Charter as constitution of the international community', *Columbia Journal of International Law*, vol. 36, no. 3, 529–619.

Fassbender, B. (2007). 'We the peoples of the United Nations, constituent power and the constitutional form in international law', in M. Loughlin & N. Walker (eds), *The paradox of constitutionalism, constituent power and constitutional form*, Oxford: Oxford University Press, p. 269.

Faull, J., & Nikpay, A. (2014). *The EU law of competition*, Oxford: Oxford University Press.

Ferejohn, J. (1998). 'Independent judges, dependent judiciary: explaining judicial independence', *Southern California Law Review*, vol. 72, no. 2–3, 353–84.

Ferejohn, J. & Kramer, L. (2002). 'Independent judges, dependent judiciary: institutionalizing judicial restraint', *NYU Law Review*, vol. 77, no. 4, 962–1039.

Ferrera, M. (2003). 'European integration and national social citizenship changing boundaries, new structuring?', *Comparative Political Studies*, vol. 36, no. 6, pp. 611–52.

Ferrera, M. (2005). *The boundaries of welfare: European integration and the new spatial politics of social protection*, Oxford: Oxford University Press.

Figueiredo, J. & Tiller, E. (1996). 'Congressional control of the courts', *Journal of Law and Economics*, vol. 39, no. 2, 435–61.

Fisher, L. (1988). *Constitutional dialogues: interpretation as political process*, Princeton: Princeton University Press.

Fligstein, N. (2008). *Euroclash. The EU, European identity, and the future of Europe*, Oxford: Oxford University Press

Foster, N. (2014). *EU law*, Oxford University Press.

Garrett, G. (1992). 'International cooperation and institutional choice: the European Community's internal market', *International Organization*, vol. 46, no. 2, 533–60.

Garrett, G. (1995). 'The politics of legal integration in the European Union', *International Organization*, vol. 49, no. 1, 171–81.

Garrett, G. & Tsebelis, G. (2001). 'The institutional foundations of intergovernmentalism and supranationalism in the European Union', *International Organization*, vol. 55, no. 2, 357–90.

Garrett, G. & Weingast, B. (1993). 'Ideas, interests, and institutions: constructing the European Community's internal market', in J. Goldstein and R. O. Keohane (eds.), *Ideas and foreign policy: beliefs, institutions, and political change*. Ithaca, NY: Cornell University Press, pp. 173–206.

Garrett, G. (1995). 'The politics of legal integration in the European Union', 49 *International Organization* p. 171.

Garrett, G. and Tsebelis, G. (2000). 'Legislative politics in the European Union', *European Union Politics*, vol. 1, no. 1, 9–36.

Garrett, G., Kelemen, D. R. & Schulz, H. (1998). 'The European Court of Justice, national governments, and legal integration in the European Union', *International Organization*, vol. 52, no. 1, 149–76.

Genschel, P. (2007). 'Why no mutual recognition of VAT? Regulation, taxation and the integration of the EU's internal market for goods', *Journal of European Public Policy*, vol. 14, no. 5, 743–61.

Genschel, P. (2011). 'One trap, many exits, but no free lunch: How the joint-decision trap shapes EU tax policy', in G. Falkner (ed.), *The EU's decision traps: comparing policies*, Oxford: Oxford University Press, pp. 54–73.

Genschel, P., & Jachtenfuchs, M. (2011). 'How the European Union constrains the state: multilevel governance of taxation', *European Journal of Political Research*, vol. 50, no. 3, 293–314.

Genschel, P. & Jachtenfuchs, M. (eds). (2013). *Beyond the regulatory polity? The European integration of core state powers*, Oxford: Oxford University Press.

Genschel, P., Kemmerling, A., & Seils, E. (2011). 'Accelerating downhill: How the EU shapes corporate tax competition in the single market', *Journal of Common Market Studies,* vol. 49, no. 3, 585–606.

Geradin, D. (2005). 'The EC fining policy for violations of competition law: An empirical review of the Commission decisional practice and the Community courts' judgments', *The Global Competition Law Centre Working Papers Series*, 03/05, College of Europe.

Gerkrath, J. (1997). *L'émergence d'un droit constitutionnel pour l'Europe*, Ed. de L'Université de Bruxelles.

Ginsburg, T. (2005). 'Bounded discretion in international judicial lawmaking', *Virginia Journal of International Law*, vol. 43, no. 3, 631–73.

Glick, D. (2009). 'Conditional strategic retreat', *The Journal of Politics*, vol. 71, no. 3, 800–16.

Gofas, A., & Hay, C. (eds). (2010). *The role of ideas in political analysis: a portrait of contemporary debates*, London: Routledge.

Golub, J. (1996). 'The politics of judicial discretion: rethinking the interaction between national courts and the European Court of Justice', *West European Politics*, vol. 19, no. 2, 360–85.

Gormley, J. W. (1985). 'Prohibiting restrictions on trade within the EEC, The theory and application of articles 30-36 of the EEC treaty', The Hague, T.M.C. Asser Instituut.

Gormley Jr, W. T. (1986). 'Regulatory issue networks in a federal system', *Polity*, vol. 18, no. 4, 595–620.

Granger, M.-P. (2004). 'When governments go to Luxembourg ... the influence of governments on the Court of Justice', *European Law Review*, vol. 29, 3–31.

Granger, M.-P. (2015). 'The Court of Justice's dilemma – between more Europe and constitutional mediation', in C. J. Bickerton, D. Hodson & U. Puetter (eds). (2015). *The new intergovernmentalism: states and supranational actors in the post-Maastricht era*, Oxford: Oxford University Press, pp. 208–26.

Graziano, P. R., & Halpern, C. (2016). 'EU governance in times of crisis: Inclusiveness and effectiveness beyond the "hard" and "soft" law divide', *Comparative European Politics*, vol. 14, no. 1, 1–19.

Greenwood, J. (2011). *Interest representation in the European Union*, Basingstoke: Palgrave Macmillan.

Greer, S. and Jarman, H. (2012). 'Managing risks in EU health services policy: spot markets, legal certainty and bureaucratic resistance', *Journal of European Social Policy*, vol. 22, no. 3, 259–72.

Greer, S. L. (2006). 'Uninvited Europeanization: neofunctionalism and the EU in health policy', *Journal of European Public Policy*, vol. 13, no. 1, 134–52.

Greer, S. L. (2009). *The politics of European Union health policies*, Berkshire: McGraw-Hill Education-Open University Press.

Greer, S. L. & Martín de Almagro Iniesta, M. (2014). 'How bureaucracies listen to courts: bureaucratized calculations and European law', *Law & Social Inquiry*, vol. 39, no. 2, 361–86.

Grimm, D. (2009). 'Defending sovereign statehood against transforming the Union into a state', *European Constitutional Law Review*, vol.5, no. 3, 353–73.

Grimmel, A. (2010). 'Judicial interpretation or judicial activism?: the legacy of rationalism in the studies of the European Court of Justice', Centre for European Studies, Working Paper Series, no. 176.

Grimmel, A. (2011). 'Integration and the context of law: why the European Court of Justice is not a political actor', Les Cahiers européens de Sciences Po, 3, Centre d'études européennes at Sciences Po.

Grimmel, A. (2012). 'Judicial interpretation or judicial activism? The legacy of rationalism in the studies of the European Court of justice', *European Law Journal* vol. 18, no. 4, 518–35.

Grimmel, A. (2014). 'The uniting of Europe by transclusion: understanding the contextual conditions of integration through law', *Journal of European Integration,* vol. 36, no. 6, 549–66.

Grossman, E., & Saurugger, S. (2012). *Les groupes d'intérêt: Action collective et stratégies de representation,* Paris: Armand Colin.

Guieu, J.-M. (2012). 'The debate about a European institutional order among international legal scholars in the 1920s and its legacy', *Contemporary European History*, vol. 21, no. 3, 319–337.

Haas, P. (1992). 'Introduction: epistemic communities and international policy coordination', *International Organization*, vol. 46, no. 1, 1–35.

Handberg, R. and Hill, H. (1980). 'Court curbing, court reversals, and judicial review', *Law & Society Review*, vol. 14, no. 2, 309–22.

Harding, C. (1992). 'Who goes to court in Europe?', *European Law Review*, vol. 17, 104–125.

Harlow, C. (1992). 'A community of interests? Making the most of European law', *The Modern Law Review*, vol. 55, no. 3, 331–50.

Harlow, C. & Rawlings, R. (1992). *Pressure through law*, London: Routledge.

Hartlapp, M. (2014). 'Enforcing social Europe though labour inspectorates: changes in capacity and cooperation across Europe', in *West European Politics*, vol. 37, no. 4, 805–24.

Hartley, T. (1996). 'The European Court, judicial objectivity and the Constitution of the European Union', *Law Quarterly Review*, vol. 112, 95–109.

Helfer, L. R. & Slaughter, A.-M. (1997). 'Toward a theory of effective supranational adjudication', *Yale Law Journal*, vol. 107, no. 2, 273–391.

Herzog, R. & Gerken, L. (2008). 'Stop the European Court of Justice', in EU Observer, Available at https://euobserver.com/opinion/26714. Accessed 31 July 2016.

Hillion, C. (2007). 'Negotiating Turkey's membership to the European Union. Can the member states do as they please?', *European Constitutional Law Review*, vol. 3, 269–284.

Hillion, C. (2014), 'A powerless court? The European Court of Justice and the Common Foreign and Security Policy', in M. Cremona and A. Thies (eds), *The ECJ and external relations: constitutional challenges*, Oxford: Hart Publishing, pp. 47–70.

Hillion, C. & Wessel, R.A. (2009). 'Competence distribution in EU external relations after Ecowas: clarification or continued fuzziness?', *Common Market Law Review,* vol. 46, no. 2, 551–86.

Hilson, C. (2002). 'New social movements: the role of legal opportunity', *Journal of European Public Policy*, vol. 9, no. 2, 238–55.

Hodges, C. (2009), 'European Union legislation'. *Annals of the American Academy of Political and Social Science*, vol. 622, no.1, 78–85.

Holzhacker, R. (2012). 'National and transnational strategies of LGBT civil society organizations in different political environments: modes of interaction in Western and Eastern Europe for equality', *Comparative European Politics*, vol. 10, no. 1, 23–47.

Hong, Q. L. (2010). 'Constitutional review in the Mega-Leviathan: a democratic foundation for the European Court of Justice', *European Law Journal*, vol. 16, no. 6, 695–716.

Hooghe, L., & Marks, G. (2009). 'A postfunctionalist theory of European integration: from permissive consensus to constraining dissensus', *British Journal of Political Science*, vol. 39, no. 1, 1–23.

Hornuf, L., & Voigt, S. (2014). 'Analyzing preliminary references as the powerbase of the European Court of Justice', *European Journal of Law and Economics*, vol. 39, no. 2, 287–311.

Horsley, T. (2012). 'Subsidiarity and the European Court of Justice: missing pieces in the subsidiarity jigsaw?', *Journal of Common Market Studies*, vol. 50, no. 2, 267–82.

Hoskyns, C. (1996). *Integrating gender: women, law and politics in the European Union*, London: Verso.

Howard, E. (2009). 'Equality – a fundamental right in the EU?', *International Journal of Discrimination and the Law*, vol. 10, no. 1, 19–38.

Howard, E. (2012). 'EU equality law: three recent developments', *European Law Journal*, vol. 17, no. 6, 785–803.

Hübner, D. C. (2015). The 'National Decisions' database (Dec. Nat): introducing a database on national courts' interactions with European law', *European Union Politics*, doi.1465116515613453.

Itzcovitch, G. (2009). 'The interpretation of Community law by the European Court of Justice', *German Law Journal*, vol. 10, no. 5, 537–60.

Jabko, N. (2006). *Playing the market: a political strategy for uniting Europe, 1985–2005*, Ithaca, NY: Cornell University Press.

Jacobs, F. (2006). 'The role of the European Court of Justice in the enforcement of the protection of environmental law', *Journal of Environmental Law*, vol. 18 no. 2, 185–205.

Jaklic, K. (2014). *Constitutional pluralism in the EU*, Oxford: Oxford University Press.

Jacquot, S., & Vitale, T. (2014). 'Law as weapon of the weak? A comparative analysis of legal mobilization by Roma and women's groups at the European level', *Journal of European Public Policy*, vol. 21, no. 4, 587–604.

Joerges, C., & Neyer, J. (1997). 'From intergovernmental bargaining to deliberative political processes: the constitutionalisation of comitology', *European Law Journal*, vol. 3, no. 3, 273–99.

Joerges, C., & Rödl, F. (2009). 'Informal politics, formalised law and the "Social Deficit" of European integration: reflections after the judgments of the ECJ in Viking and Laval', *European Law Journal*, vol. 15, no. 1, 1–19.

Jones, A., & Davies, J. (2014). 'Merger control and the public interest: balancing EU and national law in the protectionist debate', *European Competition Journal*, vol. 10, no, 3, 453–97.

Jones E., Kelemen R. D., & Meunier S. (2016). 'Failing forward? The Euro crisis and the incomplete nature of European integration', *Comparative Political Studies*, vol. 49, no. 7, 1010–34.

Jupille, J., & Caporaso, J. A. (1998). 'States, agency, and rules: the European Union in global environmental politics', in C. Rhodes (ed), *The European Union in the world community*, Boulder, CO: Lynn Rienner, pp. 157–82.

Jupille, J. & Caporaso, J. (2009). 'Domesticating discourses: European law, English judges and political institutions', *European Political Science Review*, vol. 1, no. 2, 205–228.

Kagan, R. (1997). 'Should Europe worry about adversarial legalism?', *Oxford Journal of Legal Studies*, vol. 17, no. 2, 165–83.

Kagan, R. 2007. 'Globalization and legal change: the "Americanization" of European Law?', *Regulation & Governance*, vol. 1, no. 2, 99–120.

Keeleng, D. (1998). 'In praise of judicial activism, but what does it mean? And has the European Court of Justice ever practised it?', in Curti Gialdino (ed) *Scritti In Onore Di G. F. Mancini*, Milano: Curti Gialdino ed.

Kelemen, D. R. (2001). 'The limits of judicial power, trade-environment disputes in the GATT/WTO and the EU', *Comparative Political Studies*, vol. 34, no. 6, 622–50.

Kelemen, D. R. (2002). 'Survey of European interest groups', Results on file with author and with Princeton University Survey Research Center.

Kelemen, D. R. (2011). *Eurolegalism: the transformation of law and regulation in the European Union*, Cambridge, MA: Harvard University Press.

Kelemen, D. R. (2012a). 'The political foundations of judicial independence in the European Union', *Journal of European Public Policy*, vol. 19, no. 1, 43–58.

Kelemen, D. R. (2012b). 'Eurolegalism and democracy', *Journal of Common Market Studies*, vol. 50, no. s1, 55–71.

Kelemen, D. R. (2012c). 'The political foundations of judicial independence in the European Union', *Journal of European Public Policy*, vol. 19, no. 1, 43–58.

Kelemen, D. R. & Schmidt, S. K. (2012). 'Introduction – the European Court of Justice and legal integration: perpetual momentum?' *Journal of European Public Policy*, vol. 19, no. 1, 1–7.

Kenney, S. (1998). 'The members of the Court of Justice of the European Communities', *Columbia Journal of European Law*, vol. 5, no. 1, 101–33.

Keohane, R. O., Moravcsik A. & Slaughter, A.-M. (2000). 'Legalized dispute resolution: interstate and transnational', *International Organization*, vol. 54, no. 3, 457–88.

Kilbey, I. (2010). 'The interpretation of Article 260 TFEU (ex 228 EC)', *European Law Review*, vol. 35, no. 3, 370–86.

Kilpatrick, C. (1998). 'Community or communities of courts in European integration? Sex equality dialogues between UK courts and the ECJ', *European Law Journal*, vol. 4, no. 2, 121–47.

Kilpatrick, C. (2009). 'Laval's regulatory conundrum: collective standard-setting and the Court's new approach to posted workers', *European Law Review*, vol. 34, no. 6, 844–65.

Kloka, M. & Schmidt, S. K. (2015). 'Legislative and judicial politics in the post-Maastricht era: the intergovernmentalist paradox in the Council', in C. Bickerton, D. Hodson & U. Putter (eds), *European politics in the post-Maastricht era: states, supranational actors and the new intergovernmentalism*, Oxford: Oxford University Press.

Kornhauser, L. and Sager, L. (1986). 'Unpacking the court', *Yale Law Journal*, vol. 96, 115–17.

Koukouris-Spiliotopoulos, S. (2008). 'The Lisbon Treaty and the Charter of Fundamental Rights: maintaining and developing the acquis in gender equality', *European Gender Equality law Review*, vol. 1, no.1, 15–24.

Kramer, L. (2012). *EU environmental law*, Oxford: Oxford University Press.

Kruper, R., (1998). *The politics of the European Court of Justice*, London: Kogan Page.

Larsson, O. & Naurin, D. (2016). 'Legislative override of constitutional courts: the case of the European Union', *International Organizations*, vol. 70, no. 2, 377–408.

Larsson, O., Naurin, D., Derlen, M. & Lindholm, J. (2016). 'Speaking law to power: the strategic use of precedent of the Court of Justice of the European Union', *Comparative Political Studies*, doi: 10.1177/0010414016639709.

Lasser, M. de S.-O. -l'E. (2009). *Judicial deliberations: a comparative analysis of transparency and legitimacy*, Oxford: Oxford University Press.

Lasser, W. (1988). *The limits of judicial power*, Chapel Hill, NC: University of North Carolina Press.

Leczykiewicz, D. (2008). 'Why do the European Court of Justice judges need legal concepts?', *European Law Journal*, vol. 14, no. 6, 773–86.

Leibfried, S. (2010). 'Social policy: left to the judges and the markets?', in H. S. Wallace, W. Wallace, M. A. Pollack, H. Wallace & A. R. Young (eds), *Policy-making in the European Union*, Oxford: Oxford University Press, pp. 253–83.

Lenaerts, K. (1991). 'Some reflections on the separation of powers in the European Community', *Common Market Law Review*, vol. 28, 11–35.

Lenaerts, K., Corthaut, T. (2004). 'Judicial review as a contribution to the development of European constitutionalism', in T. Tridimas & P. Nebbia (eds), *European Union law for the twenty-first century*, Oxford: Oxford University Press, vol. 1, pp. 17–64.

Lenaerts, K. (2007). 'The rule of law and the coherence of the judicial system of the European Union', *Common Market Law Review*, vol. 44, no. 6, 1625–59.

Leron, N. (2014). 'La gouvernance constitutionnelle des juges: l'institutionnalisation d'un nouveau mode de régulation du risque de conflit constitutionnel dans l'Union européenne' (Doctoral dissertation, Paris, Institut d'études politiques).

Leuffen, D., B. Rittberger & F. Schimmelfennig (2012). *Differentiated integration. Explaining variation in the European Union,* Basingstoke: Palgrave Macmillan.

Lichère, F., Potvin-Solis, L. & Raynouard, A. (2004a). *Le dialogue entre les juges européens et nationaux: incantation ou réalité?*, Brussels: Bruylant.

Lichère, F., Potvin-Solis, L. & Raynouard, A. (2004b). *Le dialogue entre les juges européens et nationaux: incantation ou réalité?*, Brussels: Bruylant.

Lindstrom, N. (2010). 'Service liberalization in the enlarged EU: a race to the bottom or the emergence of transnational political conflict?', *Journal of Common Market Studies*, vol. 48, no. 5, 1307–27.

Lochak, D. (1992). *La justice administrative*, Paris: Montchrestien.

Mabbett, D. (2005). 'The development of rights-based social policy in the European Union: the example of disability rights', *Journal of Common Market Studies*, vol. 43, no. 1, 97–120.

McCormick, N. (1994) [1978]. *Legal reasoning and legal theory*, Oxford: Oxford University Press.

McCormick, N. (2005). *Rhetoric and the rule of law: a theory of legal reasoning*, Oxford University Press.

McCown, M. (2001). 'The use of judge-made law in European judicial integration: precedent-based arguments in EU inter-institutional disputes', Paper read at European Community Studies Association Biennial Conference, Madison, Wisconsin, USA.

McCown, M. (2003). The European Parliament before the bench: ECJ precedent and EP litigation strategies, *Journal of European Public Policy*, vol. 10, no. 6, 974– 95.

McCown, M. (2006). 'Judicial law-making and European integration: the European Court of Justice', in J. Richardson (ed.), *European Union: power and policy-making*, Basingstoke: Routledge.

McCown, M. (2009). 'Interest groups and the European Court of Justice', in D. Coen & J. Richardson (eds), *Lobbying in the European Union,* Oxford: Oxford University Press, pp. 89–104.

McCown, M. (2002). 'The judge-made law of the European Court of Justice', Paper read at American Political Science Association Annual Conference, Boston, MA.

McCrudden, C. (Ed.). (1987). *Women, employment, and European equality law*, London: Eclipse Publications.

McNamara, K. R. (1998). *The currency of ideas: monetary politics in the European Union,* Ithaca, NY: Cornell University Press.

Madsen, M. R. (2013). 'Towards a sociology of international courts', iCourts Online Working Paper, no. 1.

Maduro, M. & Azoulai, L. (eds). (2010). *The past and future of EU law: the classics of EU law revisited on the 50th anniversary of the Rome Treaty*, London: Bloomsbury Publishing.

Malecki, M. (2012). 'Do ECJ judges all speak with the same voice? Evidence of divergent preferences from the Judgments of Chambers', *Journal of European Public Policy*, vol. 19, no. 1, 59–75.

Malmberg, J., & Sigeman, T. (2008). 'Industrial actions and EU economic freedoms: the autonomous collective bargaining model curtailed by the European Court of Justice', *Common Market Law Review*, vol. 45, no. 4, 1115–46.

Mancini, G.F. (1989), 'The making of a constitution for Europe', *Common Market Law Review,* vol. 26, 595–614.

Mancini F. & D. Keeling (1994). 'Democracy and the European Court of Justice', *The Modern Law Review*, vol. 57, no. 2, 175–90.

Mangenot, M. (2000). 'Une Europe improbable: les hauts fonctionnaires français dans la construction européenne, 1948–1992' (Doctoral dissertation, Strasbourg 3).

Mangenot, M. (2004). Le Conseil d'État et l'institutionnalisation du système juridique communautaire. In *Communication au colloque «Les juristes et la construction d'un ordre politique européen»*, CURAPP, Université de Picardie-Jules-Verne, 1 April.

Mangenot, M. (2005). 'The Conseil d'Etat and Europe: adapting the French administrative state', in H. Drake (ed.), *French Relations with the European Union*, New York: Routledge.

Mangenot, M. (2008), 'Le Conseil d'Etat et l'institutionnalisation du système juridique communautaire', halshs-00288626.

Martinsen, D. S. (2005a). 'Social security regulation in the EU: the deterritorialization of welfare?, in G. De Búrca (ed.), *EU law and the welfare state: in search of solidarity*, Oxford: Oxford University Press, pp. 89–110.

Martinsen, D. S. (2005b). 'Towards an internal health market with the European Court', *West European Politics*, vol. 28, no. 5, 1035–56.

Martinsen, D. S. (2005c). 'The Europeanization of welfare – the domestic impact of intra-European social security', *Journal of Common Market Studies*, vol. 43, no. 5, 1027–54.

Martinsen, D. S. (2007). 'The Europeanization of gender equality – who controls the scope of non-discrimination?', *Journal of European Public Policy*, vol. 14, no. 4, 544–62.

Martinsen, D. S. (2011). 'Judicial policy-making and Europeanization: the proportionality of national control and administrative discretion', *Journal of European Public Policy*, vol. 18, no. 7, 944–61.

Martinsen, D. S. (2015a). *An ever more powerful court? The political constraints of legal integration in the European Union*, Oxford: Oxford University Press.

Martinsen, D. S. (2015b). 'Judicial influence on policy outputs? The political constraints of legal integration in the European Union', *Comparative Political Studies*, vol. 48, no. 12, 1622–60.

Mattli, W. & Slaughter, A. (1995). 'Law and politics in the European Union', *International Organization*, vol. 49, no. 1, 183–90.

Mattli, W. & Slaughter, A. (1998). 'Revisiting the European Court of Justice', *International Organization*, vol. 52, no. 1, 177–209.

Mayoral, J. A. (2013). *The politics of judging EU law: a new approach to national courts in the legal integration of Europe*, European University Institute.

Mayoral, J. A., Jaremba, U., & Nowak, T. (2014). 'Creating EU law judges: the role of generational differences, legal education and judicial career paths in national judges' assessment regarding EU law knowledge', *Journal of European Public Policy*, vol. 21, no. 8, 1120–41.

Mazey, S. (1998). 'The European Union and women's rights: from the Europeanization of national agendas to the nationalization of a European agenda?', *Journal of European Public Policy*, vol. 5, no. 1, 131–52.

Mazey, S., (2001). *Gender mainstreaming in the EU: principles and practice*, London: Kogan Page.

Micklitz, H.-W. (2005). *The politics of judicial co-operation in the EU: Sunday trading, equal treatment and good faith*, Cambridge: Cambridge University Press.

Micklitz, H.-W. (2009). 'Judicial activism of the European Court of Justice and the development of the European social mode in anti-discrimination and consumer law', EUI Working Paper LAW 2009/19.

Miles, K. (2011). 'Sustainable development, national treatment and like circumstances in investment law', in M.-C. Cordonnier Segger, M. Gehring, & A. Newcombe, *Sustainable development in world investment law*, Amsterdam: Wolters Kluwer, pp. 261–94.

Miller, F.P., Vandome, A.F. & McBrewster, J. (2010). *European Court of Justice*, Saarbrücken: VDM Publishing House.

Monti, G. (2007). *EC competition law*, Cambridge: Cambridge University Press.

Moravcsik, A. (2002). '"In defense of the 'Democratic Deficit": reassessing legitimacy in the European Union', *Journal of Common Market Studies*, vol. 40, no. 4, 603–24.

Moser, P. & Sawyer, K., (2008). *Making Community law: the legacy of Advocate General Jacobs at the European Court of Justice*, Cheltenham: Edward Elgar.

Nagel, S. (1965). 'Court-curbing periods in American history', *Vanderbilt Law Review,* vol. 18, no. 3, 925–44.

Nicolaïdis, K., & Schmidt, S. K. (2007). 'Mutual recognition "on trial": the long road to services liberalization', *Journal of European Public Policy*, vol. 14, no. 5, 717–34.

Nowak, T. (2008). 'The Working Time Directive and the European Court of Justice', *Maastricht Journal of European and Comparative Law,* vol. 15, no, 4, 447–71.

Nowak, T. (2010). 'Of garbage cans and rulings: judgments of the European Court of Justice in the EU Legislative Process', *West European Politics*, vol. 33, no. 4, 753–69.

Nowak, T., Fabian A., Hertogh M., & Wissink, M. (2011). *National judges as European Union judges – experiences, knowledge and attitudes of lower court judges in Germany and the Netherlands*, Den Haag, Portland: Eleven Publishers.

Nyikos, S. (2008). 'Courts', in P. Graziano and M. Vink (eds), *Europeanization: new research agendas*, Basingstoke: Palgrave Macmillan.

O'Leary, S. (2002). *Employment law at the European Court of Justice: judicial structures, policies and processes*, Oxford: Hart Publishing.

Obermaier, S. (2008). 'Constitutionalising an overlapping consensus: the ECJ and the emergence of a coordinate constitutional order', *European Law Journal*, vol. 14, no. 6, 735–52.

Obermaier, A. J. (2008a). 'Fine-tuning the jurisprudence: The ECJ's judicial activism and self-restraint', Vienna: Working Paper No. 02/2008.

Obermaier, A. J. (2008b). 'The national judiciary – sword of European Court of Justice rulings: the example of the Kohll/Decker jurisprudence', *European Law Journal*, vol. 14, no. 6, 735–52.

Obermaier, A. (2009). *The end of territoriality? The impact of ECJ rulings on British, German and French social policy*, Farnham: Ashgate.

Opinion of the Council Legal Service (2007). 22 June 2007, 11197/07, JUR 260.

Ost, F., & Van de Kerchove, M. (2002). *De la pyramide au réseau?: pour une théorie dialectique du droit*, Brussels: Publications Fac St Louis.

Panke, D. (2007). 'The European Court of Justice as an agent of Europeanization? Restoring compliance with EU law', *Journal of European Public Policy*, vol.14, no.6, 847–66.

Panke, D. (2010). *The effectiveness of the European Court of Justice: Why reluctant states comply*, Basingstoke: Palgrave Macmillan.

Pauwelyn, J., Wessel, R., & Wouters, J. (2012). *Informal international law-making*, Oxford: Oxford University Press.

Payandeh, M. (2011). 'Constitutional review of EU law after Honeywell: contextualizing the relationship between the German Constitutional Court and the EU Court of Justice', *Common Market Law Review*, vol. 48, no. 1.

Peel, J. (2001). 'Giving the public a voice in the protection of the global environment: avenues for participation by NGOs in dispute resolution at the European Court of Justice and World Trade Organization', *Colorado Journal of International Environmental Law and Policy*, vol. 12, no. 47, 59–61.

Peers, S. (2011). *EU justice and home affairs law*, Oxford: Oxford University Press.

Pescatore, P. (1974). *The Law of Integration*, Leyden: Slijthoss.

Pescatore, P. (1978). 'L'exécutif communautaire: justification du quadripartisme institué par les Traités de Paris et de Rome', *Cahiers de droit européen*, 387.

Pescatore, P. (2005). 'Robert Lecourt (1908–2004)', *Revue trimestrielle de droit européen*, vol. 41, no. 3, 90.

Pollack, M. A. (1997). 'Representing diffuse interests in EC policy-making', *Journal of European Public Policy*, vol. 4, no. 4, 572–590.

Pollack, M. A. (1998). 'The engines of integration? Supranational autonomy and influence in the European Union', in W. Sandholz & A. Stone Sweet (eds). *European integration and supranational governance*, Oxford, Oxford University Press, pp. 217–33.

Pollack, M. A. (2003). *The engines of European integration: delegation, agency, and agenda setting in the EU*, Oxford: Oxford University Press.

Pollack, M. A. (2013). 'New EU legal history: what's new, what's missing', *American University International Law Review*, vol. 28, no. 5, 1257–310.

Pollack, M. A. (2015). 'Who supports international law, and why? The United States, the European Union, and international law', *The International Journal of Constitutional Law*, vol. 13, no. 4.

Pollack, M. (2016). 'European law stories'. *Conference Paper presented at the 23rd International Conference of Europeanists*, April 2016.

Pollicino, O. (2004). 'Legal reasoning of the Court of Justice in the context of the principle of equality between judicial activism and self-restraint', *German Law Journal*, vol. 5, no. 2, 283–317.

Posner, E. A & Yoo, J. C. (2005). 'A theory of international adjudication', *California Law Review*, vol. 93, 1–72.

Prete, L., & Smulders, B. (2010). 'The coming of age of infringement proceedings', *Common Market Law Review*, vol. 47, no. 1, 9–61.

Puetter, U., Bickerton, C. J., & Hodson, D. (eds). (2015). *The new intergovernmentalism: states and supranational actors in the post-Maastricht era*, Oxford: Oxford University Press.

Radaelli, C. M. (2008). 'Europeanization, policy learning, and new modes of governance', *Journal of Comparative Policy Analysis*, vol. 10, no. 3, 239–54.

Ramos Romeu, F. (2002). 'Judicial cooperation in the European courts: testing three models of judicial behavior', *Global Jurist Frontiers*, vol. 2, no. 1.

Rasmussen, H. (1984). 'The European Court's acte clair strategy in C.I.L.F.I.T.', *European Law Review*, vol. 9, no. 4, 242–59.

Rasmussen, H. (1986). *On law and policy in the European Court of Justice, a comparative study*, Dordrecht, Nijhoff.

Rasmussen, H. (1988). 'Between self restraint and activism: a judicial policy for the European Court', *European Law Review*, vol. 13, 28–38.

Rasmussen, M. (2008). 'The origins of a legal revolution: the early history of the European Court of Justice', *Journal of European Integration History*, vol. 14, no. 2, 77–98.

Rasmussen, M. (2010). 'From Costa v ENEL to the Treaties of Rome: a brief history of a legal revolution', in M. Poiares Maduro & L. Azulai (eds), *The classics of EU law revisited on the 50th anniversary of the Rome Treaty,* Oxford: Hart Publishing, pp. 69–85.

Rasmussen, M. (2012). 'Rewriting the history of European public law: the new contribution of historians', *American University International Law Review*, vol. 28, no. 5, 1187–221.

Rasmussen, M. (2013). 'Establishing a constitutional practice of European law: the history of the Legal Service of the European Executive, 1952–1965', *Contemporary European History,* vol. 21, no. 3, 375–99.

Reich, N. (2008). 'Free movement v. social rights in an enlarged Union: the Laval and Viking cases before the European Court of Justice', *German Law Journal*, vol. 9, no. 2, 125–61.

Robertson, C. (2015). 'EU multilingual law: interfaces of law, language and culture', in S. Sarcevic (ed), *Language and culture in EU law. Multidisciplinary perspectives,* Farnham: Ashgate, pp. 33–52.

Rosa, S. D. L. (2012). 'The directive on cross-border healthcare or the art of codifying complex case law', *Common Market Law Review,* vol. 49, no. 1, 15–46.

Rosenberg, G. (1992). 'Judicial independence and the reality of political power', *The Review of Politics*, vol. 54, no. 3, 369–98.

Rosenfeld, M. (2006). 'Comparing constitutional review by the European Court of Justice and the U.S. Supreme Court', *International Journal of Constitutional Law*, vol. 4, no. 4, 618–51.

Sabel, C. F. & Gerstenberg, O. (2010). 'Constitutionalising an overlapping consensus: the ECJ and the emergence of a coordinate constitutional order', *European Law Journal*, vol. 16, no. 5, 511–50.

Saltinyte, L. (2010). 'Jurisdiction of the European Court of Justice over issues relating to the Common Foreign and Security Policy under the Lisbon Treaty', *Jurisprudencija / Jurisprudence*, vol. 119, no. 1, 261–79.

Sands, P. (1990). 'European Community environmental law: legislation, the European Court of Justice and common-interest groups', *The Modern Law Review*, vol. 53, no. 5, 685–98.

Saurugger, S. (2013). *Theoretical Approaches to European integration*, Basingstoke: Palgrave Macmillan, The European Union Series.

Saurugger, S. (2016). 'Politicization and integration through law: whither integration theory?', *West European Politics,* vol. 39, no. 5, 933–52.

Saurugger, S. & Terpan, F. (2014). 'La Cour de justice au cœur de la gouvernance européenne', *Pouvoirs*, vol. 149, no. 2, 59–75.

Saurugger, S. & Terpan, F. (2015). 'Measuring judicial activism: is the Court of Justice of the European Union an activist court?' Paper prepared for the ECPR General Conference, Montréal 26–29 August 2015.

Saurugger, S. & Terpan, F. (2016a). 'Resisting "new modes of governance" through policy instruments', *Comparative European Politics*, 1 vol. 4, no. 1, 53–70.

Saurugger, S. & Terpan, F. (2016b). 'Do crises lead to policy change? The Multiple Streams Framework and the European Union's economic governance instruments', *Policy Sciences,* vol. 49, no. 1, 35–53.

Saurugger, S. & Terpan, F. (2016c). 'Judicial activism? Defence procurement and the European Court of Justice', *Paper Presented at the Implementation Conflicts & Judicial Politics Workshop*, WZB, Berlin, 3–4 March.

Saurugger, S. & Terpan, F. (2016d). 'Peut-on expliquer la Cour de justice de l'Union européenne par ses juges?', in G. Grandjean & J. Wildemeersch (eds), *Les Juges: décideurs politiques?*, Bruxelles: Bruylant, 199–218.

Sauvé, J.-M. (2013). 'Le rôle du Panel 255 dans la sélection du juge de l'Union', in A. Rosas, E. Levits & Y. Bot (eds.), *The Court of Justice and the construction of Europe: analyses and perspectives on sixty years of case-law,* Luxembourg: Asser Press, pp. 99–119.

Schäfer, A. (2004). 'Beyond the community method: why the open method of coordination was introduced to EU policy-making', *European Integration online Papers (EIoP)*, vol. 8, no. 13.

Scharpf, F. (1988). 'The joint-decision trap: lessons from German federalism and European integration', *Public Administration*, vol. 66, no. 3, 239–78.

Scharpf, F. W. (1999). *Governing in Europe: effective and democratic?*, Oxford: Oxford University Press.

Scharpf, F. W. (2009). 'Legitimacy in the multilevel European polity', *European Political Science Review*, vol. 1, no. 2, 173–204.
Scheingold, S. A. (2004). *The politics of rights: lawyers, public policy, and political change*, Ann Arbor: University of Michigan Press.
Schepel, H. (2000). 'Reconstructing constitutionalization: law and politics in the European Court of Justice', *Oxford Journal of Legal Studies*, vol. 20, no. 3, 457–68.
Schepel, H. & Blankenburg, E., (2001). 'Mobilizing the European Court of Justice', in G. de Búrca, & J. H. H. Weiler (eds), *The European Court of Justice*, Oxford: Oxford University Press, pp. 9–42.
Schiek, D. (2006). 'The Court of Justice decision in Mangold: a further twist of effects of directives and constitutional relevance of Community equality legislation', *Industrial Law Journal*, vol. 35, no. 3, 329–341.
Schmidt, S. K. (2000). Only an agenda setter? The European Commission's power over the Council of Ministers. *European Union Politics*, vol. 1, no. 1, 37–61.
Schmidt, S. K. (2009). 'When efficiency results in redistribution: the conflict over the single services market', *West European Politics*, vol. 32, no. 4, 847–65.
Schmidt, S. K. (2012). 'Who cares about nationality? The path-dependent case law of the ECJ from goods to citizens', *Journal of European Public Policy*, vol. 19, no. 1, 8–24.
Schmidt, S. K. (2014). 'Judicial Europeanisation: the case of Zambrano in Ireland', *West European Politics*, vol. 37, no. 4, 769–785.
Schmidt, S.K. (2015). 'The shadow of case law: the Court of Justice of the European Union and the Policy Process', in S. Mazey and J. Richardson (eds), *European Union: power and policy-making*, London: Routledge, pp. 159–88.
Schmidt, S. K. & Kelemen D. R. (2012). 'Introduction – the European Court of Justice and legal integration: perpetual momentum?', *Journal of European Public Policy*, vol. 19, no. 1, 1–7.
Schmidt, S. K. & Kelemen, R. D. (2014). *The power of the ECJ*, New York: Routledge.
Schmidt, V. A. (2000). 'Democracy and discourse in an integrating Europe and a globalising world', *European Law Journal*, vol. 6, no. 3, 277–300.
Schmidt, V. A. (2006). *Democracy in Europe: the EU and national polities*. Oxford: Oxford University Press.
Schönberger, C. (2015). 'Mi attendu, mi dissertation. Le style des décisions de la Cour de justice de l'Union européenne', *Droit et société*, vol. 91, no. 3, 505–19.
Schütze, R. (2012). *European constitutional law*, Cambridge: Cambridge University Press.
Sciarra, S. (2001). *Labour law in the courts: national judges and the European Court of Justice*, Oxford: Hart Publishing.

Scott, J. & Sturm S. (2006). 'Courts as catalysts: re-thinking the judicial role in new governance', *Columbia Journal of European Law*, vol. 13, 565–93.

Scott, J., & Trubek, D. M. (2002). 'Mind the gap: law and new approaches to governance in the European Union', *European Law Journal*, vol. 8, no. 1, 1–18.

Segal, J. A. & Spaeth, H. J. (1996). 'The influence of Stare Decisis on the votes of United States Supreme Court justices', *American Journal of Political Science*, vol. 40, no. 4, 971–1003.

Segal, J. A. & Spaeth, H. J. (1993). *The Supreme Court and the attitudinal model*, Cambridge & New York: Cambridge University Press.

Seikel, D. (2015). 'Class struggle in the shadow of Luxembourg. The domestic impact of the European Court of Justice's case law on the regulation of working conditions', *Journal of European Public Policy*, published online 2015, 1–20.

Shaffer, G. C. & Pollack, M. A. (2009). 'Hard vs. soft law: alternatives, complements, and antagonists in international governance', *Minnesota Law Review*, vol. 94, 706.

Shapiro, M. (1981). *Courts: a comparative political analysis*, Chicago: University of Chicago Press.

Shaw, J. (1999). 'Postnational constitutionalism in the European Union', *Journal of European Public Policy*, vol. 6, no. 4, 579–97.

Shaw, J. (2000). 'Importing gender: the challenge of feminism and the analysis of the EU legal order', *Journal of European Public Policy,* vol. 7, no. 3, 406–31.

Shaw, J., & More, G. (eds.). (1995). *New legal dynamics of European Union*. Oxford : Oxford University Press.

Shepherd, J. (2009). 'The influence of retention politics on judges' voting', *Journal of Legal Studies*, vol. 38, no. 1, 169–203.

Shuibhne, Niamh Nic. (2015). 'Limits rising, duties ascending: the changing legal shape of Union citizenship', *Common Market Law Review*, vol. 52, no. 4, 889–937.

Sigona, N. (2011). 'L'Union européenne et les Roms', *Cultures & Conflits,* no. 81–82, 213–22.

Skowronek, S. (1982). *Building a new American state: the expansion of national administrative capacities, 1877–1920*, Cambridge: Cambridge University Press.

Slagter, T. H. (2009). 'National parliaments and the ECJ: a view from the Bundestag', *Journal of Common Market Studies*, vol. 47, no. 1, 175–97.

Slaughter, A. M., Tulumello, A. S., & Wood, S. (1998). 'International law and international relations theory: A new generation of interdisciplinary scholarship', *American Journal of International Law*, vol. 92, no. 3, 367–97.

Slaughter, A.-M., Stone Sweet, A. & Weiler, J., (1998). *The European Court and national courts-doctrine and jurisprudence: legal change in its social context*, Oxford: Hart Publishing.

Slepcevic, R. (2009). 'The judicial enforcement of EU law through national courts: possibilities and limits', *Journal of European Public Policy*, vol. 16, no. 3, 378–94.

Smith, M. (2010a). *Centralised enforcement, legitimacy and good governance in the EU*, London & New York: Routledge.

Smith, M. (2010b). 'Inter-institutional dialogue and the establishment of enforcement norms: a decade of financial penalties under Article 228 EC (now Article 260 TFEU)', *European Public Law*, vol. 16, 547–70.

Solanke, I. (2011). 'Stop the ECJ? An empirical assessment of activism at the CJEU', *European Law Journal*, vol.6, no. 17, p. 764.

Stacey, J. & Rittberger, B. (2003). 'Dynamics and formal and informal institutional change in the EU', *Journal of European Public Policy*, vol. 10, no. 6, 858–83.

Stein, E. (1981). 'Lawyers, judges, and the making of a transnational constitution', *American Journal of International Law*, vol. 75, no. 1, 1–27.

Steiner, J. & Woods, L. (2009). *EU law*, Oxford: Oxford University Press.

Steinberg, R. H. (2004). 'Judicial lawmaking at the WTO: discursive, constitutional and political constraints', *American Journal of International Law*, vol. 98, no. 2, 247–75.

Stephan, P. B., III (2002). 'Courts, tribunals, and legal unification – the agency problem', *Chicago Journal of International Law*, vol. 3, 333–52.

Steunenberg, B. & Toshkov, D. (2009). 'Comparing transposition in the 27 member states of the EU: the impact of discretion and legal fit', *Journal of European Public Policy*, vol. 16, no. 7, 951–970.

Stirn, B. (2009). 'Le Conseil d'Etat et les juridictions communautaires : un demi-siècle de dialogue des juges', *La Gazette du Palais*, 13–14 février 2009, pp. 3–7.

Stone Sweet, A. (1999). 'Judicialization and the construction of governance', *Comparative Political Studies*, vol. 32, no. 2, 147–84.

Stone Sweet, A. (2000). *Governing with judges: constitutional politics in Europe*, Oxford: Oxford University Press.

Stone Sweet, A. (2004). *The judicial construction of Europe*, New York: Oxford University Press.

Stone Sweet, A. (2010). 'The European Court of Justice and the judicialization of EU governance', *Living Reviews in European Governance*, vol. 5, no. 2, available at http://europeangovernance.livingreviews.org/Articles/lreg-2010-2/ (accessed 8 September 2011).

Stone Sweet, A. (2012). 'A cosmopolitan legal order: Constitutional pluralism and rights adjudication in Europe', *Global Constitutionalism*, vol. 1, no. 1, 53–90.

Stone-Sweet, A. (2013). 'The structure of constitutional pluralism: review of Nico Krisch, Beyond Constitutionalism: The Pluralist Structure of Post-National Law', *International Journal of Constitutional Law*, vol.11, no. 2, 491–500.

Stone Sweet, A. & Brunell, T. L. (1998). 'Constructing a supranational constitution: dispute resolution and governance in the European Community', *The American Political Science Review*, vol. 92, no. 1, 63–81.

Stone Sweet, A. & Brunell, T. L. (2012). 'The European Court of Justice, state non-compliance, and the politics of override', *American Political Science Review*, vol. 106, no. 1, 204–13.

Stone Sweet, A. & Caporaso J. A. (1998). 'From free trade to supranational polity: the European Court and integration', in W. Sandholtz & A. Stone Sweet, *European integration and supranational governance*, Oxford: Oxford University Press, pp. 92–133.

Stone Sweet, A. & McCown, M. (2004). 'Free movement of goods in the European Union', in A. Stone Sweet (ed.), *The judicial construction of Europe*, Oxford: Oxford University Press.

Stone Sweet, A. & Stranz, K. (2012). 'Rights adjudication and constitutional pluralism in Germany and Europe', *Journal of European Public Policy*, vol. 19, no. 1, 92–108.

Sunstein, C. (2001). *Designing democracy, what constitutions do*, Oxford: Oxford University Press.

Syrpis, P. (2012). *The judiciary, the legislature and the EU internal market*, Cambridge: Cambridge University Press.

Tallberg, J. (1999). *Making states comply: the European Commission, the European Court of Justice, and the enforcement of the internal market* (Vol. 109), Lund University.

Tallberg, J. (2000). 'Supranational influence in EU enforcement: the European Court of Justice and the principle of state liability', *Journal of European Public Policy*, vol. 7, no. 1, 104–21.

Tallberg, J. (2002). 'Delegation to supranational institutions: why, how, and with what consequences?', *West European Politics*, vol. 25, no. 1, 23–46.

Tamm, D. (2013). 'The history of the Court of Justice of the European Union since its origin', in *The Court of Justice and the construction of Europe: analyses and perspectives on sixty years of case-law – La Cour de Justice et la Construction de l'Europe: Analyses et Perspectives de Soixante Ans de Jurisprudence*, Luxembourg: Asser Press, 9–35.

Terpan, F. (2015a). 'Soft law in the European Union – the changing nature of EU law', *European Law Journal*, vol. 21, no. 1, 68–96.

Terpan, F. (2015b). 'Le constitutionnalisme européen: penser la Constitution au-delà de l'Etat', *Mélanges en l'honneur du Professeur Oberdorff*, Lextenso, pp. 181–192.

Thym, D. (2009). 'In the name of sovereign statehood: a critical introduction to the Lisbon judgment of the German Constitutional Court', *Common Market Law Review*, vol. 46, no. 6, 1795–822.

Thym, D. (2015). 'The elusive limits of solidarity: Residence rights of and social benefits for economically inactive Union citizens', *Common Market Law Review*, vol. 52, no. 1, 17–50.

Tizzano, A., Kokott, J., & Prechal, S. (2013). 50ème anniversaire de l'arrêt / 50th anniversary of the judgment in: Van Gend en Loos, Actes du Colloque de Luxembourg 13 Mai 2013, Conference Proceedings Luxembourg 13 May 2013.

Toshkov, D., (2007). 'In search of the worlds of compliance: culture and transposition performance in the European Union', *Journal of European Public Policy*, vol. 14, no. 6, 933–59.

Trabucchi, A. (1974). 'L'effet "erga omnes" des décisions jurisprudentielles de la Cour de justice des Communautés européennes', *Revue trimestrielle de droit européen*, vol. 10, 56.

Trachtman, J. P. (2006). 'The constitution of the WTO', *European Journal of International Law*, vol. 17, no. 3, 623–46.

Tsebelis, G. (2002). *Veto players*, Princeton: Princeton University Press.

Türk, A. (2009). *Judicial review in EU law*, Cheltenham: Edward Elgar.

Van den Herik, L. & Schrijver, N. (2008). 'Eroding the primacy of the UN system of collective security: the judgment of the European Court of Justice in the cases of Kadi and Al Barakaat', *International Organizations Law Review*, vol. 5, 329–38.

Van der Mei, A. P. (2003). *Free movement of persons within the European Community: cross-border access to public benefits* (Vol. 30), Oxford: Hart Publishing.

Van der Vleuten, A. (2010). 'Judges or lawmakers? The European Court of Justice and gay, lesbian and transgender rights', Paper presented at the 51st Annual Convention of the International Studies Association (ISA), New Orleans, 17–20 February 2010.

Van der Vleuten, A. (2014). 'Transnational LGBTI activism and the European courts: constructing the idea of Europe', in P. M. Ayoub & D. Paternotte, *LGBT activism and the making of Europe*, Basingstoke, Palgrave Macmillan, pp. 199–144.

Vanberg, G. (2005). *The politics of constitutional review in Germany*, Cambridge: Cambridge University Press.

Vanberg, G. (2008). 'Establishing and maintaining judicial independence', in K. Whittington, R. D. Kelemen & G. Caldeira (eds), *The Oxford Handbook of Law and Politics,* Oxford, Oxford University Press, pp. 99–118.

Vanhala, L. (2009). 'Anti-discrimination policy actors and their use of litigation strategies: the influence of identity politics', *Journal of European Public Policy,* vol. 16, no. 5, 738–54.

Vanhala, L. (2010). *Making rights a reality?: Disability rights activists and legal mobilization,* Cambridge: Cambridge University Press.

Vanhala, L. (2011). *Making disability rights a reality?* Cambridge: Cambridge University Press.

Vanhala, L. (2012). 'Legal opportunity structures and the paradox of legal mobilization by the environmental movement in the UK', *Law and Society Review*, vol. 46, no. 3, 523–56.

Vanhala, L. (2016). 'Legal mobilization under neo-corporatist governance', *Journal of Law and Courts,* vol. 4, no. 1, 103–30.
Vara, J. S. (2011), 'The consequences of Kadi: where the divergence of opinion between EU and international lawyers lies?', *European Law Journal*, vol. 17, no. 3, 252–274.
Vauchez, A. (2007). 'Judge-made law. Aux origines du modèle politique communautaire (retour sur Van Gend en Loos et Costa c. ENEL)'. In A.Cohen & A. Vauchez (eds), *Une Europe des élites? Réflexions sur la fracture démocratique de l'Union européenne*, Bruxelles, Presses de l'ULB, pp. 139–166.
Vauchez, A. (2008). 'The force of a weak field: law and lawyers in the government of the European Union (for a renewed research agenda)', *International Political Sociology,* vol. 2, no. 2, 128–144.
Vauchez, A. (2010). 'The transnational politics of judicialization. Van Gend en Loos and the making of EU polity', *European Law Journal,* vol. 16, no. 1, 1–28.
Vauchez, A. (2012). 'Keeping the dream alive: the European Court of Justice and the transnational fabric of integrationist jurisprudence', *European Political Science Review*, vol. 4, no. 1, 51–71.
Vauchez, A. (2013). 'Le prisme circulatoire. Retour sur un leitmotiv académique', *Critique internationale*, vol. 13, no. 2, 9–16.
Vauchez, A. (2014). *L'Union par le droit: l'invention d'un programme institutionnel pour l'Europe*, Paris: Presses de Sciences Po.
Vauchez, A. (2015). *Brokering Europe. Euro-lawyers and the making of a transnational polity,* Cambridge: Cambridge University Press.
Verschueren, H. (2015). 'Preventing "benefit tourism" in the EU: a narrow or broad interpretation of the possibilities offered by the ECJ in Dano?', *Common Market Law Review*, vol. 52, no. 2, 363–90.
Versluis, E. (2007). 'Even rules, uneven practices: opening the "black box"of EU law in action', *West European Politics*, vol. 30, no. 1, 50–67.
Vink M., M. Claes & C. Arnold. (2009). 'Explaining the use of preliminary references by domestic courts in EU member states: a mixed-method comparative analysis', Paper presented at the 11th Biennial Conference of the European Studies Association.
Voeten, E. (2007). 'The politics of international judicial appointments', *International Organization,* vol. 61, no. 4, 669–701.
Volcansek, M. L. (1992). 'The European Court of Justice: supranational policymaking', *West European Politics*, vol. 15, no. 3, 109–21.
Vollaard, H., Van de Bovenkamp, H., & Martinsen, D. S. (2015). 'The making of a European healthcare union: a federalist perspective', *Journal of European Public Policy* (ahead-of-print), 1–20.
Vries, S. A. D., Groussot, X. & Petursson, G. T. (2012). *Balancing fundamental rights with the EU treaty freedoms: The European Court of Justice as 'tightrope' walker*, The Hague: Eleven International Publishing.

Walker, N. (2002). 'The idea of constitutional pluralism', *The Modern Law Review*, vol. 65, no. 3, 317–59.

Walter, M. & Slaughter A.-M. (1998), 'Revisiting the European Court of Justice', *International Organization*, vol. 52, no, 1, 177–209.

Wasserfallen, F. (2010). 'The judiciary as legislator? How the European Court of Justice shapes policy-making in the European Union', *Journal of European Public Policy*, vol. 17, no. 8, 1128–146.

Weatherhill, S. (1996). After *Keck*: some thoughts on how to clarify the clarification', *Common Market Law Review*, vol. 33, no. 5, 887–908.

Weiler, J. H. H. (1981). 'The community system: the dual character of supranationalism', *Yearbook of European Law*, vol. 1, 257–306.

Weiler, J. H. H. (1986). 'Eurocracy and distrust: Some questions concerning the role of the European Court of Justice in the protection of fundamental human rights within the legal order of the European Communities', *Washington Law Review*, vol. 61, 1103–1142.

Weiler, J. H. H. (1991), 'The transformation of Europe', *The Yale Law Journal*, vol. 100, no. 8, Symposium International Law, 2403–2483.

Weiler, J. H. H. (1993). 'Journey to an unknown destination: a retrospective and prospective of the European Court of Justice in the arena of political integration', *Journal of Common Market Studies*, vol. 31, no. 4, 417–46.

Weiler, J. H. H. (1994). 'A quiet revolution. The European Court of Justice and its interlocutors', *Comparative Political Studies*, vol. 26, no. 4, 510–34.

Weiler, J. H. H. (2001). 'The judicial après Nice', in G. de Búrca, & J. Weiler, *The European Court of Justice*, Vol. 10, Oxford: Oxford University Press.

Weiler, J. H., & Haltern, U. R. (1998). 'Constitutional or international? The foundations of the community legal order and the question of judicial Kompetenz-Kompetenz', in J. Weiler, A. Stone Sweet & A.M. Slaughter (eds) *The European courts and national courts: doctrine and jurispudence*, Oxford: Hart, pp. 331–64.

Weiss, M. & Blauberger, M. (2016). 'Judicialized lawmaking and opportunistic enforcement: explaining the EU's challenge of national defense offsets', *Journal of Common Market Studies*, vol. 54, no. 2, 444–62.

Wernicke (2009). 'Au nom de qui? The European Court of Justice between member states, civil society and Union citizens', *European Law Journal*, vol. 13, no. 3, 380–407.

Wessel, R. A. (2015). 'Resisting legal facts: are CFSP norms as soft as they seem?', *European Foreign Affairs Review*, vol. 20, no. 2, 123–145.

Whittington, K. (2003). 'Legislative sanctions and the strategic environment of judicial review', *International Journal of Constitutional Law*, vol. 1, no. 3, 446–74.

Wigger, A. & Nölke A. (2007). 'Enhanced roles of private actors in EU business regulation and the erosion of Rhenish capitalism: the case of antitrust enforcement', *Journal of Common Market Studies*, vol. 45, no. 2, 487–513.

Wincott, D. (2001). 'The Court of Justice and the European policy process', in J. Richardson (ed.), *European Union, power and policy-making,* London: Routledge, pp. 179–97.

Wind, M. (2001). *Sovereignty and European integration: towards a post-Hobbesian order*, Basingstoke: Palgrave.

Wind, M. (2010). 'The Nordics, the EU and the reluctance towards supranational judicial review', *Journal of Common Market Studies*, vol, 48, no. 4, 1039–63.

Wind, M., Martinsen, D. S. & Rotger, G. P. (2009). 'The uneven legal push for Europe questioning variation when national courts go to Europe', *European Union Politics,* vol. 10, no. 1, 63–88.

Wollenschläger, F. (2011). 'A new fundamental freedom beyond market integration: Union citizenship and its dynamics for shifting the economic paradigm of European integration', *European Law Journal,* vol. 17, no. 1, 1–34.

Woods, P. J. and Hilbink, L. (2009). 'Comparative sources of judicial empowerment: ideas and interests', *Political Research Quarterly*, vol. 62, no. 4, 745–52.

Wyatt, D., Dashwood, A., Dougan, M., Rodger, B., Spaventa, E., (2011). *European Union law*, Oxford: Oxford University Press.

Zahn, R. (2008). 'The Viking and Laval cases in the context of European enlargement', *Journal of Current Legal Issues*, vol.3 http://webjcli.ncl.ac.uk/2008/issue3/zahn3.html. Accessed 31 July 2016.

Index

www.ingramcontent.com/pod-product-compliance
Ingram Content Group UK Ltd.
Pitfield, Milton Keynes, MK11 3LW, UK
UKHW021033150926
475561UK00003B/81